To three compassionate and inspiring physicians: Dr Hugh Dawson, Dr Julie Draper and Dr Jim Waddell.

Acknowledgements

I am indebted to Laura Fleminger for pointing out the need for this book and then convincing me I should write it; Hilary Bradt also lent encouragement and support and gave helpful and wise advice on the text. Another great motivator has been Shane Winser who gave lots of useful advice when I was young and green and planning various expeditions and most recently has commented on the book. Some of the material in the book was first published in *Wanderlust* magazine.

I did most of the work on this book whilst living in west Nepal, many hours from even the most basic library. My already too-busy, long-suffering friends and relations, particularly Dr Mary Styles, Jill Sutcliffe and Dr Mark Howarth, were generous in giving their time to ensure I received information I needed to complete the manuscript. Dr Hugh Dawson, Dr Jim Waddell, Dr Mark Howarth, Jill Sutcliffe, Dr Mary Styles, Sally Crook, Louise Hatton, Andy Robinson, Lorna and John Howell, and Dr David Wilks read drafts of the book and greatly contributed by freely sharing their experience and wisdom. Dr Anne Denning, Dr Angus McCrae, Paul Stewart, Professor David Bradley and Dr John Scott made invaluable comments on parts of the manuscript.

Thanks to others for promptly answering specific enquiries or for making helpful suggestions: Dr Jo (AR) Bradwell (Birmingham Medical School), Dr Charles Bangham (Oxford), Dr John Richens (London), Kate Cooper (La Paz), Dr Christopher J Ellis (Birmingham Heartlands Hospital), Dr Glen Chandler (Melbourne), Karen Shimada (Kathmandu and Tokyo), Dr David Shlim (Kathmandu), Joseph Wilson (my long-suffering Dad), Mary Kenny (Kathmandu), Dr Marianne Janosi (of VSO), Dr Marjory Foyle (London), Dr Glen Chandler (Melbourne), Karen Shimada (Kathmandu) and Dr Peter Brock (of Lederle). And thanks to my editor, Dominique Shead, at Cadogan Books.

Lots of others have unwittingly contributed during the processes of my ecological, parasitological and medical education. It will be clear that I have also gleaned all kinds of useful information from travellers and most of all from my patients who continue to educate me.

Without the unfailing support of my husband, Simon Howarth, who has read various versions of the text *ad nauseam* and protected me from distractions at critical points, the book never would have been finished; he prefers quiche to bread.

Contents

CADOGAN
guides

Dr Jane Wilson Howarth

HEALTHY TRAVEL
BUGS, BITES
& BOWELS

Cadogan Books plc
London House, Parkgate Road, London SW11 4NQ, UK
Distributed in North America by
The Globe Pequot Press
6 Business Park Road, PO Box 833, Old Saybrook,
Connecticut 06475–0833
Copyright © Dr Jane Wilson Howarth 1995
Illustrations © Marcus Patton (cartoons), Betty Levene
Book and cover design by Animage
Cover illustrations by Toby Morrison
Maps © Cadogan Guides, drawn by Map Creation Ltd
Series Editors: Rachel Fielding and Vicki Ingle
Editing: Dominique Shead
Copyediting: Carol Quarini   Indexing: Jan Morris
Production: Rupert Wheeler Book Production Services

A catalogue record for this book is available from the British Library
US Library of Congress Cataloging-in-Publication Data available
ISBN 0-86011-045-2
Output by Bookworm, Manchester. Printed and bound in Finland by Werner Söderström oy.

About the Author

Since qualifying as a doctor, Dr Jane Wilson Howarth has received postgraduate training in General Practice, Family Planning and Child Health (DCH and DCCH). She has worked on health projects in Asia (Ladakh, Sri Lanka, Indonesia, Pakistan and Bangladesh) for most of the past seven years as well as acting as general practitioner to fellow expatriates, travellers and (in Sindh) North American missionaries. Her fascination in natural history and formal training in zoology (BSc from Plymouth) led to her first expedition to the Himalayas. This six-month trip provoked a particular loathing of leeches and parasites and stimulated a desire to work towards their control. Research in Oxford (MSc parasitology) and a medical qualification (BM Southampton) has given her a sound academic training but fieldwork abroad (including three expeditions to Peru and Madagascar) has also allowed her to develop a practical approach to both zoological and medical research and other work in remote regions where proper resources are wanting; her book *Lemurs of the Lost World* describes some of these experiences. She has served as a cave rescue warden and is a trained scuba diver, cave diver and life saver (ASA Award of Merit).

Dr Wilson Howarth is a fellow of the Royal Society of Tropical Medicine and Hygiene, has published a range of papers in academic medical journals, lectures widely (including at the Royal Geographical Society) and writes a regular medical feature for *Wanderlust* magazine. She is presently a medical adviser to British VSO and US Peace Corps volunteers in Nepal. She has chosen to be host to only the more benign parasites including *Ascaris* worms, amoebae, histoplasmosis and leeches. She lives with her young family in the lowlands of west Nepal, which is also the home to four species of highly venomous snakes, plus scorpions, malaria mosquitoes and mugger crocodiles.

Introduction

More and more people are travelling to unhealthy places. About two million UK residents travel to the tropics each year and half become ill, mostly with travellers' diarrhoea. Each year, more than 2000 travellers return with malaria and about half a dozen or so people die of it. Generally the travelling public are poorly informed about how to avoid exotic diseases and what to do when they are taken ill abroad. This book is aimed at intrepid, and not-so-intrepid, travellers to the tropics, sub-tropics, mountainous and other remote areas of the developing world where standards of medical care are often poor. It should appeal to tourists, travellers, people travelling on business and expatriates including those who live abroad with children.

I have been consulted by many people who have become dehydrated, ill and frightened from simple travellers' diarrhoea. This is the most common tropical ailment, yet few know that they can be rehabilitated within hours by drinking a home-made sugar and salt solution. It saddens me that the information that would have stopped them becoming infected, or at least eased their suffering, is not

Table 1: Serious Tropical Diseases and Where They Occur

DISEASE or HAZARD	ASIA			AFRICA
Key to symbols: Risk high ☠☠☠ Risk low ☠☠ Risk present ☠ V vaccine available	**Southeast & East** Burma, Indo-China, Indonesia, Phillipines, Japan, China etc.	**South** Pakistan, India, Nepal, Bangladesh, Sri Lanka	**Middle East** inc. Afghanistan	**Sub-saharan**
Diarrhoea & filth-to-mouth diseases inc. cholera, typhoid etc. (*see* p.20)	☠☠☠	☠☠☠	☠☠☠	☠☠☠
Food-borne flukes (flatworms) (*see* p.42)	☠☠☠	☠	☠	☠☠
Malaria (*see* p.54)	☠☠☠	☠☠	☠	☠☠☠
Leishmania (*see* p.61)		☠	☠☠	☠
Elephantiasis (filariasis) (*see* p.59)	☠☠	☠	☠	☠
Japanese encephalitis (*see* p.9)	☠	☠		
Trypanosomiasis (*see* p.62)				☠
River blindness (*see* p.82)				☠
Yellow fever (*see* p.8)				V
Dengue fever (*see* p.60)	☠☠☠	☠☠☠	☠	☠☠
Dengue haemorrhagic fever (*see* p.60)	☠	☠		
Scrub typhus (*see* p.137)	☠☠	☠☠		
Tick-borne fevers (*see* p.66)	☠	☠	☠	☠
Sand-fly fevers (*see* p.61)			☠	☠
Loa-loa (*see* p.135)				☠☠
Bilharzia/schistosomiasis (*see* p.81)	☠☠		☠☠	☠☠☠
Rabies (*see* p.11)	☠☠☠	☠☠☠	☠☠	☠☠☠

This table is not definitive: situations change and it should be used only

Table 1: Serious Tropical Diseases (continued)

AFRICA	AMERICA		PACIFIC		EUROPE	
North	Caribbean	South & Central	Australasia	Islands	Medit	East
Morocco to Egypt			Australia, New Zealand	Fiji, Solomons, Papua New Guinea etc.		
⚠⚠⚠	⚠⚠⚠	⚠⚠⚠	⚠	⚠⚠⚠	⚠⚠	⚠⚠
⚠	⚠⚠	⚠⚠⚠	⚠	⚠⚠	⚠	⚠
⚠	⚠⚠	⚠⚠⚠		⚠⚠⚠		
⚠	⚠	⚠⚠⚠			⚠	
	⚠	⚠		⚠⚠		
		⚠				
		⚠				
	⚠⚠⚠	⚠⚠⚠	⚠	⚠⚠⚠		
	⚠			⚠		
			⚠⚠	⚠⚠		
⚠	⚠	⚠	⚠	⚠	⚠	⚠
⚠		⚠			⚠	⚠
⚠⚠	⚠⚠	⚠⚠		⚠⚠		
⚠⚠	⚠⚠	⚠⚠⚠		⚠⚠	⚠⚠	⚠⚠

as a guide to seeking further information in the text or from a travel clinic common knowledge. I have written this book to share this—and much more—information, so that people do not find their trip-of-a-lifetime turns into a nightmare.

If you love poring over books which set you pondering on all the excruciating illnesses which may cause your slow and painful demise in some horribly uncomfortable mud hut somewhere, this is not the book for you. Many of the hazards from tropical diseases and noxious animals are rather overstated. The diseases which commonly afflict travellers are diarrhoea, colds and sore throats; the most common killers are accidents, pre-existing disease and malaria. Half of the deaths in travellers, tourists and expatriates are due to heart attacks in people who probably would have suffered from them whether they had travelled or not. These notes are aimed at people without medical problems. Diabetics, asthmatics and people with other long-standing health problems should seek specific advice before travelling. Malaria is the only 'tropical' disease you need worry about and is largely avoidable with sensible precautions.

It is worth knowing which problems you are most likely to encounter at your destination. Until very recently, nearly all malaria imported into Britain came from Africa; now numerous cases are arriving from the Indian subcontinent too. Most British cases of hepatitis A, typhoid and other filth-to-mouth diseases in travellers are contracted in the subcontinent. Americans bring home their faecal–oral diseases from Peru and neighbouring countries. Read on so that you know which few problems you do need to be aware of and how to avoid them, and then go forth and enjoy your explorations.

Tropical diseases are not so much diseases of the tropics, but rather diseases which are rife where sanitation and standards of housing and hygiene are poor. In many places I have used 'tropical' as shorthand for somewhere with a warm climate and poor housing and infrastructure. Using that definition, Nepal (which is not in the tropics) is covered in the book, but I have not said much about health problems in Queensland, Florida or Singapore. There is also information on the hazards of cold climates and the problems an intrepid back-packer might encounter in any remote place, whatever the climate.

The book is not intended to be comprehensive, but rather a simple guide to the health precautions and treatment necessary in remote places. It should also be an anxiety-defuser for those who worry about tropical diseases. The first aid that the book contains is of the kind needed in situations where second aid might be poor or completely absent. It is intended to supplement, but not replace, proper first aid training.

Styles of medical practice in developing countries may be very different from those we are used to in the West. We expect our doctors to offer a diagnosis and explain the purpose and possible side effects of prescribed treatment. Many doctors practising abroad may be unused to patients who know enough about their bodies to discuss medical conditions and their treatments. Patients commonly consult doctors to be given medicine to take which will make them feel better. Foreign doctors may not volunteer the information you expect. Tactfully ask what you would like to know, and realize that linguistic difficulties may make him (or you) seem rude. This book includes tips to enable people to discuss alternatives with doctors and check that their prescribing is rational. Sometimes antibiotics may be prescribed in inadequate amounts, even when the right treatment is offered, or several treatments may be suggested when one will do.

Doctors practising in the developing world not only have to cope with diseases which are rife in insanitary conditions, they are often also hampered by lack of facilities (the budget to run a 150 bedded hospital in Uganda is one-tenth the salary of some US consultants), but this means that very often their pure clinical skills are sharp and impressive. Unfortunately, because in some countries medical students bribe their way through their final exams, doctors' skills may also be very poor. If you need a medical consultation, ask around first. Hotel staff, expatriates and embassy staff may know who is competent and, perhaps as important, which doctors are used to dealing with foreigners.

The book is intended to be primarily preventative; it is not a Do-It-Yourself Doctor Kit. Although some treatments are given, where this seems appropriate, it is wise to seek a medical opinion if this is possible. If you are going somewhere remote ensure that one member of your group has at least some para-medical training. This book aims to tell you what to do, rather than baffle you with long medical names.

It has been a tough task condensing the essentials of several mighty medical tomes into this book (the index alone of one of my main source books runs to 114 pages), but I hope that I have succeeded in presenting the most useful points simply and accessibly. If, in simplification, you feel there are deficiencies or omissions do write and let me know. I would also be interested to receive any travellers' tales and stories about encounters with noxious animals which might go into the next edition of this guide.

Take care, keep well and *bon voyage*!

J.M.W.H.
Rajapur, Nepal

Homework

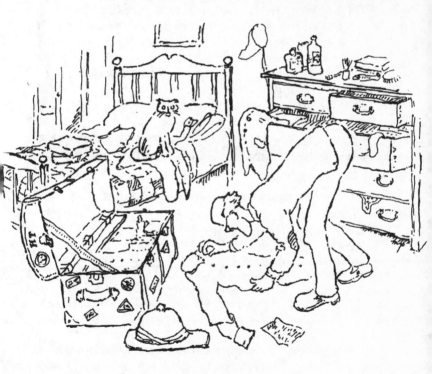

What needs to be done to ensure a disease-free trip? Are there any special preparations beyond buying malaria tablets and seeing your family doctor for a couple of immunizations? Most people, particularly novice travellers, would be wise to prepare themselves a little better than this since it is not possible to be immunized against most of the health hazards which harm travellers. Give some thought to appropriate clothing which will protect you from biting insects and too much sun, for example. Bear in mind that adopting a healthy approach to road safety, food preparation and eating habits, avoidance of biting insects, and safe sex will do you far more good than having an arm full of injections.

It is worth seeking impartial information about health and other risks, since travel agents are sometimes rather lax about warning of the hazards involved in travelling. It is not really in their interests, for example, to say much about the high risk of catching malaria in some regions. General practitioners (GPs) are increasingly aware of necessary preparations before travel, but few have the time to keep completely up to date; some, though, may now have on-line access to travel information. Travel clinics are excellent sources of reliable, up to the minute, impartial health information; ask them for advice or use the MASTA phone line (*see* p.211).

Pre-trip Chores

Is Your Destination Safe?

Your first pre-trip chore should be to ensure that your destination is safe. Despite the speed with which news travels the world, a surprising number of travellers get caught up in riots, civil unrest, or are held at the mercy of dacoits (armed robbers) or terrorists. It can be difficult to sort out whether the particular area of the country you intend to visit is dangerous. Sources like newspapers and embassies or the Foreign and Commonwealth Office (London) can help even if diplomats are rather over-cautious much of the time; they do not want the hassle of baling out foolish tourists. Some travel clinic printouts include security warnings and information.

Case History (**Pakistan**)

Some naive Japanese expeditioners were kidnapped by dacoits while canoeing down the Indus. Any enquiries they had made should have warned them that they were entering a risky area where dacoity (lawlessness) is rife and dacoits see foreigners as rich and vulnerable. They were eventually released after a ransom was paid. In Pakistan kidnapping, mainly of locals for a ransom demand, is common.

Probably the best source of information is returning expatriates, expeditioners or travellers, although they may not always be up to date. Some informants may be contacted through the Royal Geographical Society's (RGS) Expedition Advisory Centre (*see* useful addresses appendix) which publishes country briefs covering much useful information, including up-to-date sources. Otherwise, organizations like the South American Explorers Club (which has bases in Lima, Quito and New York State), or the London-based Anglo–Malagasy, Anglo–Peruvian, Anglo–Indonesian or the Britain–Nepal Societies can be very helpful.

Insurance

Ensure that you take out adequate insurance to cover medical care and accidents. If you are evacuated by 'air ambulance' the initial cost is at least three **full price** seats, plus nursing care, etc. You actually need to be quite well to make a long flight home so the insurance must cover possible medical expenses before you are fit to travel. If, for example, you have a very bad car smash, you may be in intensive care in Bangkok and then be flown home by air ambulance. This is an expensive business; make sure the worst possible case is covered. Check carefully that the policy that you buy gives you what you need, for example, a helicopter rescue from Everest Base Camp. Travel insurance policies are available through banks, insurance companies, travel agents and tour operators. High street insurers and travel agents generally refuse cover, even for short trips, if you have some long-standing medical problems or are heavily pregnant, for example, and in this case you will need to find a specialist firm. Self-help medical groups (which your GP should know about) have often negotiated special deals and are worth approaching for advice. The RGS can advise on companies willing to insure expeditions.

In European Union countries a certain amount of emergency medical treatment is offered free or at considerably reduced cost to EU residents who have an E111 form. The UK Department of Health booklet *Health Advice for Travellers* explains how to get medical treatment inside and outside the European Union (call freephone © 0800 555777 and ask for booklet T5). It may be wise to take out medical insurance in addition to this. There are various reciprocal arrangements whereby certain foreign nationals can receive some free or subsidized treatment in certain countries (e.g. at the time of writing Australians in UK, Italy, Malta, Netherlands, Greece, New Zealand, Sweden and Finland) so enquire about your particular journey.

First Aid and a First Aid Kit

Guidelines on what medicines to take are given on p.186. Do not forget the crucial items: sun-screen, sun glasses, insect repellent and anti-itch creams for insect bites.

If you are travelling to somewhere remote or are planning a long trip, try to attend a first aid course before you go.

In Britain, if you ask your GP to prescribe medicines to take abroad, Health Service rules say that a private prescription fee should be charged. A specialist service like Nomad (*see* **Useful Addresses**, p.212) might be a cheaper option.

Teeth

Have a dental check-up. Dentists may not charge very much abroad but the standard of treatment is sometimes poor and if equipment sterilization is inadequate there is a risk of acquiring hepatitis B or HIV. Stones in rice and lentils often cause dental trouble so consider taking temporary fillings or a dental 'first aid kit'; travel clinics often sell them. Meat in the developing world is often very stringy so pack some dental floss too (it can also be used as a washing line when travelling).

Drinks

If you are going somewhere hot, pack one or two large (one litre) water bottles. Thermos flasks are also useful, even in the tropics (*see* p.27).

Clothes

Think about what you will wear while travelling. Ensure you have at least one long-sleeved 100 per cent cotton shirt and long loose trousers; these will help protect you from mosquitoes, barbed vegetation and also intense sun. Dark clothes attract insects and they also absorb sunlight radiation, so they are hotter than light colours. Jeans are unsuitable travel wear because they are heavy and take ages to dry; they are hot and clingy in hot weather and yet not warm enough in cold climates.

T-shirts are also not particularly comfortable tropical wear. They are much hotter than ordinary cotton shirts and do not protect the back of the neck from sunburn. They are, however, very useful additional layers if the weather is cool. One (or more) T-shirts under a long sleeved shirt is quite warm, if you ascend to cooler conditions from a hot low area, for example. I have shivered through a few very cold nights on mountains in Java and Sri Lanka, islands where year round temperatures at sea level seldom change from around 31°C, for example. Several layers of clothes are warmer than one thick garment and they are also more adaptable if you are travelling through several climatic zones.

It is common for the girth to shrink dramatically on tropical trips: women's waists seem particularly variable. The heat reduces the appetite, there are fewer tempting snacks and there are bouts of diarrhoea. I now always pack a belt so that I can keep my trousers up despite shrinking.

Remember that in many cultures it is unacceptable to be scantily clad. In some Moslem countries and many Asian cities it would be considered almost obscene for men to be out in public bare chested or wearing shorts. Men and women wear loose-fitting garments which cover all but the head, hands and feet. In Pakistan I have even been chastised for allowing my eighteen-month-old son to run about naked in an enclosed garden.

If women dress as they would at home while travelling they may encourage problems. In much of the tropics, where tourists are a rarity, stripping down to a bathing costume is never done and if women bathe at all they bathe fully clothed. Until recently, women in Malawi were not allowed to wear trousers at all, and figure-hugging garments in many parts of the world may attract unwanted attention—even if they do cover most of your skin. Consider buying some longer-than-average skirts to travel in. Reasonably full, longish skirts have the additional advantage of allowing a discreet pee in public without revealing the bare essentials. Ask several people who have travelled to your intended destination about local dressing customs.

A Pre-trip Check-up?

A routine medical check-up is rarely useful in people who feel fit and well, even if your proposed trip is to somewhere very remote. However, when planning any journey, consider the level of fitness required for what you plan to do and ensure that you are fit enough. A surprising number of people, who have taken little or no recent exercise, book trekking holidays in the high mountains. At best they are in pain from aching muscles for much of their holiday and at worst they put themselves at risk of serious mishap.

You should try to ensure that you do not leave home without sorting out any recurrent medical problems that have been bothering you. An exotic trip may well make them considerably worse. Even athletes foot can become a misery.

Immunization

It is inappropriate in a book such as this to give detailed immunization schedules for each and every region of all countries, during all seasons, since situations change. However, I have provided some information here about the immunizations which are available and who should have them. Advice on the immunization and malaria tablets required for your particular journey is best obtained through a specialist travel clinic. They offer exceptionally good, up-to-date, immunization advice and those that are linked to a computer database can give you a printout specific to the area of the country that you are visiting and also details of health risks at different seasons. Information on any recent outbreaks will be available so that protection can be as full as possible. Addresses are given on p.18.

Once you have determined what immunization you need, British readers should be able to organize some vaccines (but not all) free or at much less cost from their GP. Special vaccines such as Japanese encephalitis are not usually available and even BCG is only available from the National Health Service (NHS) at special hospital clinics. Travel clinics can provide everything, but they charge the full rate for all that they give, even if it can be prescribed on the NHS. However, it may be much more convenient to get all immunizations done at the same travel clinic. So, at least 2 months before departure, go to a travel clinic, find out what you need, then decide (depending on time and money available) who will give the vaccine. Several new vaccines are being developed (including one which may be effective against travellers' diarrhoea, one against bacillary dysentery, another against *Campylobacter* diarrhoea and another against malaria) which may become available in the coming years. Travellers' clinics will probably hear about the availability of these before GPs.

Australians will probably arrange their pre-trip immunizations through their local doctors, although it may be wise to contact a travel clinic (*see* p.212) if your destination is somewhere unusual (i.e. not Bali, Java or Fiji). The cost of a consultation with a local doctor and in a travel clinic is comparable ($29.50 per visit plus the cost of vaccines) and claimable on Medicare (Australian health insurance). Most local doctors carry a stock of vaccines and antimalarial tablets, but it would be sensible to check that these are available when you make the appointment to visit the doctor.

Immunization Against Tropical and Other Diseases

There are no vaccines yet to protect against the most common (diarrhoea) and the most serious (malaria) diseases of travellers. Precautions against these should be taken seriously and wherever you are travelling it is wise to avoid insect bites, *see* p.49.

Immunization Required for Trips to Developing Countries

Tetanus, Polio and Diphtheria

You will probably have been immunized against these very serious diseases as a child, but check if you need a booster: all three only need boosting every 10 years. Tetanus and polio are a danger to all travellers. Diphtheria is still prevalent in Africa, Asia, Central and South America; there have also been an increasing number of cases of diphtheria in the Russian Federation and Ukraine. It can be unpleasant to have a full strength diphtheria immunization if you already have good immunity from previous immunization; a special low dose version is therefore available for boosting diphtheria immunity. There is now also a low dose diphtheria vaccine combined in a single injection with tetanus toxoid so that both can be boosted at once. You do not have to go very far afield to contract polio. An unimmunized British tourist on a one-week holiday to Morocco suffered from paralytic polio recently.

Tuberculosis and BCG

Tuberculosis (TB) is on the increase worldwide. Notes on the disease are to be found on p.179. Most British adults will have been immunized against TB with BCG at about the age of 13 years. Check whether this was done. It is unlikely to need boosting again. Children under the age of 13 should been given BCG if they are living abroad in high-risk areas. This can be given any time after the first day of life. American physicians are not so convinced of the efficacy of the BCG vaccine. BCG can confuse the diagnosis of TB and so if you are seeing an American doctor about possible TB you must mention that you have had BCG.

Hepatitis A

Viral hepatitis is one of the most common groups of diseases travellers acquire. Perhaps 5 per cent of all travellers to the developing world contract it. The most common form is hepatitis A. Since 1992 there has been a very effective vaccine (Havrix) against hepatitis A. A course of two injections provides 10 years' protection.There is also now a version suitable for children (Havrix junior). It largely supersedes gamma globulin which gives immediate but only very temporary protection. Gamma globulin relies for its protective effect on donors having been exposed to hepatitis A; since this is now an uncommon disease in the West, its efficacy is probably waining. Nevertheless gamma globulin would be useful in someone travelling at very short notice to a high risk area for 3 months or less.

The disadvantages of Havrix are expense and the fact that it takes 2–4 weeks for it to stimulate a protective immune response. A course costs just over £40 (1994 prices) as compared to £3–6 for gamma globulin.

If you have had hepatitis A (this can be checked with a blood test), you will have life-long immunity and neither Havrix nor gamma globulin is necessary thereafter.

Typhoid

The first typhoid vaccine was given in 1896 and all British soldiers were immunised against typhoid before going to fight in the Boer War. Typhoid is rare in travellers and some would argue that it is not strictly necessary for travellers to subsaharan Africa or Southeast Asia since the likelihood of contracting the disease in these regions is small; similar to that in southern and eastern Europe. An overall figure of risk in travellers (from the US) is six cases per million journeys. The risk is higher in travellers to the Indian subcontinent (around 100 cases per million travellers) and to some areas of tropical South America, most notably Peru (174 per million). The best precaution against typhoid is to avoid raw or inadequately cooked food and raw water (*see* p.22).

The old vaccine used to provoke quite an unpleasant sore area around the injection site as well as fever and headache, but there are now two good alternatives. One is a new vaccine which has very few side effects and rarely leaves you with a sore arm. There is now also an oral vaccine which comes as three capsules which have to be swallowed on different days. The capsules need refrigeration and are expensive at £24.81 (the intra-muscular version is £4.11) but many will think this is a small price to pay for avoiding an injection. Immunization whether by injection or capsule generally needs boosting every 3 years. However, people over the age of 35 who have had four or more courses do not need further typhoid immunization, unless they are at exceptional risk. The available vaccines give similar degrees of protection against typhoid (this has not been thoroughly field tested, but it seems to be only about 70–80 per cent protection) so even immunized travellers need to take care to avoid infection via contaminated food and water.

Immunization Required for Some Geographical Areas

Malaria

There is no immunization against malaria, although a promising vaccine is being tested. Antimalarial tablets need to be taken in a great many developing countries; travel clinics will give advice on what is best for which area. Antimalarial tablets do not give absolute protection and precautions against being bitten by mosquitoes are also essential.

Yellow Fever

This is a very serious and untreatable mosquito-borne disease which is endemic in much of sub-saharan Africa, Central America and parts of South America. There is a good vaccine which gives 10 years' protection. Many countries require an international vaccination certificate if you are travelling from an endemic area, the reason for this is that a good part of the world is inhabited by mosquitoes capable of spreading this devastating disease and no one wants to see it spread beyond its present range. The vaccine is not recommended for people with a severe allergy to eggs, in those under 9 months of age, in pregnancy or in people who are immunosuppressed (e.g. cancer sufferers, or people on high dose steroids), but you should discuss all this with your doctor before travelling. You cannot enter a yellow fever area without being vaccinated.

Japanese Encephalitis

This is a problem in Sri Lanka and south India up into Nepal and as far north as the maritime province of Russia; it also occurs sporadically in Southeast and East Asia (including Korea and China) particularly where pigs are kept. It usually only infects those living in rural areas in close contact with pigs and paddy-fields. It was said to be rare or absent from Moslem communities, but there have been recent reports from Pakistan, where egrets rather than pigs may be acting as the intermediate hosts. The transmission season in seasonal climates is mainly April to October (the peak is at the onset of the monsoon); closer to the equator, transmission is less pre-dictable.

It is a very serious mosquito-borne disease but it is unusual for expatriates or trav-ellers to acquire it. There were only three proven cases among all the many Australians travelling to South and Southeast Asia from 1970 to 1991. Only about one in every 50 infected bites transmits the disease, but the death rate in those who develop it is 10–30 per cent and even higher in epidemics. Of those who sur-vive, 30 per cent are left with long-term disability, much of it neurological. It is a nasty disease, and since it is incurable, those travelling to, or more particularly working in, rural Asia may wish to take the precaution of having the vaccine. The course is two injections a week apart. There have been some reports recently of quite severe reactions up to 48 hours after the second dose of vaccine so discuss with your doctor whether you are at particular risk and if you decide to be vacci-nated, make sure that you have the last dose at least a week before departure. This vaccine seems to give some cross-protection against dengue fever, which is a much more common problem in travellers and for which there is not yet a vaccine.

Meningococcus

This vaccine, for some types of bacterial meningitis, is indicated for travellers to India, Pakistan, Nepal, Saudi Arabia and the 'meningitis belt' of Africa which is mainly between the latitudes of 15°N and 5°N, but extending down to the equator in Kenya and Uganda. The area includes the sub-saharan parts of Senegal, Mali, Chad and Sudan; all of Gambia, Guinea, Togo and Benin; southwest Ethiopia, northern Sierra Leone, Liberia, Ivory Coast, Nigeria, Cameroon and Central African Republic. In the African 'meningitis belt' epidemics occur at the onset of the dry season (December–February) and usually stop with the onset of the rains in May–June. The vaccine can be given to anyone over the age of 18 months and is a single injection. It is entirely different to the recently introduced routine Hib vaccine to protect children under 4 years of age from a different kind of meningitis. Neither vaccine protects against all forms of meningitis.

Pneumococcus

Pneumococcus vaccination is required once in a lifetime for those who have lost their spleen or have sickle cell disease. A few doctors advise it for all travellers, since pneumococcal pneumonia is not uncommon in the tropics. The incidence of pneumoccal infection in travellers is hard to research, but it does seem unusually common in otherwise healthy people who would not be expected to be at special risk while at home. Your GP or travel clinic can arrange this.

Tick-borne Encephalitis

This is a risk for people walking, orienteering or camping in areas of lowland forest in parts of Scandinavia, the Commonwealth of Independent States (former USSR), central Europe particularly Austria, Czechoslovakia, West Germany and former Yugoslavia; April to August are the high risk months. The virus can also be transmitted through unpasteurized dairy products from cows, sheep or goats. There is also a post-exposure vaccine which can be given up to 4 days after a tick bite in high risk areas. The vaccines are not available in the USA and they do not protect against tick-borne diseases other than the European tick-borne encephalitis.

Cholera

Cholera is very rare in travellers, even in epidemic areas. The best way to remain cholera free is to avoid contaminated food and water (*see* p.22). Travellers are no longer routinely vaccinated against cholera, even for travel to endemic and epidemic areas, and this policy has not led to an increase in travellers contracting cholera. An effective oral vaccine may soon be developed, which should give much better protection.

Cholera vaccine is not worth having unless the country you are visiting demands it for entry and even then it is debatable whether it is necessary. It is not only an unpleasant vaccine, but it is an ineffective protection against cholera. If you have to have it just to get past the bureaucrats (and thus avoid being immunized at a border post with a dirty needle), one dose should be sufficient for the certificate. In many developing countries you will be able to buy the vaccination certificate without having the injection.

Immunization for Those with Special or Occupational Risks

Hepatitis B

Immunization against hepatitis B is worthwhile for expatriates and health workers; it is probably not indicated for short-term tropical travel, but its value can be discussed with your GP or travel clinic. It has few side effects, gives good immunity and protects you from acquiring hepatitis B from blood transfusions or dirty needles in the possible event of a road accident. The primary course is three doses at 0, 1 month and 6 month intervals; immunity can be checked (by a blood test) to determine whether a fourth dose is required. Boosters are required after about 5 years. It does not protect against other forms of hepatitis nor from AIDS. In adults, the injection should be given in the arm and in small children into the thigh.

Rabies

Rabies vaccine is an innocuous immunization and is sensible for people living in the Indian subcontinent (including Pakistan and Sri Lanka) or other regions where there are a lot of stray dogs; it would be wise for anyone travelling to very remote places and for anyone intending to enter caves in the Americas. Thailand has a particularly high prevalence of rabies (although not in the major cities); there are 200–300 human deaths a year and about 100,000 people receive post-bite immunization. Rabies vaccine is a must for veterinary surgeons or zoologists doing field work in the developing world; indeed, these professionals can usually get vaccinated on the NHS in the UK. The incubation period for rabies (and thus the amount of time you have available to get treatment after a bite) depends on the distance the bite is from the brain. Small children and toddlers often get bitten on the face and so there is very little time to get medical help in the case of a bite. It is important for young children visiting endemic areas to be vaccinated.

The course is two doses a month apart with a reinforcing dose after 6–12 months then boosters every 3 years. The cheapest way to be immunized is to have a part dose (eight people can be immunized intra-dermally from a 1ml. vial) and travel clinics can often arrange this if you are not travelling in such a group. If an intramuscular immunization is given, this must be in the arm and not the buttock. It may be that the efficacy of rabies vaccine is reduced if you are taking *chloroquine* (an antimalarial tablet) at the time of immunization so either get immunized well before departure and before you need to start your antimalarial treatment or (if this is not possible) have the intramuscular (larger) dose of rabies vaccine.

Plague

Few travellers will need immunization against plague. It is not a particularly effective vaccine. Those who may find immunization a useful precaution are zoologists intending to handle rodents in areas where plague is rife in animal populations or those travelling to help during plague epidemics, particularly nurses and medical laboratory technicians. There have been recent outbreaks in Bolivia, Brazil, Madagascar, Tanzania, Uganda, Mozambique, China, Myanmar, Vietnam, India and sporadic cases in the US. Plague responds to prompt antibiotic treatment.

Influenza

'Flu vaccination protects people at special risk of respiratory diseases from influenza. It does not protect against all influenza strains nor against the common cold. Ask your GP for advice.

People Who May Have Special Health Problems Abroad

Smokers and inexperienced travellers are more likely to become ill when travelling abroad, so those who are new to tropical travel should be particularly cautious. It is impossible to give comprehensive guidelines on who is and who is not fit to travel. Given two people with identical medical problems, one may manage travelling rough for months and the other may get into trouble on a short package tour. Clearly if you have some medical problem it would be wise to discuss your travel plans with your doctor.

Diabetics

Diabetics may need help rescheduling their medicines, for example, and should be aware of the special problems they face when they get travellers' diarrhoea. It is safe for diabetics to take oral rehydration solutions containing glucose, but a diarrhoeal illness may upset normally good diabetic control so it would be wise to discuss danger signs with your doctor. Tablets which control diabetes (and a range of other medicines) can cause sunlight-sensitive rashes (*see* pp.70 and 191) which can lead to sunburn.

Those on Anticoagualants

People who are taking anticoagulants should avoid intramuscular immunization; it will probably cause bleeding into the injected muscle which will be at best sore and uncomfortable. Many immunizations may be given subcutaneously to avoid this problem, but it is important to consider other risks. If anyone taking anticoagulants is unfortunate enough to be involved in a car crash, they are much more likely than others to bleed to death. They are also more likely to need blood transfusions in emergency situations; the risks of this are described in p.126.

Will Reduced Oxygen Harm You?

Most aircraft are pressurized to the equivalent of about 2000m; people with long-standing heart or lung disease may therefore suffer from the reduced oxygen availability and become unwell during a flight. Children with cystic fibrosis may also have problems due to decreased oxygen availability in the plane but paediatricians at the Royal Brompton Hospital in London are researching ways of predicting which children will have problems while flying. (The Brompton test is of no use in predicting how asthmatics will cope with altitude and flights.) People with cystic fibrosis lose more salt in sweat than normal and so this may cause problems in acclimatizing to hot climates.

Kidney Stones, Recent Surgery and Pacemakers

Those who have had kidney stones in the past are likely to get them again when in hot climates; they must make a special effort to drink plenty (*see* p.26). It may not be advisable to travel after very recent surgery, so ask your surgeon if it is wise. If you fly soon after laparoscopy you may feel very uncomfortable; gas left in the abdomen expands at the low cabin pressures. Those who have their jaws wired (after a fracture) are advised to avoid situations where they may be travel sick. Pacemakers may be affected by aircraft electronic and radar devices.

Obesity, Eczema, Asthma and Allergies

Over-weight people will be at higher risk of heat exhaustion than their slim friends and they may find the heat makes them feel miserable. Severe eczema and acne may worsen in the heat, although eczema may improve in sunshine especially if you continue to use plenty of moisturizers. Asthma may emerge as a new problem in travellers to large, polluted, third-world cities. Some asthmatics find their condition improves when they escape from the pollen of temperate plant species. Anyone who has experienced a severe allergic reaction (that is difficulty breathing, swelling of the face or collapse) to insect stings or other substances may wish to carry an *adrenaline* (*epinephrine* in the US) injection with them which they can administer themselves in case of a repeat allergic reaction. The alternative, inhaled *adrenaline* (e.g. Medihaler-Epi), is not as effective but would be an option for those unable to face learning how to inject themselves. A Medicalert bracelet or neck pendant would also be a sensible precaution (ask your GP or practice nurse, or *see* **Useful Addresses**, p.212). Those at high risk of repeat stings may consider a series of hyposensitization injections. These are especially effective in people over 30 years of age, but they involve 2–3 years of monthly injections at a specialist allergy clinic (e.g. the Department of Allergy and Allied Respiratory Diseases, Guys Hospital, London) so the treatment requires a great deal of commitment.

Some conditions may be helped by a trip to the tropics. Sufferers from aches and pains in joints and muscles, or fibrositis or arthritis may feel better in a warm climate. Psoriasis also improves with plenty of sunshine.

If you have a medical problem, travel with a written professional summary of it and also make a careful note of the medicines you are on with their *generic* (medical) names, not their trade names. Carry enough medicines with you to last your trip and remember that luggage often gets lost, so do not pack it in your suitcase or all in one place if your life depends upon it.

If in doubt, ask your GP whether you are fit to travel. Some medical conditions undoubtedly make travel hazardous, but also be aware that some doctors may be more cautious than is strictly necessary. Listen to the advice that your GP offers you; if you do not like what you are told get a second opinion from a travel clinic. Be informed and assess the risks that you are taking.

Children and Pregnant Women

Children and pregnant women are highly susceptible to malaria and are more likely to die if they contract it. Travel to highly malarious regions (especially parts of Africa) when pregnant or with children would be considered by some to be totally reckless, so think seriously about whether the trip is necessary and take advice before travelling. Take meticulous precautions against being bitten in addition to your antimalarial tablets. Pregnant women who contract hepatitis E can also become desperately ill and so these people need to be meticulous about avoiding filth-to-mouth diseases (see pp.22 and 180).

Many expatriates return home in the late stages of pregnancy to deliver their babies. For most airlines the deadline for flights is 32 weeks. New mothers understandably want to rush back to rejoin their families very quickly after the birth. It is surprisingly difficult to diagnose even serious diseases in early infancy so there is a lot of sense in being at home for 4–6 weeks before travelling back to the tropics. The safest age to take small children to the tropics is while they are exclusively breast fed. In Britain breast-fed babies are seven times less likely to be admitted to hospital (with any illness) than bottle-fed babies. In the tropics, bottle-fed babies are at even greater risk. If you are travelling to the developing world, try to breast feed rather than bottle feed your baby.

When travelling, young babies are easier to manage than young children. The most difficult age is between 1 and 3 years when children are easily bored on long flights and are not interested in sitting-down activities. Asian airlines are often more child friendly than Western ones.

The Flight

Fear of Flying?

More than three-quarters of people who fly admit to more than a little nervousness and some people are so scared that they cannot fly at all. You are more likely to die on the journey to the airport than on the flight (flying is one of the safest modes of travel), but such facts do nothing to defuse the terror in those who have a true phobia. Britannia Airways (✆ 01582 424155) and British Airways (✆ 0161 832 7972) run one-day courses aimed at helping people cope with flying phobia and these culminate in a flight with a specially selected and trained crew. The Britannia

Airways course costs £95 and the British Airways one costs £109 or £149 depending on whether the course is held in Manchester or London.

You will feel better during long flights if you move around every hour or so and abstain from alcohol. Dehydration is common on long flights and aggravates symptoms of jet lag; make an effort to drink plenty of fruit juices. Coffee and alcohol are both dehydrating and should be avoided. Fizzy drinks can make you feel uncomfortable as the gases in your stomach expand when atmospheric pressure falls.

Pressure Effects

Pressure changes (which are most rapid on take off and landing) bother some adults and many children; they are more likely to be noticeable if you have a cold or sinus problems. If you are suffering from ear or sinus symptoms it may be worth taking a decongestant such as *pseudoephedrine* (e.g. Sudafed in UK and US; Actifed in UK; Drixoral in US) a couple of hours before take off (but athletes beware: *pseudoephedrine* is a banned drug). Sucking a sweet, chewing gum, yawning or swallowing equalizes the pressure on each side of the eardrum. If you experience earache on take off or while in the air, grasp the nose, close the mouth and suck in to reduce the pressure in the ears as the pressure drops in the aircraft. If the pain is on descent, grasp the nose, close the mouth and gently blow to slightly increase the pressure in the ears. Giving babies a drink during ascents and descents will stop them suffering earache.

It is customary to be offered cotton wool to stuff in your ears on flights in Nepal and India; this is of no help in protecting your ears from pressure changes. The sweets you will be offered do help though.

The reduced pressure within the aircraft makes bottle tops pop off and sun-creams ooze out of their containers, which can be messy. Squeeze out any air before sealing the container and it will be less of a problem. Roll-on deodorants and some cheap ball-point pens also leak so need to be packed in plastic bags.

Eating, Drinking and Exercising on the Flight

Long flights may cause the ankles to swell. Loose-fitting clothes, moving about the plane, ankle-flexing and calf-tensing exercises help to reduce this. These activities also help guard against another rarer, but more serious, risk of long flights which is a thrombosis or blood clot in the leg.

Alcohol and smoking definitely aggravate the effects of jet lag and long-flight fatigue, but sleeping tablets can be very useful; *temazepam* is one that I have used. If you are poor at sleeping naturally on overnight flights these can ensure that you are not deprived of sleep. They take about half an hour to work and are effective for 6–8 hours. Some are good mind and body relaxants too, so are helpful if you are tense about flying or if you have had a frenetic departure and are concerned about leaving ends untied or business undone. Try to sleep on the plane, stick to a light diet, take plenty of fluids and try to organize a relaxed schedule for the first 48 hours after arrival.

A little-recognized effect of long flights is that some people notice hair loss about 3 months after the flight. This is effectively a moult, which is given the fancy name *telogen effluvium*. I suspect that this may be an effect that some people blame on antimalarial tablets.

Jet Lag

I am not convinced that there are any really effective 'treatments' for jet lag. It is a problem which must just be allowed for. If you have crossed more than five time zones, do not expect to be at your most alert for some days. It is said to take one day to adjust to each hour of time difference. Your bowels may take even longer to get back into equilibrium. It is said to take much longer to adjust to time differences when flying eastward, than when flying west.

The timing of flights makes some difference to jet lag and long-flight fatigue and it may be worth paying more to avoid particularly inconvenient times. Personally, I find the best timing for eastward flights is an evening departure so that you arrive the following afternoon—in time for a light meal and a bit of relaxation before bed. If you are tired before your journey you can expect jet lag to hit you harder. There are complicated routines which are said to reduce the effects of jet lag (*see* Bezruchka's *The Pocket Doctor* for example, p.216), but it is hard to imagine that they are much better than adequate rest and pacing yourself initially.

There are two areas which may be worth exploring to see whether they work for you. The first is the influence of a hormone called melatonin. This is usually produced by the body in the late evening and its secretion is inhibited by exposure to light. Getting outside in the sunlight when you arrive at your destination should help control this (but beware of too much sun) and improve the disturbed sleep patterns experienced by long-haul travellers. It may be possible to give melatonin as a kind of sleeping pill in the future.

The other approach is dietary. Some physiologists think that if you eat protein-rich meals (which are high in tyrosine) at breakfast and lunchtime these will allow the body to manufacture the hormones you need to have a dynamic day. A light evening meal with plenty of carbohydrates helps provide tryptophan for the hormones necessary for sleep. Some experts also advocate giving artificial tyrosine and tryptophan supplements.

Motion Sickness

Where you sit in any vehicle affects the amount of motion sickness you will experience; choose the position which rolls and pitches least. The most comfortable place in a plane is between the wings. In ships the least movement is felt in the middle, amidships. Lying down with your eyes shut, if at all possible, will also help all types of motion sickness.

Sufferers will feel better in the front seat of a car or bus, looking forwards (not sideways) and not reading or trying to navigate. Avoid the back seat of buses if you are prone to travel sickness. Adult locals travelling by bus in the developing world are by no means immune to travel sickness and I now try to get a seat as near the front as possible to avoid the vomit being blown in through the window from someone sitting further forward than me. The great disadvantage of sitting near the front, though, is that you can see how many near-crashes there have been.

If you are prone to travel sickness stick to a minimum of light, non-greasy, easily digested food, do not drink too much (volume aggravates travel sickness) and avoid alcohol.

Cures for Travel Sickness

Elasticated wrist bands called Sea Bands press on acupuncture points and seem to work well in preventing travel sickness even in children; they have no side effects.

The most effective drug in preventing travel sickness is *hyoscine* (e.g. Kwells in UK, but note that Kwell in the US is a treatment for lice!). This also has more side effects than other anti-sickness medicines, namely dry mouth, drowsiness and blurred vision, although these are dose dependent (the more you take, the worse the side effects) so it is good for short trips when only one dose is required. There is also now a skin patch which releases *hyoscine* over 72 hours (Scopoderm 500mg in UK, Transderm-scop in US); this should be placed behind the ear 5 hours before the start of the journey and can be left on for 3 days; it is only available on prescription in the UK.

Antihistamine drugs also help prevent travel sickness; their main side effect is sedation, so be aware that you may not be safe to drive after taking any of these drugs. A third possibility *cyclizine* (e.g. Valoid) 50mg acts for about 8 hours and is less likely to cause drowsiness than *hyoscine* or antihistamines.

All these anti-sickness preparations need to be taken well before travelling (2–4 hours before, depending on the drug) and are seldom of much use once the symptoms of travel sickness have begun. Injected preparations are active after about 15 minutes.

In the US and Canada there are a variety of clinics and information centres which will help with immunization advice. The American Society of Tropical Medicine maintains a list of North American travel clinics. These and others are listed by local public health departments. The Public Health Centers for Disease Control in Atlanta, Georgia are the central source and have a touch-tone phone line and fax service. They also publish each summer the invaluable *Health Information for International Travel*. Single copies are available from CDC (Attention Health Information), Center for Prevention Services, Division of Quarantine, Atlanta, GA 30333, ℡ (404) 332 4559. There are local (county and state) public health clinics and special travellers' medicine clinics now appearing in most large cities in North America; most universities have medical centres which can also help. *The Medical Guide for Third World Travelers* includes a list of clinics (*see* **Bibliography**, p.215). For a list of Australian travel clinics, *see* p.212.

Some UK Travel Clinics

British Airways Travel Clinics, (℡ 0171 831 5333 for the nearest); there are 30+ throughout the UK.

Thomas Cook Travel Clinic, 45 Berkley Street, London W1A 1EB (℡ 0171 408 4157/8).

Hospital for Tropical Diseases, 4 St Pancras Way, London NW1 0PE has a touch-tone phone line (℡ 0891 600350) giving advice relevant to specific destinations.

Independent Medical Centre/Bridge the World, 47 Chalk Farm Road, Camden, London NW1 (℡ 0181 444 4070).

Nomad Travel Pharmacy and Vaccination Centre, 3–4 Wellington Terrace, Turnpike Lane, London N8 0PX (℡ 0181 889 7014).

MASTA, Medical Advisory Services for Travellers, at the London School of Hygiene and Tropical Medicine, Keppel St, London WC1 7HT (℡ 0891 224 100 or 0171 631 4408) offer immunization advice and individual health printouts but have no travel clinic.

Summary

✚ Have a dental check before your trip so that you avoid, as far as possible, dental treatment abroad (and thus a possible AIDS risk).

✚ Ensure that you know whether your intended destination is malarious and take precautions as necessary.

✚ Allow lots of time and slow down to the pace of the country you are in.

Travel Broadens the Mind...

...and Loosens the Bowels

*The English—ah the English. They are renowned for the
frailty of their digestive systems and their preoccupation with
drains and plumbing. They have a talent for diarrhoea... if an
Englishman hasn't got it, he's looking for somewhere to have it.*

Peter Mayle, *A Year in Provence*

Diarrhoea is responsible for about five million children's deaths in
the tropics every year; these deaths are mostly the culmination of
recurrent bouts of diarrhoea in association with malnutrition.
Although diarrhoea kills by dehydration, it is easily corrected by
drinking home-made sugar and salt solution. Fortunately, because
most travellers are well nourished and capable of fighting the
infection, they are unlikely to become especially ill. They often catch
diarhhoea, though, because all the local sick children excrete a large
quantity of bacteria into the environment and, since standards of
sanitation are so bad, they can easily end up inside a traveller.
Travellers' diarrhoea, then, is common, but rarely dangerous.

What is Travellers' Diarrhoea?

Diarrhoea, gastroenteritis, food poisoning, the squits, Montezuma's Revenge,
Gippy Tummy, Delhi Belly, the Kathmandu Quickstep, Tandoori Trots, the Aztec
Two-step, *turista*, the runs or whatever you wish to call it, is the most common
medical problem for travellers. On average, half of those travelling to the developing world will suffer from travellers' diarrhoea. The common cause of diarrhoea
in visitors to the tropics is ETEC (enterotoxigenic *Escherichia coli*) which are nasty
forms of normally friendly intestinal bacteria; there are many other causes (*see*
below) Do not be put off by the long list of diseases, though; sensible precautions
will protect you from them all.

Why Do You Get Travellers' Diarrhoea?

Infection is acquired by getting other people's faeces into your mouth, usually via
dirty hands or food. Travellers' diarrhoea is a bad hygiene disease. A common mis-
conception (even among doctors and public health engineers) is that most travellers'
diarrhoea comes from drinking contaminated water. Dirty water can be a source, but
it is much less risky than eating contaminated food. The risk of developing disease is
related to the number of 'germs' consumed, and bad food contains very large numbers of pathogens. As you travel more, you develop some immunity to some kinds of
diarrhoea (notably ETEC diarrhoea). But only the foolish do not continue to take precautions (*see* below) since the transmission route for ETEC diarrhoea is the same as
for many other diseases. In a recent survey of visitors to East Africa only 2 per cent
were taking adequate protective dietary precautions.

A host of filth-to-mouth pathogens cause diarrhoea in careless travellers and stay-at-homes alike.

- Enterotoxigenic *Escherichia coli* (ETEC).

- Rotaviruses, which are responsible for the winter epidemics of diarrhoea in Britain; also the most common cause of diarrhoea affecting tropical children.

- Entero-adherent and other nasty strains of *Escherichia coli.*

- *Campylobacter* causes a lot of griping pains with the diarrhoea.

- *Shigella*, such a powerful pathogen that only 10 need to get into your mouth for you to be struck down with a devastating bacillary dysentery (severe bloody diarrhoea).

- Other bacterial causes of diarrhoea, like *Salmonella* food poisoning.

- *Giardia* (*see* p.39)

- A variety of other parasites and worms (*see* p.35).

- Amoebic dysentery.

- *Cryptosporidium* which causes a tedious type of diarrhoea which lasts for 2 weeks with a lot of cramps; there is no specific treatment.

- A catalogue of rarer diarrhoea-causing viruses.

- Cholera.

- *Cyclospora*, an illness caused by pathogens like blue-green algae with no specific treatment (*see* pp.27 and 216).

Diarrhoea is not the only disease you may catch by getting other peoples' faeces into your mouth. You are also at risk of:

- Typhoid

- Paratyphoid A, B and C

- Hepatitis A and E (*see* p.180)

- Polio

- Cystocercosis (worm cysts in the brain) (*see* p.38)

Where are Filth-to-Mouth Diseases a Hazard?

Diarrhoea and the other filth-to-mouth diseases are a problem in any region where sanitation is poor. Although much more common in warm, humid climates, they are not restricted to tropical countries. Cholera was a problem in Victorian London until there were improvements in the city's housing and sanitation.

Prevention

How to Avoid Travellers' Diarrhoea (and Other Filth-to-mouth Diseases)

There is not yet a vaccine to protect you from travellers' diarrhoea; it is avoided by eating sensibly. Although there are many causes of diarrhoea, avoidance strategies are essentially the same for each type. Ensure that your food is prepared and stored in a hygienic manner, that you maintain scrupulous standards of personal hygiene, and that your drinking water is safe. Food is the main problem: expatriates who cook for themselves, or who employ reliable servants can quite easily ensure that it is safe. Travellers staying in hotels have less control over the way their food is prepared, so they are at much greater risk. Ordering cook-to-order meals in restaurants is safer than eating ready-made dishes. Be at your most cautious when staying in large centres of population since the more people that there are around you the more faeces there will be. The star ratings of hotels are no guide to hygiene.

Travellers can reduce the risk by taking some simple precautions.

- ☉ Piping hot foods that are freshly cooked or thoroughly reheated are safe; sizzling hot street snacks are therefore safer than luke-warm foods served at buffets, even in expensive international hotels.

- ☉ Avoid salads, especially lettuce and watercress.

- ☉ Vegetables are usually safer than meat dishes.

- ☉ Any meat that you eat must be thoroughly cooked and steaming hot.

- ☉ Avoid ice and ice cream.

- ☉ Refuse soft fruits which cannot be peeled, like strawberries.

- ☉ Be wary of sea food; make sure it is properly cooked (*see* p.44).

- ☉ Obviously soiled cutlery, plates, cups and glasses should be avoided.

- ☉ Only drink safe water (*see* below, p.26).

If you are on an expedition or camping with friends do not allow anyone who is ill to do the cooking. It is especially tempting to expect an ailing expedition member to cook while recuperating in base camp, but this is the best way to ensure that the whole team goes down with the same tummy-bug. If you employ a cook when trekking, for example, make sure that he understands the basic principles of hygiene and check that he washes his hands with soap after defaecating and before preparing food. Short finger nails are easier to keep clean than long ones.

If you find yourself consuming something that you suspect is unsafe, do not think 'in for a penny, in for a pound'. The less you consume the less likely you are to become ill. Most pathogens need to invade you in considerable numbers to make you sick and in many cases, the number that get inside will determine how ill you become. Never assume that you are immune to all pathogens. The body is never able to build up an immunity to *Shigella* which causes bacillary dysentery, for example, so it is possible to suffer from dysentery several times a year; and in some unhealthy environments people do.

Which Foods are Unsafe?

Uncooked foods are unsafe. Food can be contaminated with human faeces while it is growing, during transport, cooking, storage or serving. 'Nightsoil' is a traditional fertilizer in Nepal and China, and in some parts of Peru and Bolivia, for example, irrigation water is at such a premium that farmers break into sewage mains to water their crops with untreated effluent. Even with all this contamination, though, thorough cooking will sterilize food.

+ boil it
+ peel it
+ cook it
+ shell it
...*or forget it!*

Salads are always a likely source of diarrhoea and lettuce can only be rendered safe by being vigorously boiled. If you pine for crunchy salads, stick to tomatoes, cucumber and similar smooth-skinned items which can be washed then, preferably, soaked in chlorine ('Milton' or dilute bleach) or iodine (12 drops/litre) for 30 minutes.

Ice is often made with contaminated water. It may then have travelled from the ice factory uncovered on the back of someone's bicycle and then been deposited at the roadside on the way to your drink. If you want a cold drink, pack ice around the outside of the glass or bottle, rather than putting suspect ice in the drink. Although ice cream is usually unsafe, the acidity of sorbets kills many bacteria (including *salmonella*) and so sorbets are much less risky.

Milk

Make sure that any milk you drink has been boiled, even if it claims to be pasteurized. I have found wood shavings and buffalo hair in 'pasteurized' milk. In the Indian subcontinent, milk is usually boiled, but check before drinking cold milk that it has been previously boiled. Unboiled milk (or the water used to adulterate it) can give you TB, brucellosis, Q-fever, typhoid and polio as well as diarrhoea. Powdered and tinned milk are safe as long as the water added to them is clean. Yoghurt is usually safe as long as the milk it was made with was boiled first. Goats' milk is not much safer than cow or buffalo milk; it can carry brucellosis and other disease organisms.

Eggs

A great deal of publicity has been given to the risk of acquiring *Salmonella* food poisoning from eggs in Britain. Third-world, free-range eggs are less likely to be infected, but clearly it is safest to eat them well cooked (especially if you are pregnant).

Flies

Flies can be infuriating guests at the dinner table and different people react to them in different ways. In some parts of the world flies are repelled by candles. Try lighting a candle to see if it dissuades them from sharing your food.

Those who are new to tropical travel are often revolted by flies feasting on their food, but with experience people tend to become increasingly blasé so that it is possible to grade the length of time an expatriate has lived abroad by his reaction when a fly lands in his beer. The new expatriate will throw the beer away and pour himself another. An expatriate who is well settled into life abroad will fish out the fly and continue drinking, but the truly hardened expatriate will drink the beer, eat the fly and extol the virtues of this readily available source of protein. 'The chicken is so stringy, you see!'

In Sindh, villagers know that flies carry disease but believe that each fly has a dirty wing and a clean wing. When a fly falls into their tea, they believe that they must ensure both wings are submerged so that the clean wing neutralizes the dirty one. I have no idea how this custom arose; it is not a practice that I would recommend.

One of the most important survival mechanisms travellers must develop is a sensible approach to keeping themselves healthy. Some people make themselves thoroughly miserable by trying to surround themselves with absolute sterility. My approach is to be careful but not to spend every waking moment contemplating disease risks. Whether or not you catch a disease depends in part on the quantity of pathogens which get inside your insides. A fly landing in your drink may theoretically infect you but, especially if you evict the fly promptly, the number of bugs it will introduce will be comparatively small and the risk of an infection unlikely. It makes sense to follow the example of the well-settled expatriate and evict the fly before drinking more.

Case History (Indonesia)

An expatriate family living in a smart suburb of Jakarta were meticulous about sterilizing food: they soaked all fruit, tomatoes and cucumbers in soap powder, then bleach, then rinsed in boiled water, dried and stored it in the refrigerator. They also boiled their water for a full 20 minutes before filtering it. All the food came from a very plush ultra-clean supermarket used almost entirely by expatriates. The family came down with typhoid. The disease was attributed to locally manufactured ice cream bought at the supermarket.

The family's measures to protect themselves from infection were mostly sound, even verging on the obsessional, yet they had not realized that ice cream—even ice cream from an apparently hygienic supermarket—is very risky stuff. Many tropical countries suffer frequent power cuts. Frozen food may have been allowed to thaw and then been refrozen, making it dangerous to consume. Several Jakarta residents said that they avoided buying frozen foods for a week or so after any long power cut; this may reduce the risk as long as the whole shopping community is not acting in the same way!

Case History (Nepal)

We went into a restaurant on the edge of Thamel, the tourist area of Kathmandu. The place lacked something: decor and clientele. It was stark but rather pretentiously laid out. Was there a good reason for lack of customers? I wondered whether we should eat somewhere else, but it was getting late so we ordered. I decided on a Mexican dish. The menu described that it would be served on a bed of lettuce and covered in sour cream. It sounded delicious but I said that I did not like lettuce. It arrived topped with chopped raw tomatoes, and was accompanied by a little dish of cold sour cream. I had expected the cream to be cooked in some kind of sauce, since although fresh cream in Nepal is said to be pasteurized, I am not convinced that the process would render the cream safe (people take short cuts and quality control is poor). Sadly, I rejected the cream but ate the rest including the tomatoes thinking that if they had been thoroughly washed and if they had not been cut up in the same place as the raw meat, they would be reasonably alright. (In fact I was hungry and thus justified eating what otherwise I might not).

It was not long before I realized I had to pay for ignoring my own rules. I awoke in the small hours with that feeling I was about to be very ill and then lay awake all night feeling awful. I did not start vomiting until the next morning by which time my body had very cleverly selected out the tomatoes for rejection. By lunch time I had drunk six glasses of hot lemon (which I had allowed to cool a little and to which I had added a pinch of salt and plenty of sugar) and a Coke to which I had added a pinch of salt. I felt a lot better. That evening I was nibbling a few crackers with my hot lemons and was fine again by the following morning, although I stuck to only a light plain diet for the rest of the day.

Diarrhoea from Dirty Water

The vast majority of diarrhoea episodes come from contaminated food and poor food hygiene, but water is sometimes so heavily contaminated that drinking it untreated is likely to make you ill. The biggest risks are probably in towns and cities with intermittent piped water supplies. Sometimes water is cleaner at source than it is after it has been treated and delivered to the taps. Even though it is not the main cause of diarrhoea, drinking dirty water is risky and it is unnecessary. It is easy to make your water safe.

Safe Drinking Water

Ideally, drinking water should be brought to a vigorous rolling boil and kept there for a full minute; at high altitude (e.g. 5800m/19,000ft where water boils at 178°F) water should be boiled for 5 minutes. Pressure cookers reduce boiling times and save on fuel. At sea level, merely bringing water to the boil makes it safe enough for most purposes. Boiled water tastes flat because the dissolved gases have been driven out, but if it is left standing for several hours in a partly filled covered container, or shaken vigorously for a minute in a container with an air gap, the taste improves. Bottled water (which is often just treated tap water) is usually safe if the seal is in tact, although it is expensive and can taste of plastic. Boiled water is much safer than water treated with iodine. Iodine is safer than using water sterilization tablets or other forms of chlorine. Iodine comes in several forms but produces drinkable water in 10 minutes. If the water is very cloudy or cold either double the iodine concentration or leave to stand for 20 minutes. Add 4 drops of 2% tincture of iodine to a litre of water, shake and leave to stand for 10 minutes. Iodine crystals may be better for longer term travellers. Make a saturated solution of iodine by roughly quarter-filling a 20ml screw-topped bottle with iodine crystals (but note that this form of iodine eats through plastic). Top up with any water. Shake for a few seconds (the crystals settle and nothing appears to disolve) and leave for at least half an hour. Shake again. Pour about 10ml of the solution (but not the crystals) into a 1 litre bottle; shake and leave for 10 minutes. Top up the 20ml bottle ready for the next time it is needed. This should make up to 1000 litres. If you can find a 20ml bottle with volume marks on the side, it makes estimating the 10ml volume easy.

It is safe to use iodine for 6 months continuously unless possibly you have a thyroid problem or are pregnant, or are treating water for children under 16 years. But note that consuming a whole 30ml/1oz bottle of concentrated iodine at once or swallowing iodine crystals will do you no good.

Cryptosporidium and amoebae survive in chlorine and *Cyclospora* is resistant to both iodine and chlorine. This recently discovered illness is most common during the monsoon in Nepal and only seems to be a problem between May and

November there. During this season, water should be boiled, since chemical sterilization methods are inadequate. *Cyclospora* is caused by pathogens which resemble blue-green algae. Not surprisingly, doctors are so far stumped on how to eradicate something which is more likely to succumb to weed-killer than antibiotics, but *co-trimoxazole* (e.g. Bactrim or Septrin) may help. *Cyclospora* causes diarrhoea which lasts for 6 to 12 weeks. It is now turning up in Sri Lanka, Pakistan, India, Indonesia, southeast China, Peru and Bolivia.

If you need water to be completely sterile (for example for feeding small infants) ask the restaurant or hotel for boiling water and fill a thermos flask with it; the water will be sterile in 15 minutes. Water purification devices are described below.

Other Safe Drinks

When travelling in the Indian subcontinent lately, I have abandoned drinking plain water altogether, but drink tea, coffee or hot lemon. In Indonesia, most eating houses offer *air putih* (literally white water: boiled water which is often served warm, but beware of added ice). In Madagascar *ranovola* (water boiled with a little burnt rice) is a tasty and safe accompaniment to food and camomile tea (*manzanilla* in South America) is also excellent.

Filters and Water Purification Units

Ceramic water filters designed for use in the kitchen are readily available in the Indian subcontinent, (but not in Indonesia) and these allow expatriates to organize a ready supply of safe water. The filter removes sediment and some larger 'germs'. Check the filter candles regularly for cracks and clean the filter by scrubbing, then boil them for 20 minutes once a week, otherwise you may introduce more bugs than were in the original water supply. Ideally you should filter the tap water first, boil it in a large covered saucepan, then allow it to cool a little before pouring into bottles for refrigeration. In fact most expatriates boil and then filter; the danger here is that if the filter is contaminated, pathogens may be introduced during the filtering process.

Filtered water is not necessarily safe water. Hotels and restaurants in Asia commonly advertise that their drinking water is filtered which usually means that is has only been passed through a large-pore porcelain filter. Even if these filter candles are cleaned regularly and they are not cracked, they are not capable of removing all diarrhoea-causing organisms. There are a variety of sophisticated portable filters and water purification devices designed for travellers. The newer pump-action devices are a huge improvement on the original, heavy, slow gravity filter versions, but they are all rather expensive. Many of the bacteriological filters work well, but check that they remove viruses as well as bacteria. In some situations viruses cause more than half of the cases of diarrhoea and since hepatitis viruses can also be present in water, filters which do not remove viruses do not render it completely safe, unless they also include a form of chemical sterilization. PUR filters with iodine matrixes do seem to produce completely safe water, but these range in price from £50 to £180 so you have to pay for truly sterile water. Nomad and Cotswold (*see* **Useful Addresses**, p.212) stock a range of purification devices.

Why Diarrhoea Prevention with Medicines is Unnecessary

Taking medicines to prevent diarrhoea can create more problems than it solves. Unpleasant and protracted diarrhoea can actually be caused by taking antibiotics which wipe out the friendly bacteria inhabiting the bowel. Some doctors feel that very short-term prevention of diarrhoea with an antibiotic is occasionally justified where it is essential that someone is fit for some crucial meeting.

The US Navy is particularly active in researching ways to avoid travellers' diarrhoea since they have experienced debilitating outbreaks which, most recently, stopped marines going into battle during the Gulf War. Interestingly even they (who are perhaps less interested in the long-term health of their servicemen than civilian doctors) do not recommend prevention with antibiotics, even on short missions.

The best protection against diarrhoea in infants is breast feeding so if you plan to travel with small children try to ensure that they are breast fed rather than being offered formula milk from a bottle. Ideally expatriate children should not be weaned off the breast until the age of a year. Local children are often breast fed for 2 or 3 years and this is an excellent and healthy practice.

Treatment of Diarrhoea

Diarrhoea is a good thing. It is the natural process of expelling the poisons which cause disease. By stopping this process, recovery may be slowed. My dislike of 'blocking' medicines puts me at odds with some other doctors, but my justifications are given on p.32. A healthy adult is unlikely to come to any great harm from travellers' diarrhoea. Starvation and clear fluids will settle the symptoms of simple travellers' diarrhoea quickly enough for you to continue working. In those very few travellers who become especially ill, it is adequate fluid replacement that saves life not antibiotics or anti-diarrhoeal medicines. Passing blood and/or mucus and/or having a fever with diarrhoea probably means you have dysentery, which will require treatment in addition to fluid replacement; *see* below.

Replacing Lost Fluids

The normal processes of food and fluid absorption are upset in diarrhoea, yet simple mixtures of sugar, salt and water continue to be well absorbed by the stomach and upper intestine. Indeed their absorption is even more efficient than plain water. Complex carbohydrates (in the form of salty crackers, dry bread, plain rice or boiled potatoes) also aid absorption of the fluids you need to replace those that are pouring out of your bottom end. The fastest road back to health, then, is to stop eating normal meals for 24–36 hours, take lots of clear fluids. Avoid milk and alcohol. If you do not feel like eating, do not eat.

Good drinks to take are clear soups, young coconut, drinks made from Marmite, Bovril or stock cubes, herbal infusions, Malagasy *ranovola*, hot lemon, lemon tea and fizzy drinks (like Coke or Fanta) which have been allowed to go flat; weak black tea and coffee may also be taken but do not drink too many, since these make you pass more urine. Combinations of sugar and salt are absorbed best so add a little salt to sweet drinks or sugar to savoury drinks. Alternatively drink oral rehydration salts (ORS). These are available in most countries and marketed as *Dioralyte*, *Rehidrat*, *Rapolyte*, *Gluco-lyte* and *Electrolade* in the UK, as *Oralit* in Indonesia and *Jeevan Jal* (literally water of life) in Nepal. It is safest to use ORS (rather than home-made solutions) for children, the very old, adults with long-standing medical problems and also anyone with very profuse (12 times a day) diarrhoea. Most travellers will be safe making and drinking their own sugar and salt solution (*see* below).

Children with Diarrhoea

When children have diarrhoea, dehydration is even more of a danger. Like adults, they should be encouraged to drink each time they open their bowels; half a glass of fluid is enough for small children. Oral rehydration sachets mixed with boiled and cooled water are the safest remedy. Children can get into trouble with the balance of salts in their blood especially if they have profuse diarrhoea. Some brands of commercial ORS taste awful, though, so it is often more realistic to offer flat Coke with a pinch of salt in it. Otherwise offer home-made solutions flavoured with Ribena or some other tempting cocktail; lemon or orange squash or cordials, although not strictly clear fluids, are also suitable. Getting children to drink is the crucial issue.

Important Note for Parents

Infants and very small children have died from being given too much salt, so if in doubt give too little salt or no salt at all. Sugar or glucose and water alone make an acceptable rehydration solution. Small children should continue to be breast fed, although it may be wise to reduce the amount of cows' milk offered, and solid foods should be given as usual.

Home-made Oral Rehydration Solutions (ORS)

Two heaped teaspoons of glucose (or sugar) and a three-finger pinch (less than a quarter of a teaspoon) of salt should be mixed in a glass of boiled cooled water or 8 level tablespoons of sugar and a level teaspoonful of salt in a litre. Otherwise use a sugar and salt measuring spoon (which may be bought from TALC, p.213, or British Airways Travel Clinics, p.211).

The solution you make should taste no more salty than tears. If glucose is not available, good substitutes are raw sugar or molasses (*ghur* in Hindi/Urdu); these are rich in potassium which is lost from the body during diarrhoea and vomiting. Otherwise use palm syrup or honey. Adding a little fresh lemon, lime or orange juice improves the taste and also adds useful potassium to the solution.

How Much Do You Need To Drink?

People with diarrhoea need to drink a great deal otherwise they become dehydrated. Dehydration makes diarrhoea sufferers feel really awful. Most people make the mistake of not drinking enough. To maintain fluid balance, a healthy person of normal build who is not eating needs to drink about three litres a day. Fluid requirements are greater in hot climates, at altitude, when in high winds or travelling in cars with the windows open or on a motorbike, or when breast feeding. If you are ill with diarrhoea or a fever you need even more fluids. Drink two glassfuls of fluids each time the bowels are opened. Drink more if you are thirsty. Those who are vomiting can still absorb fluids, but they will need to drink slowly, and take fluid in sips.

One symptom of being depleted of fluid is to feel dizzy (or you may even faint) when getting out of bed or a chair. Drink more, and in the meantime move more slowly and sit for a minute with your legs over the side of the bed before rising. If you are passing only a scant amount of dark-coloured urine you should also drink more.

The Gastro-Colic Reflex

Very hot or very cold drinks and foods tend to provoke a reflex bowel action and abdominal pain. This gastro-colic reflex can be useful if you are constipated; a hot drink first thing in the morning will often encourage a bowel action. However, if you have diarrhoea with a lot of abdominal crampy pains take only tepid food and drink to avoid making your bowel even more active. Cramps are more likely if you are continuing to eat. Try to stick to a minimal, fat-free diet.

Some people get unpleasant irritable bowel symptoms and crampy abdominal pain during or just after an attack of diarrhoea. *Hyoscine* (e.g. Buscopan) two 10mg tablets when needed (up to eight in a day) or *mebeverine* (e.g. Colofac) one three times daily or peppermint oil (e.g. Colpermin) 1–2 capsules three times daily can help.

What to Eat When Diarrhoea Strikes

Drink plenty, but if you have no appetite, eat nothing. Otherwise eat only a little light food; solid greasy foods are not well tolerated and can cause colicky abdominal pains as the bowel tries to expel them. Bananas help stop diarrhoea and also contain plenty of potassium which is lost in diarrhoea. Yoghurt can help settle the stomach by replacing diarrhoea-causing bacteria with friendly ones. Dry biscuits or bread can be comforting to an aching empty stomach. Continue to feed children who have diarrhoea.

Case History (Peru)

A phone call announced 'My colleague looks awful, feeling dizzy, can hardly get out of bed, terrible diarrhoea, splitting headache. Could it be cholera? There was a cholera epidemic in the country wasn't there? Should he fly home?' I asked a few questions. Most of this chap's symptoms seemed to be due to fluid loss and fear that he was desperately ill since he did indeed feel so awful. Why else could he hardly stand up? They had some rehydration salts (ORS) in the house and I told him that he needed to drink a lot to replace the diarrhoeal losses. 'See if you can drink at least a litre of clear fluids in the next hour; slow the drinking rate if you feel nauseated.'

An hour and a half later I called round to find a stocky man in his late twenties looking extremely sorry for himself. I estimated that he had lost 5 per cent of his body fluids—he was quite markedly dehydrated. 'How are you getting on with the drinking?'

'Well the fresh orange juice gives me stomach ache, but I have drunk half a glassful.' I explained that since a lot of fluid comes from food and he had not eaten all day he needed to drink 3 litres; in addition I estimated from his state of dehydration that he had lost 1.5 litres to a fairly dramatic diarrhoea so he needed to replace 4.5 litres, plus an additional two glassfuls every time he opened his bowels again. He was surprised at the volume, but was then convinced enough to settle down to some more enthusiastic drinking. (Diluting the orange drink made it considerably more tolerable to his aching belly and he made some glucose and salt solution to make up the volume this time. He could not stomach the ORS.) Two hours later he phoned to say the headache and dizziness had gone and he felt much better.

Case History (Nepal)

Two Nepalis supported a middle-aged American man on a horse. They all stopped at the same teashop as me and so I offered help. The American reported a sleepless night disturbed by diarrhoea, combined with the exhaustion of trekking the Annapurna circuit.

'You are probably quite dehydrated; that makes you feel awful. You need to drink three litres a day to keep your body's fluids topped up—as well as replace all that you have lost to diarrhoea and breathing hard at altitude,' I said.

'I drank a quart this morning and also one of those rehydration salt packets so I'm not dehydrated.' He ordered a Coke and I suggested adding a pinch of salt to it. 'No I got all the salts I need from that packet.' I explained that the salt would help him absorb the water in the Coke but he did not want my advice and he struggled on. This poor chap suffered unnecessarily. He was dehydrated and needed to drink a lot more. He also misunderstood the role of the rehydration packets. They are not a once-only medicine, but a vehicle for fluid transport into the body. They also give a glucose-fired burst of energy which makes you feel really good and provides the enthusiasm for some serious (non-alcoholic) drinking.

When to Use Medicines to Treat Diarrhoea

Blockers

'Blocking' medicines such as Imodium, Lomotil and *codeine phosphate* are not the cure for diarrhoea that they may appear. Blockers work by paralysing the bowel and so trap noxious bugs and poisons within the body, when what is needed is to expel them as fast as possible. Nor do blockers effectively stop the loss of vital fluids from the parts of the body which need them. Instead these fluids become pooled in inaccessible pockets. Many people remain convinced that these drugs are useful and effective, but although they are convenient, they slow recovery. Blockers may be useful if you cannot postpone a bus journey for 24 hours, but they tend to make sufferers feel ill for longer.

It is positively dangerous to give blockers to children and no one with dysentery (diarrhoea with fever and the passing of blood and/or slime) should use them.

Enterovioform was banned as a dangerous drug in Britain years ago, but it is still available in some countries. It should be avoided.

Antibiotics

Travellers' diarrhoea in British soldiers in Belize was successfully treated with a single 500mg dose of the antibiotic *ciprofloxacin*. The time the diarrhoea lasted was reduced by the treatment from an average of 50 hours (untreated/no anti-biotic) to an average of 21 hours. The subjects were fit young men.

Diarrhoea is generally very short lived and so careful consideration should be given to whether it should be treated with an antibiotic—even with a single dose. *Ciprofloxacin* has some side effects. The most worrying is that it can cause major problems in people who are dehydrated; a problem which is common in those suffering from diarrhoea in hot climates. If you want to take *ciprofloxacin*, you should (as a precaution) drink a litre of clear fluids half an hour before taking it and ensure that you drink at least a further two litres within the next 8 hours. If you have very profuse diarrhoea you need to drink *in addition to this* two glasses of fluid every time you open your bowels. *Ciprofloxacin* should not be taken by children or growing adolescents, in pregnancy, and probably not by epileptics or people with other neurological problems. Reported side effects of courses of treatment with *ciprofloxacin* include diarrhoea and vomiting. It also commonly causes confusion and disorientation in the elderly.

Research published in 1993 suggests that a new drug, *zaldarine maleate*, reduces the release of water and body salts which happens during diarrhoea. This may become a useful treatment to control the symptoms of travellers' diarrhoea. Further research on this medicine will be needed before it can be prescribed.

Treatment of Diarrhoea with Fever, Bloody Diarrhoea and Dysentery

If diarrhoea is accompanied by fever and/or blood in the faeces, rehydration is still an important part of treatment, but it would be reasonable to take an antibiotic as well. Whether, for example, you take one dose of *ciprofloxacin* or a one-week course should be decided by the severity of your symptoms.

Ciprofloxacin 500mg twice daily for 3 days is an effective treatment for severe bloody diarrhoea. As is *norfloxacin* (which carries the same cautions as *ciprofloxacin*) 400mg twice daily for 3 days. *Nalidixic acid* (1g four times daily for 7 days), is particularly effective for travellers' diarrhoea acquired in Nepal. The World Health Organization (WHO) recommends treating bloody diarrhoea with a 5-day course of *cotrimoxazole*; the adult dose is 960mg twice daily. The advantages and disadvantages of taking antibiotics are discussed on p.190.

Even if you have treated yourself with antibiotics, it may be wise to consult a doctor. If symptoms do not seem to be settling, if you have persistent abdominal pain, the diarrhoea becomes bloody or a fever begins (probable dysentery), confusion sets in, or the diarrhoea goes on for more than a week, seek medical help.

Diarrhoea that Goes On and On

Diarrhoea which goes on for more than 4–5 days should be treated; if no doctor is available try one of the antibiotics suggested above. Occasionally diarrhoea can persist for 2 months or more and this is often labelled tropical sprue. Sufferers tend to lose a lot of weight. It is not a very well-understood disease but it often responds to *tetracycline* (250mg four times daily) and folic acid (15mg daily for a month). Experiment to see whether avoiding milk and foods containing milk, fatty or oily foods, alcohol and spicy foods help reduce the symptoms. Persistent diarrhoea often gets better when you get home, even without treatment.

Nearly all diarrhoea in travellers is due to bacteria and viruses, but a tiny minority is due to some other cause. Protracted diarrhoea could be the start of another, non-tropical problem which will need proper medical assessment.

Summary

A Travellers' diarrhoea usually comes from eating contaminated food.
O Eat piping hot, thoroughly cooked food.
Avoid salads and other raw foods; do not take ice or ice cream.

A It is dehydration which makes you feel bad when you have diarrhoea.
O Drink at least three litres of clear fluids a day.
Drink in sips if you are vomiting or nauseated.

A Headache and dizziness are symptoms of dehydration.
O Try drinking more if you have these problems. The body's thirst mechanisms are poor at encouraging you to drink enough.

O Starvation or taking a very light, plain, diet will usually cure the abdominal cramps of travellers' diarrhoea and will reduce nausea too.
O Avoid fatty and oily foods (e.g. cheese, milk, nuts and fried foods) if your stomach is upset.

A Taking very hot or very cold drinks or food will often stimulate a reflex bowel action (the gastro-colic reflex) which can be accompanied by abdominal pain.
O If this is a problem, allow your hot food and drink to cool down; do not put ice in drinks.

O If you have diarrhoea and have no appetite, listen to your body and realize that it may be telling you it is best not to eat.

O In the absence of medical advice, the only safe remedy for childhood diarrhoea is oral rehydration solution.

O Babies who travel abroad should be breast fed. Breast feeding protects against diarrhoea and should be continued throughout any attack.

O If you use iodine crystals to sterilize water, you need to pack one 20ml screw top, non-plastic bottle, a 10ml measure (e.g. a syringe) and a one litre water bottle.

A Diet of Worms?

Worms are more alarming than dangerous. The most common is the roundworm *Ascaris lumbricoides*; it looks like a large earthworm and is about 30cm long. They rarely cause problems unless they are present in very large numbers (100 or more), and since travellers seldom acquire more than a couple, infestations are generally no trouble. They may cause vague abdominal symptoms, but most people are unaware of the worms' presence until one which has died of old age emerges a year or so after it stowed away.

Where are Worms a Problem?

Worms infest people wherever disposal of faeces is inadequate. Although they are common in the tropics, they are also found in plenty of non-tropical countries.

Hookworm occurs throughout the moist, hot parts of the world. Roundworms are especially hardy parasites and can survive the particularly harsh freeze-drying of high cold deserts like those in Tibet. They are also prevalent in nearly all unhygienic temperate environments. *Trichinella* and tapeworms exist wherever cattle or pigs can eat fodder contaminated with human excreta. Threadworms are universal. Other worms, including a selection of unpleasant flukes, are acquired from eating raw or lightly cooked fish and shellfish or water plants like watercress which have been contaminated with excrement.

First Catch Your Worm

Roundworms and sometimes hookworms and tapeworms are acquired from contaminated food via some of the same transmission mechanisms as diarrhoeal diseases (*see* p.22). Worm life cycles, though, are more complex than the diarrhoeal diseases, since roundworms and hookworm cannot be passed directly from person to person. Worm eggs need a period of maturation in soil before they can infect people. Tapeworm and trichinella usually need to pass through an intermediate animal host before they can infect man. Threadworms can be transmitted directly from hand to mouth—they are most common among people who live in close contact with children. These, and some tapeworms, are the only worms which are spread directly from one person to another.

Although there are differences in the ways each type of worm is acquired, they (with the exception of hookworm) can be avoided with good food hygiene. All of them are destroyed in food by thorough cooking. Hookworm is avoided by wearing shoes.

What Type of Worm?

There are a great variety to choose from, but those described below illustrate most of the problems.

Roundworm

Roundworms are common; in the developing tropics and sub-tropics they inhabit 80–90 per cent of children. Passing a roundworm can be a thoroughly horrible experience, but it does not necessarily mean that you need treatment. In many cases the worm you pass is a lonely hermit and so no treatment is necessary. It is dangerous to take some worm tablets if you are pregnant and some treatments are unsafe in children under the age of 2 years, so be careful if you decide to treat yourself. Waiting to take treatment is unlikely to do any harm and is a safe option if you are pregnant.

Hookworm

Hookworm can be acquired through contaminated food. The worms are also able to penetrate the skin. They are usually picked up by walking barefoot in damp shady places where people have defecated; the pollution need not be obvious. Sunshine and dryness kill hookworm eggs so it is not a disease of open deserts. Wearing shoes in likely hookworm habitats stops the worms penetrating the skin. Short-term travellers need not worry about them, since any hookworm colonists will die out on returning to a temperate climate. I would not bother to get them treated.

The only group of travellers who are likely to suffer significantly from hookworm are expatriate children. They like playing barefoot and are probably open to repeated infestations for long enough to acquire a largish resident population. If worms are present in sufficient numbers (as they so often are in local children) they cause leaking of blood from the gut and eventually anaemia. When treatment is necessary, worm tablets cure infestations. It is better to prevent infestations by discouraging children from playing barefoot.

Threadworm

These are tiny and cause intense anal itching especially at night. They are a hazard of family life (both at home and abroad) since they are usually acquired from children and are readily transmitted between family members. Expatriates need to treat each member of the household.

Treating Threadworm

You will probably want to treat threadworm because they cause such intolerable itching. *Piperazine* (Antepar, Pripsen in UK; Antepar, Vermizine in US) is a good safe medicine to use, but it must be given as a 7-day course. Cure rates are improved if a second course is given after a week. *Mebendazole* (Vermox, Ovex in UK; Vermox, Wormin in US) given as a single 100mg dose, repeated 2–3 weeks later, is a better medicine but it must not be given in pregnancy (so it would be inadvisable for expatriates to treat female staff members) nor to children under 2 years of age. Personal hygiene must be scrupulous while the infestation is present. Hands must be washed and nails scrubbed with a nail brush before meals and after each visit to the toilet. Finger nails must be kept short. Otherwise those who are infected will reinfect themselves and they may also infect others.

Tapeworms, Trichinella and Toxoplasma

Tapeworm segments look like flat white pieces of ribbon in the stools which have an alarming ability to crawl about. Tapeworm infestation can be dangerous since cysts occasionally settle in the brain. They come from inadequately cooked pork or beef. Avoid infestation by eating thoroughly cooked meat; reject rare steaks. Because the pork tapeworm, *Taenium solium*, can also be acquired from eating foods contaminated with human excreta, lettuce if irrigated with human sewage (as it may be in Bolivia, Peru, Nepal and many other places) can be a source of infestation. Cystocercosis occurs when cysts settle in the brain, eyes or other parts of the body. It is a problem well worth avoiding. Seek medical advice if you think you are infected.

Trichinella worms are also acquired from eating inadequately cooked pork. Like tapeworms, these are by no means confined to the tropics. If you eat under-cooked wild boar in the Arctic you can become infested with *Trichinella.*

Toxoplasma (not a worm but a protozoan parasite) is also acquired from eating under-cooked meat, especially pork and lamb. It may also be contracted by contact with cat faeces. Toxoplasma is a relatively unimportant infection unless it is caught for the first time during pregnancy when it can cause a lot of harm to the foetus. It is quite a common problem, even in Europe, so take care if you are pregnant or trying to conceive. Avoid rare meat and wash your hands after contact with cats.

Case History (Bolivia)

Sara was 20 and teaching English for a year in La Paz. She often enjoyed eating out and had a particular liking for salads including lettuce; she was careful to avoid drinking tap water. Although usually very fit and well she suddenly started suffering from fainting fits. She also noticed that she had developed numerous little lumps under her skin. There was another inexplicable symptom too: she experienced shadows passing before one eye. A friend noticed that during one of Sara's 'faints' she was twitching slightly. They realized that this was something more serious than a faint and went to hospital for investigations.

Tests showed that she had cystocercosis: cysts of the pork tapeworm, *Taenium solium*, holed up in her brain, eyes and under her skin. She responded quickly to treatment in hospital and is now completely well.

She later discovered that much of the lettuce which is sold in La Paz is irrigated with water contaminated with the city's effluent.

Guinea Worm (Dracunculiasis)

Guinea worm (or Medina worm) is caught by swallowing 1–2mm long freshwater 'fleas' so drinking boiled or strained water will protect you. It is an unpleasant affliction but it is rapidly nearing extinction throughout much of its range: equatorial Africa, eastern India, Pakistan, southwest Saudi Arabia and southern Iraq. Do not worry about it.

Giardia

Giardia are elegant, heart-shaped, microscopic creatures which swim around in the contents of the small intestine propelled by a pair of splendid whiskers. A lot of travellers self-diagnose *Giardia* when they get an upset stomach which seems to be the source of a lot of sulphurous gas emerging as foul-smelling belches and odiferous farts. The gas causes abdominal distension too and there is often diarrhoea. These are indeed symptoms of giardiasis, but other infections also cause them. Before rushing to swallow a course of *metronidazole* tablets (e.g. Flagyl), therefore, try 24 hours on clear fluids and a bland, fat-free diet (*see* p.28); untreated giardiasis will do little harm except make you an unwelcome guest and cause some loss of weight. One symptom that is fairly specific to giardiasis is passing stools which stink and are difficult to flush away because they float (there are other causes of producing recalcitrant, foul-smelling stools but these are quite uncommon in travellers).

The treatment for giardiasis is *metronidazole* (e.g. Flagyl) 2g (e.g. 5x400mg) daily for 3 days. Do not drink alcohol with Flagyl or you will feel ill.

As with other intestinal parasites, you need three negative stool checks each taken several days apart before you can be sure you are not infected. However, if you feel well, do not bother with the tests.

Feeling Queasy

Episodes of nausea, poor appetite and feeling vaguely unwell are common in the tropics. These symptoms are often due to a mild assault by diarrhoea-causing pathogens; 24 hours starvation or eating a minimal and bland diet will help settle the problem.

Proguanil (Paludrine) antimalarial tablets also cause nausea if taken on an empty stomach so take them after a meal.

Constipation

Constipation is a common problem in the tropics since it can be difficult to arrange a diet high enough in fibre. Wholemeal flour is rarely available in the developing world, but local coarse wheat flour (known as *atta* in the Indian subcontinent) which is used to make chapattis is wholemeal and I have made very good bread with it. Dehydration and immobility make constipation worse (going for a run often gets things moving). Many pain-killing medicines cause constipation. Bananas and eggs exacerbate constipation but other fruits help relieve it.

An uncomfortable level of constipation can be caused by anti-diarrhoea preparations, especially Paregoric. Even without taking 'blockers' it is quite common for travellers to oscillate between having diarrhoea and constipation. I first came across *ispaghula husk* in India 18 years ago while looking for something to soothe my intestines as they lurched from diarrhoea to constipation during my first tropical trip. It is called flea seed husk or *saat ispagol* in India and it attracted my attention because it claimed to cure both constipation and diarrhoea. Strangely, it worked. Later this South American cure arrived on the list of medicines that British GPs can prescribe and it is indeed a useful regulator. Although if you are profoundly constipated it will take some days and several doses to have a useful effect. Trade names for the preparation in the UK are Fybogel and Regulan.

If eating more fruit and increasing the amount you drink does not get the bowels moving, and you cannot get bran or *saat ispagol*, then take *lactulose* syrup 15ml with breakfast. This syrup is a gentle, natural laxative and takes a day or two to work. In severe constipation you can take twice this dose twice a day (i.e. 60ml/day) but build up the dose gradually or you may be caught short somewhere far from a toilet. Lactulose syrup is rather bulky and heavy and not an ideal medicine for backpackers, but if constipation is really getting you down you may wish to stop and rest for a few days. If you decide to use bran or *ispaghula husk* or *lactulose* to cure constipation, you also need to increase the amount you drink because they both act by drawing water into the bowel to loosen and soften the stool.

Senna is a more powerful stimulant laxative, but is not so good at 'retraining' the bowel back into a normal pattern. Once you have started to re-establish a normal pattern try to ensure that you go to the toilet whenever the urge strikes (usually after food or hot drinks). Travellers may find this difficult since facilities are not always available when needed and the constipating effects of dehydration are exacerbated by 'hanging on' too long.

Piles

Haemorrhoids or piles sometimes begin during tropical travel. Mountaineers sometimes get them, perhaps because of the heavy packs that they carry combined with the effect of exercising and breathing hard at altitude. Piles are small bulges in the lining of the rectum. Some of them hang out through the anus like the fleshy end of a little finger. Most of them itch and some bleed. They are harmless, but can be very painful, or at least uncomfortable. Treatment while travelling can be difficult. Keep them clean (their awkward shape and position means that they are easily soiled with stool and this makes them even more itchy and uncomfortable), keep them lubricated with some bland cream (e.g. Anusol) and try to ease them back inside the rectum. If they are very painful you will need to rest (lying on your side or with buttocks uppermost, raised above the abdomen, propping the bottom up on a pillow). Warm baths or cold compresses (crushed ice in a condom) may help.

Piles can be caused by anything which increases the pressure within the abdomen. A common factor in tropical piles is constipation so attention to that problem should help to reduce them. Drink plenty of fluids, eat lots of fruit, avoid constipating food (like eggs and bananas) and take some regular exercise. Obesity can also bring piles on or make them worse, so keeping slim and fit is advisable. Spending a long time reading on the toilet is also said to encourage piles.

Occasionally a small blood vessel can leak into a pile so that it becomes intensely painful and looks purple. Purple piles which are more than 2cm in diameter need to be lanced with a scalpel (perhaps surprisingly, it brings great relief) and smaller ones which are very painful may also be lanced. If there is no-one around capable of doing this, it will take some time (more than a week) for the pain to subside completely, but no long-term damage will occur.

Abdominal Pain

Pains in the abdomen frequently accompany diarrhoea, but they are often relieved by passing wind or a motion. If diarrhoea is the cause, the pain usually comes in waves. If pain is severe, constant, of sudden onset, worsens rapidly, is associated with a high fever, long lasting (more than 4 hours) or not accompanied by diarrhoea, it may be a sign of serious disease and a doctor should be consulted.

Appendicitis often starts as a central, umbilical pain which moves to the right lower corner of the abdomen and settles there. Diarrhoea and constipation can both cause spasms of pain in the lower left corner of the abdomen. A competent medical opinion should sort out the trivial from the serious.

Stomach or duodenal ulcers tend to cause a gnawing pain between the tummy button and the bottom of the rib cage, in the pit of the stomach. If simple antacids do not give relief, *ranitidine* or *cimetidine* should help. When you return home consult your doctor since some ulcer sufferers benefit from a combination of medicines to eradicate the bacteria which cause recurrent ulcers. New or persistent symptoms are always worth a consultation.

Heart Burn and Indigestion

A burning pain at the bottom of the rib cage should respond to antacids (for example, simple *magnesium trisilicate*, e.g. Gaviscon in the UK and e.g. Amphojel, Maalox, Tums and Magalan in the US); milk or yoghurt is sometimes settling too. Reducing the amount of alcohol drunk and cigarettes smoked usually helps. Try *ranitidine* or *cimetidine* if antacids do not work.

Stomach acid is the body's first line of defence against pathogens that you have swallowed; taking antacids will reduce stomach acid and so make you more prone to diarrhoeal disease. There is no evidence (nor has there been any systematic research yet) to suggest that *ranitidine*, *cimetidine* or related drugs increase the susceptibility to intestinal or other infections.

Vomiting Blood

Vomited blood can look like coffee grounds; it is a serious symptom which needs prompt medical attention. If the blood has been swallowed after a nose bleed, however, this need cause no concern and no treatment is required.

Problems from Bad Food

The term food poisoning usually suggests the contamination of food with the bacteria or viruses which cause diarrhoea and vomiting; such travellers' tummy problems are covered on p.20. Other 'germs' can also reach you through bad food. An outbreak of streptococcal tonsillitis, for example, was traced to poorly prepared food. In addition to bacterial food poisoning, it is also possible to become ill by consuming foods containing chemical poisons.

Chemical Food Poisoning

There is such a range of possible chemical poisons which can contaminate food that it is impossible to mention them all. However, since most naturally occurring food toxins are well recognized wherever they are consumed, local culinary habits have evolved to deal with them.

Cassava

Tapioca is made from the cassava tuber; it is also called manioc. In its raw form it contains sufficient cyanide to kill, but local methods of preparation (boiling, soaking, washing in running water and pounding) reduce the amount of cyanide to a non-toxic level. Do not prepare cassava yourself but get a local person to cook it for you. It is only a risky food during disasters or famine when there is insufficient time or fuel for traditional methods of preparation.

Strychnine Fruits

In Madagascar, people eat wood-encased, cricket-ball-sized fruits of *Strychnos* trees. Although they are very tasty, eating too many induces a headache. A tree from the same genus, *Strychnos nux-vomica*, is the source of strychnine so perhaps the headache is a symptom of mild intoxication. Interestingly, overindulgence in the Sri Lankan 'wood apple' (which looks superficially similar to *Strychnos*) also induces a headache and I wonder whether it also contains some tiny amount of toxin.

Local Alcohol

A more predictable poison is alcohol. Even in its purest, Highland Malt form, it is toxic, but when its origin is some still in a shack somewhere, it is likely to contain additional poisons. Be ready to face the consequences if you drink too much. Beware of spirits; distilled drinks can contain extremely dangerous toxic methanol which can cause permanent blindness. Undistilled drinks of lower alcoholic content (less than 40 per cent) are unsafe if (as they usually are) they are prepared with dirty water (e.g. Tibetan *chang*). An exception is Nepali *toongba*, where boiling water is poured over fermented millet, but make sure that the water is boiling and the pot pre-heated.

Notes on sensible levels of alcohol consumption are given on p.202.

Pesticides

Expatriates who live abroad for years increasingly worry about the profligate use of pesticides on crops. In some regions farmers spray fruit and vegetables with pesticides just before sending them to market as this makes them look shiny and attractive. There are large numbers of people who suffer from pesticide poisoning (about 40,000 people die and a million are made ill or permanently disabled annually) but these casualties are the result of unsafe crop-spraying techniques or suicide attempts. I have not heard of any significant poisoning of expatriates or travellers through foods contaminated with pesticides. Even so, it is probably sensible to peel or thoroughly wash any fruit or vegetables in order to reduce the amount of harmful chemicals ingested, especially if you live abroad long term.

Food for Free

It can be tempting, especially when camping in a remote place, to go foraging for free foods such as fungi, berries and salad stuffs. Take great care what you eat when travelling since some plants which are highly poisonous may resemble familiar edible plants at home; ask local advice. There is a plant, for example, which provides succulent berries to foragers in Madagascar and looks almost identical to European deadly nightshade (*Atropa belladonna*). Consequently there are numerous hospital admissions and some deaths in Malagasy people who have consumed deadly nightshade berries in France.

Avoid eating red or brightly coloured fruits and berries unless you know them to be harmless. Never eat anything which looks like a tomato (unless you know it is one) even if it smells pleasant. Do not eat roots, fruits or vegetables with a bitter, stinging or otherwise disagreeable taste. Try them with the tip of your tongue if in doubt. Consuming wild watercress in many geographical regions carries a risk of liver fluke infestation. Seaweeds are all edible as long as you are not in a highly polluted area. The tastiest kinds are generally the pink, purple, reddish or green types.

'Sea-sickness': Diseases from Seafood

Shellfish

Shellfish are efficient concentrators of faecal bacteria so should only be eaten if you can be sure that they were caught far from sewage outfall. Seafood caught in Louisiana and Texas has been identified as a source of cholera. For crab to be safe, for example, it should be boiled for 10 minutes (8 minutes is not enough) or steamed for 30 minutes (25 minutes is not enough). Shellfish, including crabs, often harbour parasites and it is not uncommon for travellers to acquire worms in Southeast Asia as a souvenir of all the delicious seafood they have enjoyed. Most routine cooking does not render heavily contaminated seafood safe. In addition, there are cases of a ciguatera type of poisoning (*see* below) in people who have consumed crabs and king crabs in Southeast Asia and the Pacific. The exact nature of this toxin has not yet been sorted out.

Seafish

Fish may also be contaminated, although they are not as common a source of disease as filter-feeding shellfish. One of the delicious specialities of the coastal regions of Peru is *cerviche* which is raw fish marinated with lemon and chillies; this has been identified recently as a source of cholera. *Sushi*, a Japanese raw fish dish may give you herring worms (anisakiasis due to fish nematodes) and these may also be acquired from undercooked, salted or pickled fish, specialities of Holland and California. Fortunately the worms find man rather an unsuitable host and usually die fairly promptly after causing at most a little stomach ache and nausea. There is no specific treatment.

Red Tides

From time to time in tropical seas there are dramatic blooms of tiny dinoflagellate animals which make the water look red. This dangerous season is signalled by the deaths of large numbers of fish and sea birds. It is more common along polluted coasts. Local fishermen usually know not to catch fish during these red tides since they are poisonous. Shellfish, being filter-feeders, are particularly adept at concentrating the red tide poisons and so must also be avoided at these times. Symptoms develop within half an hour of eating contaminated fish and may progress to fatal paralysis in 12 hours. There is no specific treatment.

Ciguatera Fish Poisoning

This is more difficult to recognize and occurs when there is no obvious change in the sea. No doubt this is why it causes several deaths a year. Like red tide poisoning, it is also due to fish accumulating dinoflagellate toxins from their food. The liver, viscera and sexual organs or roe of large and also scaleless warm water shore or reef fish are most likely to contain the toxin. Moray eels should not be eaten because of the high risk of ciguatera poisoning. One early sign that a fish is affected is that it causes tingling or numbness of the mouth. There is no specific treatment.

Scombrotoxic Poisoning

This occurs when the red flesh of tuna, mackerel and their relatives (including albacore, skipjack and bonito), and the flesh of tinned fish such as sardines and anchovies or others including mahi-mahi, blue fish, amberjack and herring are decomposed by bacteria to produce histamine poisons. These toxins often cause a tingling or smarting sensation in the mouth, or a peppery or bitter taste in the fish. If you do not stop eating at this point you will go on to experience flushing, sweating, itching, abdominal pain, vomiting and dizziness which usually goes away within 24 hours. This kind of poisoning is avoided by eating fresh fish or by removing the guts and freezing fish as soon as possible after being caught. The problem seems to be most common in hot climates, presumably because decomposition begins so quickly. Treatment is not necessary.

Puffer Fish

This *fugu* beloved of the Japanese is said to be outstandingly delicious but if improperly prepared is lethal. There are 250 cases of poisoning per year in Japan with 60 per cent mortality. There are other fish which may also be toxic in Southeast Asia and the Indo-Pacific so it may be sensible to get a local cook to prepare fish for you.

Other Hazards of Eating Exotic Dishes

Thailand is renowned for its delicious food and it is also well known for the great variety of exotic parasites you can catch from eating it. Freshwater crabs, raw tadpoles, frogs and snakes are frequent sources of gnathostome worms. Raw freshwater fish harbour *Clonorchis* liver flukes in Southeast and East Asia. Eating raw freshwater crabs in Nigeria and Zaire may give you worm cysts and abscesses in the neck. Consumption of raw Chinese beetles and grubs may give you worm-filled lumps in the bowel. Eating under-cooked Giant African land snails and freshwater shrimps in Asian and Pacific countries and also in Central and South America carries the risk of angiostrongyliasis: a nasty little worm that occasionally sets up home in the brain or eyes. Avoid this by eating your shrimps and snails well cooked.

A serious source of travellers' health advice has warned that armadillo tacos in Mexico and the Southwest USA have been implicated in some cases of leprosy in travellers. These animals undoubtedly are prone to leprosy but it is hard to believe that a little cooking would not destroy the bacteria. So eat your armadillos well done.

The only birds known to be poisonous are three species of pitohuis, thrush-like perching birds from Papua New Guinea. They produce a powerful toxin very similar to that of South American poison arrow frogs so that licking the feathers makes your mouth go numb and tingly. Presumably eating their flesh would do you no good so do not eat small wild birds in PNG. Fruit bats are tasty, however.

Nutrition

Vitamin Pills and Diet

Some people take vitamin pills while travelling. It is better practice (and often considerably cheaper) to take a good varied diet including fresh fruit or vegetables every day. If this is not possible, realize that real vitamin deficiency states are enormously rare in those taking anything approaching a normal diet. It takes months and months of a very poor and unvaried diet before vitamin deficiencies will show themselves, unless you have some long-standing disease of the intestine.

One cause of protracted diarrhoea is tropical sprue (*see* p.33). The treatment for this is to take antibiotics and folic acid. This is one time when nutritional supplements have a place. Another is when planning a pregnancy. There is some evidence that congenital abnormalities are less likely in children born to women who take vitamins and *folic acid* supplements before and around the time of conception. In addition, women who are pregnant (or planning a pregnancy) and are taking *proguanil* (Paludrine) antimalarial tablets also need to take *folic acid* 5mg daily (*see* pp.56 and 124).

Salt Needs and Salt Tablets

Salt tablets are unnecessary and are not a good way of increasing salt intake. If your body requires more salt your taste for it will increase and you should shake more on your food. If you are very salt depleted, salt will not taste salty so drink slightly salty drinks until they taste salty again.

Fluoride

In some regions (including parts of Pakistan) water contains naturally high levels of fluoride. If this is the case, and you are a long-term resident, fluoride supplement drops for children or others are not a good idea. You may be able to find out what is in local drinking water by asking engineers working on water projects, but if in doubt it is best not to give supplements. Supplements are usually recommended for children when water fluoride is less than 0.2 parts per million.

Summary

⚠ Diarrhoea and a great variety of fascinating and spectacular parasites are acquired from contaminated food which has been inadequately cooked.

✚ Eat piping hot, thoroughly cooked food.

✚ Avoid salads (especially lettuce and watercress).

⚠ Never eat rare or raw steak when in regions where sanitation is poor.

✚ Pay attention to local culinary methods and eating habits. Local methods of preparing foods have generally been developed to minimize any risks to health; the exception is foods which are served raw.

✚ Seafood, freshwater crustacea and fish must be thoroughly cooked before eating; most routine cooking will not render them safe.

✚ Avoid eating seafood if you are a long way from the sea.

✚ Reject fish with a peppery or bitter taste or which cause a tingling or smarting sensation in the mouth (but note that some tinned fish prepared in Southeast Asia has pepper or chilli added!).

⚠ Never eat brightly coloured fruits and berries unless you know them to be harmless; things which look like tomatoes are often highly poisonous.

⚠ Vegetables or fruits with a bitter, stinging or otherwise disagreeable taste may well be toxic; if in doubt, taste with the tip of your tongue before eating.

Getting Bitten to Death?

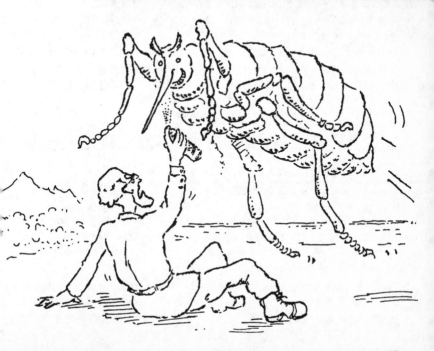

Vectors and Vector-borne Diseases

An array of creatures bite for a living and as a side effect pass on some disease: these are disease vectors. Mosquitoes are the most important of the vectors, but ticks, sand-flies, black-flies and others must not be forgotten. The best precaution against any vector-borne disease is to avoid being bitten.

There are an enormous number of vector-borne diseases, from tick-borne Omsk haemorrhagic fever to the wonderfully named Inkoo virus (a mosquito-borne infection peculiar to Finland). They are by no means all tropical diseases, but most are enormously rare and only fascinating to parasitologists. Tables 2 and 3 summarize the main dangerous ones. Malaria is a real risk, though. You must know about it if you are venturing into the malaria belt and take precautions against it.

Mediterranean Fevers

Malaria was a major problem in Italy only 50 years ago and it still occurs in Turkey. There have been a rash of reports lately describing holiday-makers returning from Cyprus suffering from a nasty fever, muscle aches and severe headache. They had contracted a range of viruses which all cause sand-fly fever (*see* below for bite avoidance). All victims recovered without specific treatment, but these cases highlight the good sense in avoiding insect bites even when as close to home as the Mediterranean region.

There is a Mediterranean spotted fever (also called Boutonneuse fever) which is occasionally unpleasant and sometimes causes dangerous haemorrhagic (bleeding) disease. It is rare, and spread by the dog tick (*see* below for safe tick removal techniques). Similar tick-borne diseases actually occur as far south as South Africa, and in southern Russia, India and northeast Australia.

Mosquitoes

Recognizing Mosquitoes Which Carry Disease

There are many mosquito species; only some transmit disease. Even so, the mosquito is the most deadly animal known to man. It transmits malaria, elephantiasis, dengue, yellow fever and Japanese encephalitis (the last two are incurable and often fatal) as well as a host of exotic diseases like O'nyong-nyong, Eastern, Western and Venezuelan equine fevers and several other types of encephalitis. The best way to avoid all of these diseases is to avoid being bitten.

When most mosquitoes settle on walls, their bodies lie parallel to the wall or they stand with their bottoms closer to the wall than their heads. *Culex*, the common house mosquito which transmits elephantiasis but not malaria, rests parallel to the

Table 2: Geographical Distribution of Vector-borne Diseases

Malaria	Widespread throughout the tropics and sub-tropics except at altitude
Dengue fever	Spreading throughout the tropics and sub-tropics
Dengue haemorrhagic fever	Presently known mainly from SE Asia, the Philippines, the Pacific Islands, India and Indian Ocean, Caribbean
Elephantiasis	Humid tropics or costal regions
Yellow fever	Tropical Africa, Central and South America; not in Asia
Japanese encephalitis	A problem only in Asia mainly where pigs are kept and rice is grown
Plague	A disease of unpredictable outbreaks in very poor living conditions (so unlikely to affect travellers); cases have been reported recently from the US, Madagascar, China, Myanmar, Vietnam and India
Bilharzia (urinary and intestinal schistosomiasis)	Savannah and semi-arid regions of Africa, the Middle East and South America
Oriental schistosomiasis	Patchy distribution in Southeast Asia, China and the Philippines
River blindness	W.Africa, South and Central America and a few small areas in E. and Central Africa
Sleeping sickness (African trypanosomiasis)	Only in Africa in suitable scrubby habitats between the Sahara and the Zambezi
Chagas' disease (American trypanosomiasis)	Lowland Mexico, Central and South America
Tick-borne fevers	All continents, temperate and tropical
Scrub typhus	East and Southeast Asia including the Philippines, the Pacific Islands including Papua New Guinea, Australia and South Asia (*see* p.137)
Leishmania	Dangerous forms in lowland forests of tropical Central and South America

Culex   *Anopheles*   *Aedes*

wall and sports splendid bushy antennae. Malaria-carrying *Anopheles* mosquitoes characteristically rest on walls with their bottoms as far from the wall as they can get. They are evening and night-time biters.

Day-biting *Aedes* mosquitoes which spread dengue fever and yellow fever rest parallel to the wall but are more easily distinguished by their striking black and white striped legs.

Mosquito Bites

Mosquito bites itch most in people visiting a new area. After about 6 months of being bitten by the same mosquito species, a kind of immunity to the bites develops so that they hardly raise a bump. The 'immunity' effect which makes bites non-itchy is quite localized so that, for example, Peruvians posted from one lowland jungle region to another within their native country complain of the itching and grief the mosquitoes cause for their first 6 months in a new place. Just because you are not covered in itchy bites, do not assume that you are not being bitten. If your skin is exposed between dusk and dawn you risk malaria in much of the world.

If you live abroad, try to reduce mosquito breeding sites near your house, by draining away any standing water and emptying or covering any water containers. Travellers will get bitten less if they select hotels away from collections of standing water. Foul black water is where *Culex* house mosquitoes like to breed.

I have not yet found a preparation which completely takes the itch out of bites but the following creams help a little: tiger balm, calamine, alcohol, crotamiton (Eurax) and even toothpaste (antihistamine creams and potions containing local anaesthetic are not particularly effective and often cause allergic rashes). Anything that cools the area of inflammation is helpful. Try to avoid scratching bites or you may get a nasty skin infection. If you do scratch a hole in the skin, clean it with antiseptic and cover with a sticking plaster (*see* p.105).

Some unfortunate people are hypersensitive to some insect bites which erupt into large watery blisters; these should not be deliberately punctured. If you suffer from this problem in one geographical region, it will not necessarily be a problem elsewhere. South American sand-flies are particularly potent provokers of these unpleasant blisters.

Avoiding Mosquito Bites

Recent research in Africa has shown that using permethrin (insecticide) impregnated bed nets protects people from being attacked by night-biting mosquitoes. In fact a screen of impregnated cloth dangling around the bed is also effective: mosquitoes choose not to fly over the screen to bite their victims. Bed-nets (costing from around £20) are a good investment and if treated with permethrin will kill any mosquito which touches them. This avoids the problem (particularly of conical mosquito nets) of being bitten through the net if you roll against it in your sleep. Nets only need to be treated every 6 months. Permethrin sprays with which you can treat your own net, or any tatty hotel net, are available from Nomad or MASTA (*see* pp.57, 211 and 212).

Electric Devices to Repel Mosquitoes

Small electric hotplates are available which heat up insecticide-impregnated vaporizing mats. The vapour repels or knocks down mosquitoes. They work well unless you are sleeping in a very large room with a high ceiling (common in hot climates) when there is just too large an air space for them to be effective. They do not work well if there is a through draught. Most types work in a room of 30m^3 (about 1000cu ft); they are less efficient if the device is a long way from you. If the hotel has provided only one mosquito mat for a large room, ask for another or use repellent too. The best vaporizing mats contain synthetic insecticides, such as esbiothrin.

Where there is no electricity you can burn incense coils. These are readily available in most places where mosquitoes are a problem. Very long-term use may carry some hazards similar to cigarette smoking.

Electric buzzer devices are useless against mosquitoes, cockroaches, and (as far as I know) all other insects. Ceiling fans may help to baffle mosquitoes a little, although strains are evolving now which are experts at flying in turbulent air (they have no difficulty in flying backwards in a rainstorm).

Repellents

Insect repellents not only deter six-legged assailants, but they also repel leeches, ticks and chiggers. The best repellents are based on DEET (diethyltoluamide), but be careful because it dissolves plastic (including some watch-glasses) and ruins all kinds of synthetic materials. It also irritates those with sensitive (or sunburnt) skin and is not advised for children. Oasis (*see* **Useful Addresses**, p.212) market Gurkha repellent which is milder. Applying DEET repellent to shoes will also deter leeches from climbing on to your skin.

Mosquito repellent anklets soaked in DEET (available from MASTA, *see* p.211) protect quite well from mosquitoes which 'hunt' at ankle level, as long as you are upright. However, when the mosquito density is high they only reduce biting rates and do not stop bites completely. They do not repel *Aedes* mosquitoes which do not hunt at ankle level. This is a pity since *Aedes* bites are painful and they are a great nuisance even in regions where there is no risk of disease transmission. The lemony smelling citronella plant and also the Chinese quwenling natural repellent work moderately well, but are not as good at repelling mosquitoes as DEET. There is no evidence that taking vitamin B_1 tablets gives protection against mosquito bites.

Wearing baggy cotton clothing with trousers tucked into socks and shirt tucked into trousers will also help protect you. When there are a great number of small flying insects about I also wear a cotton neckerchief (donned like a cravat) to seal the neck opening of my shirt. Only a relatively small area of naked skin then remains to be doused in repellent.

Tips for Avoiding Night-biting Mosquitoes

- ✪ At dusk, either retreat to a screened room or put on long clothes and a DEET-based insect repellent, especially around the ankles.

- ✪ Sleep under a mosquito net (preferably a Permethrin-treated net) or use electric mosquito mats or burn mosquito coils at night.

- ✪ Try to stay only in screened buildings and use insecticides regularly to dispatch the resident biters.

- ✪ Wear light coloured clothes since dark colours attract mosquitoes.

- ✪ Avoid using scented soaps or perfumes or wearing shiny jewellery as mosquitoes like these too.

Malaria

More than 2000 travellers return to Britain with malaria and on average seven die of it each year. Drug-resistant cerebral malaria is on the increase. Between 1976 and 1986 the number of cases of malaria treated in Britain rose by 50 per cent. It is more important than ever, then, to take precautions against being bitten by mosquitoes and to take antimalarial tablets meticulously. It is reckless to do otherwise. Protecting yourself against bites from malaria mosquitoes also has the side effect of helping you avoid other rarer insect-borne diseases.

What is Malaria?

People acquire malaria when they are bitten (and only one bite is necessary) by an *Anopheles* mosquito which has previously bitten someone with malaria. Symptoms then follow at least 7 days after being bitten. Often malaria starts as a 'flu-like illness (fevers, chills, aches and pains), but it can appear in various guises, such as as diarrhoea, abdominal pain or a cough.

Malaria is caused by *Plasmodium*, a fastidious parasite which lives within the red blood cells of animals and also inside the body of the mosquito. Bats, rats, deer, monkeys, birds and even reptiles have their own species of malaria—there are over 100 different kinds—but only four prefer to inhabit man. The nastiest of the four, *Plasmodium falciparum*, can cause cerebral malaria and also black water fever. In this extreme form of the disease so many blood cells become full of parasites that when they rupture in unison, the body (particularly the kidneys) is overwhelmed with blood cell debris and death often results however high-tech the medical care is. The death rate from *falciparum* malaria is fairly consistently 1 per cent whether treatment is given in developed or developing countries, although in countries like Japan where they are not used to recognizing and treating the disease the mortality rate can be as high as 10 per cent.

The other three kinds of malaria are less dramatic and do not kill, but they can be difficult to clear from the body completely. Unfortunately it is the dangerous form which is on the increase and it is the dangerous form where resistance to medicines is the biggest problem.

Malaria used to be a problem in temperate regions including on Long Island and in Britain. There are five species of *Anopheles* mosquitoes capable of spreading the disease in the UK and Oliver Cromwell certainly suffered from the 'ague'. The last cases in this country were in Romney Marsh just after the First World War—probably spread by local mosquitoes from convalescing soldiers who had returned with malaria. Now the only cases contracted in England are from infected mosquitoes which have disembarked at Gatwick or Heathrow airports.

Where is Malaria a Hazard?

Malaria kills about one million Africans annually. Over 1 per cent of travellers to West Africa, for example, contract malaria. Most (92 per cent) of the travellers who return to Britain with malaria have caught it in Africa: it is particularly important to be aware of the dangers of the disease in this continent. In Southeast Asia around Cambodia and Vietnam the malaria which is rampant is often resistant to treatment. Malaria is a very widespread disease which occurs in much of Asia (including parts of Turkey but excepting Israel), sub-saharan Africa (except most of South Africa), South and Central America. Polynesia and Micronesia are malaria-free. Melanesia (Papua New Guinea, Solomon Islands and Vanuatu) is a high risk area. It can be acquired (albeit rarely) at altitudes as high as 2000m (6500ft), so mountainous areas are not necessarily safe. Get up-to-date information about the risks before departure.

Most capital cities in Southeast and East Asia and South America are free from malaria at present, as are the popular Caribbean resorts. Most of South Africa is free although there are a few areas (e.g. the Kruger National Park) where there is still some risk.

If you are pregnant, both you and the baby are likely to die if you get *falciparum* malaria. Avoid high risk areas if you can, and be extra vigilant wherever you travel.

How to Avoid Malaria

The mosquitoes which transmit malaria bite from about 5.30pm until dawn. At dusk put on long clothes and repellents. Sadly gin and tonic does not contain enough quinine to protect you.

Three A's will help you remember how to avoid malaria:

▶ **Awareness** (knowing whether or not the region you are visiting is malarious)

▶ **Avoidance** (of mosquito bites)

▶ **Antimalarial** (tablets)

Ensure that you know whether you are in a malarious region. Tips for bite avoidance are given above. Antimalarials are considered below.

Antimalarial Tablets

Who Should Take Antimalarials?

A vaccine for malaria is presently undergoing field trials, but it will be a long time before it is generally available. At present, taking antimalarial tablets and preventing bites are your only protection from malaria. Anyone visiting a malarious region needs to take advice on antimalarial precautions. It is particularly important for children and pregnant women to take antimalarials and avoid being bitten. Although antimalarial medicines are passed into breast-milk, breast fed babies also need to be given *chloroquine* syrup or some suitable alternative.

People born and/or brought up in malarious regions and who suffer from malaria repeatedly build up a partial immunity to the parasite so that if they contract the disease they are less likely to become seriously ill with it. However, this immunity wanes so that natives of malarious countries who have been away for a year or more become as susceptible as other travellers and children. These people must also protect themselves.

Which Antimalarial and How to Take It

Malaria tablets must be started one week before departure and continued for at least a month after returning. The reason for this is that there is no drug yet known which can prevent the malaria parasite from infecting people. Antimalarials merely slow down the process of multiplication and inhibit the penetration of the parasites into the red blood cells. By taking the tablets for long enough the supply of parasites is exhausted.

Patterns of drug resistance change constantly so seek up-to-date advice about what antimalarial tablets to take. *Mefloquine* (Larium), a weekly preparation, is now recommended for many trips of up to a year. *Chloroquine* (e.g. Nivaquine, Avloclor in the UK; Aralen, Resochin in US) two a week and *proguanil* (Paludrine in UK; not available in US) two a day is the best combination for most travellers unless they are visiting areas with multiple drug resistance. The antibiotic *doxycycline* is also now being taken by some travellers to the border regions of Thailand and Cambodia, because resistance to the standard drugs is becoming so common; *mefloquine* and *doxycycline* are both prescription only medicines.

Take up-to-date advice from a computer-linked travel clinic or phone the Centres for Disease Control, Atlanta, GA 30333 or in the UK:

> **Malaria Reference Laboratory**: countries of risk and prophylaxis, ✆ 0891 600350; advice on avoiding bites, ✆ 0891 600274; or
>
> **MASTA**, Medical Advisory Services for Travellers, at the London School of Hygiene and Tropical Medicine, Keppel Street, London WC1 7HT, ✆ 0891 224 100 or 0171 631 4408. Calls cost 36p/min cheap rate or 48p/min at all other times (in 1994).

No antimalarial is infallible but those few unfortunates who acquire malaria while taking antimalarial tablets (perhaps because some doses are forgotten or are poorly absorbed during a period of diarrhoea) are extremely unlikely to get severe and dangerous malaria. Even so, seek medical help if you think you have malaria.

Side Effects

Those who are concerned about the side effects of taking antimalarials must keep in mind the major effect of malaria: rapid death. *Chloroquine* can affect the eyes, but this is only after taking it for a total of at least 6 years. *Proguanil* (Paludrine) can cause two troublesome side effects. If it is taken on an empty stomach it can cause nausea so take it after a meal. It often causes mouth ulcers so pack something to ease them (e.g. Teejel or Bonjela).

Hair loss is sometimes blamed on antimalarials but prolonged flights provoke a moult up to 3 months later so this may be the explanation for hair loss. Menstrual irregularities are also blamed on antimalarials: this may be the case, or more likely it is an effect of all the changes that happen during travelling.

A British engineer was working for 3 years in Surabaya and knowing that Java is almost completely free from malaria, he did not take antimalarial tablets. He spent a weekend on neighbouring Lombok, and took no precautions against malaria there either. Three weeks later he died of cerebral malaria.

This man had spent most of his working life in the tropics and had contracted malaria in Africa on one occasion. This attack had made him only slightly unwell and the treatment had soon got the mild symptoms under control. He was not keen to take antimalarials because of side effects and because he was sure that malaria was not a particularly serious disease. His decision not to take malaria tablets while living in the big city of Surabaya was entirely reasonable since his risk of catching the disease there was minuscule. However, he needed some protection in Lombok. The new international hotels at Senggigi Beach, Lombok are not keen to advertise the fact that there is a significant risk of contracting serious *falciparum* malaria in the area; if word got out it would be bad for business.

Diagnosing Malaria

It can be difficult to diagnose malaria, even for a doctor with experience of the disease, but if you feel unwell, with fever over 38°C or have 'flu (prostration, aches and pains) 7 days or more after arriving in a malarious region or within 3 months of returning, you may have malaria and must seek local medical help immediately. If you are far from medical help, self treatment is fairly safe, unless pregnant or under 12 years of age. Remember that there are many causes of fever, and notes to help diagnose them are on p.177. The risk of acquiring malaria is very high in sub-saharan Africa, Melanesia and parts of Southeast Asia around Cambodia and Vietnam.

Cure and Treatment

Try to get a blood film examination if possible (it is useful to establish a diagnosis and know the malarial type) before taking any treatment for malaria. If you are travelling to remote tropical regions anywhere in the malaria belt, you should probably be carrying a course of treatment to take if you suspect malaria; you should then get to a doctor as soon as possible. Emergency treatments include a course of *quinine* or Fansidar (take three Fansidar tablets at once) or *mefloquine.* Travel clinics sell treatment kits. If you are pregnant, consider delaying your trip or going to a lower risk area. Get specialist advice before travelling since these drugs (and malaria itself) harm the foetus. Most doctors would advise against travel to malarious regions during pregnancy because it is so dangerous.

Artemether, an active component of a drug known and used in China for more than 2000 years, seems to be effective and safe in treating severe malaria and should soon become available for widespread use. Seek up-to-date advice on the particular area you are visiting to ensure that the emergency drug that you are carrying is likely to be effective.

Most travellers who acquire the dangerous form of malaria become ill within 2 or 3 months of returning home and most have acquired the parasite in Africa. If you are taken ill within 3 months of returning from Africa, Melanesia or Indo China (milder forms may take up to a year to reveal themselves) seek medical help at once. If you cannot contact a GP, take yourself promptly to a hospital accident and emergency department. Remember that antimalarial tablets are not an absolute protection and you could contract malaria even if you have been careful in taking them.

Many experienced travellers will tell you that they have had malaria and that it was trivial; many undoubtedly have contracted it, many more will have been misdiagnosed. The disease is changing, and more travellers are now acquiring the dangerous and deadly form. Malaria is not a trivial illness.

Case Histories (Africa)

A British businessman had been visiting various sub-saharan countries over the previous 26 years and no longer took antimalarial tablets since he thought that after so much time in Africa he must be immune to malaria. He returned from one trip with fever and chills, but delayed seeing his doctor for 3 days. He developed cerebral malaria and renal failure and needed 3 weeks' treatment in an intensive care unit. He recovered completely.

A Canadian woman living in Uganda stopped taking antimalarials because she was pregnant and feared that the tablets might harm the baby. She contracted cerebral malaria and both she and the baby died, despite emergency treatment in a hospital with a great deal of expertise in treating severe malaria.

Avoiding Other Insect-borne Diseases

Elephantiasis

Elephantiasis is a disease which every man fears, for there are stories about sufferers whose scrotum becomes so distended that they need a wheelbarrow to transport their sorry member. Fluid does indeed build up around the testes in men with elephantiasis but this process takes more than a decade. Any sane traveller will seek treatment long before the disease has become so advanced. Long-standing disease also causes massive swelling of the legs in both sexes.

These are mosquito-borne diseases which are also known as filariases since filarial worms cause them. They can be spread by both day- and night-biting species. Elephantiasis is most rampant in the Pacific Islands, East and Southeast Asia, but it is also in sub-saharan Africa, West Asia, south and east India, central America and the east of South America. Elephantiasis is treatable. It has an incubation period of between a few weeks and 15 months depending on the type.

Arboviruses

Arboviruses (viruses which are spread by mosquitoes and other insects or ticks) are a hazard in many places: 80 are known to cause disease in humans. There is no specific treatment for them and few vaccines, so prevention is all important. This means avoiding insect bites by wearing repellents and long clothes and knowing how to get ticks off quickly and safely (*see* p.65).

Arbovirus diseases may not be seen as a problem in regions where they occur. Local people (who will have survived an attack of the disease in childhood) develop good immunity to their local arboviruses—or die young from them—so that adults do not fear them. But travellers and children are at high risk and these are the ones who can get very ill if infected. There is little point describing each disease in detail but realise that preventing insect and tick bites is wise.

Classical Dengue Fever (DF) and Dengue Haemorrhagic Fever (DHF)

Dengue is the most common arbovirus in man. There are about 40 million cases of dengue fever worldwide annually. Of these about two million are caused by DHF, the haemorrhagic form of the disease which is responsible for 35,000 deaths almost entirely in the local population of children. The risk of travellers contracting the dangerous form are minimal. There have been major outbreaks of classical dengue fever in the US, Greece, Australia and Japan, but these are sporadic and rare. The Greek outbreak in 1927–8, for example, made more than a million people ill; the virus may have arrived in birds migrating from Africa.

The virus is spread by day-biting *Aedes* mosquitoes, which breed in clean water. Classical dengue or 'breakbone fever' usually occurs between the latitudes of about 30° north and 40° south. It is endemic in parts of South and Southeast Asia, the Pacific, Africa, and the Americas. The incubation period is 2–7 days. Classical dengue fever causes severe muscle pains (hence 'breakbone' fever), high fever (40°C) of abrupt onset and a characteristic measles-like rash, but it lasts for no more than a week and is seldom fatal. The disease is caused by one virus which comes in four serotypes. The illness confers complete immunity to further attacks of the same serotype, but not to the other three.

The dangerous variant is dengue haemorrhagic fever (DHF). This (but not classical dengue fever) provokes breakdown in the blood clotting system which causes uncontrolled bleeding and shock. In untreated patients, 50 per cent die but with supportive treatment the mortality rate is about 5 per cent. DHF is a big problem in Southeast Asia and it is also known from the Caribbean and the Pacific. So far, DHF has not been seen in Africa. This form of the infection is not completely understood but it used to be thought that two successive infections with different dengue serotypes, with a period of 6 months between the two infections was needed before DHF could strike. The disease is not so readily pigeon-holed, but Western travellers are at low risk. People born in endemic regions who return home do seem to be at risk, though and travellers and expatriates do contract classical dengue.

Since the mosquito vector breeds in clean standing water close to houses, emptying vessels like flower pots, old car tyres and buckets. will help reduce the bite rate. Expatriates should put fish in any outside water tanks to eat the mosquito larvae or cover them with mosquito gauze. A vaccine is being developed in Thailand which is about to be tested on people, but it will be some years before it is generally available.

Sand-fly-borne Diseases

Sand-flies are very small, brownish, hairy flies which are chiefly insects of hot climates. They are most active at twilight but bite throughout the night; in Central or South America, but also as close to home as the Mediterranean and Middle East. They transmit leishmania, a protozoan disease. This either causes painless tropical sores (see p.111) or in hot dry regions largely outside the tropics in the old world kala-azar fever. Sand-flies are able to penetrate mosquito netting when hungry although they cannot leave once engorged. Permethrin-treated nets will keep them out, though. Repellents are of some help and, since sand-flies are weak fliers, ceiling fans—if such luxuries are available—will protect you to some extent.

In the new world sand-flies are principally moist forest species and are most likely to bite during rainy seasons in the forests of Central America, Brazil, the Guyanas and Mexico. The severe and untreatable form of the lowland disease is called *espundia*. Lowland, new world leishmania is reasonably common and is difficult to treat, so precautions against being bitten must be taken seriously. In the western Andes of Peru and the Argentinean highlands, sand-flies behave differently and stay close to villages where they bite dogs, people and whoever else seems tasty. The ulcers caused by Andean leishmania or *uta* heal by themselves.

African and American Trypanosomiasis

Trypanosome parasites cause disease in man and animals and they are difficult to control and eradicate; people acquire infections from insect vectors which have previously bitten infected domestic and wild animals. In Africa, the main disease reservoirs are cattle and antelope while in America they are most often domestic dogs or forest wildlife.

Chagas' Disease (American Trypanosomiasis) and Assassin Bugs

Chagas' disease may be what finally polished off Charles Darwin, but it is a very rare disease in travellers. It is a problem of the rural poor in the lowlands from the southern USA through into Central and South America. The Chagas parasite is transmitted to man in all central and South American countries but it is most prevalent in Brazil, Argentina, Venezuela, Chile, Peru and Bolivia. It is rare in the Amazon basin of Brazil since Indian huts, having no walls, are unsuitable for colonization by the bug vector.

The trypanosome parasite grows happily in almost any mammal species and is transmitted from host to host by assassin bugs (*see* p.136). These substantial, shield-shaped, four-winged, nocturnal, cone-nosed bugs are also known as kissing bugs or *vinchuca* in Bolivia and Argentina, *chipo* in Venezuela and *barbeiro* in Brazil; they are about 2–2.5cm long. While these unpleasant insects are feeding on blood they defecate and the parasite finds its way from the bug's faeces into the victim via broken skin. By no means all American bug bites are infective. If the parasite does manage to gain entry, an inflamed swelling (a chagoma) appears at the site of entry in many people and in half there is a characteristic swelling of the eyelids. The first stage of the disease is mild and sometimes not noticed at all. Symptoms generally begin after several years by which time treatment is difficult. Avoidance of bites, then, is all important. The bug's best chance to get at you is if you sleep on floors in wattle and daub type village houses, so a hammock will help protect you, particularly if it has a built-in mosquito net; these are marketed in South America.

There are numerous species of assassin bug which bite, usually in self defence, and their bite is painful, but they do not feed on blood nor transmit Chagas' disease.

Tsetse-flies and African Sleeping Sickness (African Trypanosomiasis)

Tsetse-flies are restricted to tropical Africa and transmit sleeping sickness in a patchy distribution over sub-saharan Africa. Most transmission goes on at forested lake shores and river banks or in forest–savanna mosaic. They like leafy habitats, although one variety has been able to extend its

Getting Bitten to Death?

range almost into the Sahara desert. Local knowledge about the disease is generally good so ask if it is a problem before you venture into the bush. Tsetse-flies are active during daylight hours and their bite is painful. They are twice the size of a house-fly.

Plague

> *Traffic halted in the northern city of Lucknow after a dead rat was spotted on a busy road. Students at a nearby polytechnic immediately gulped down antibiotics and the lifeless rodent was whisked away in an ambulance.*
>
> *The Kathmandu Post,* 3 October 1994

There have been such hysterical reactions to the 1994 plague outbreak in western India that a few sentences about the disease seem worthwhile, despite the fact that it is such a minuscule risk to normal travellers. Plague simmers in wild animals and from time to time infects rats living close to those inhabiting unsanitary, poor accommodation. As the rats die from plague, they are deserted by their fleas which then seek a new host to bite. People bitten by such homeless rat fleas thus acquire bubonic plague which is treatable with antibiotics. Untreated bubonic plague can develop into septicaemia and also highly infectious and usually fatal pneumonic plague, but even in a big epidemic nearly all those infected acquire their disease from rat flea bites and so there is little risk of catching plague during normal travel. Those at risk are nurses caring for those dying of plague, laboratory technicians working with specimens from plague patients and zoologists handling infected wild animals. Although there is a vaccine, it is not very effective and has a high incidence of side effects especially after booster doses; boosters need to be given every 6 months. Those travelling into areas where a plague epidemic is going on are advised to carry forty 500mg tetracycline tablets with them and see a doctor if they develop a fever, particularly if they notice painful swellings in the groin or other body 'junction points'. The incubation period is 2–8 days.

Ticks and Tick-borne Diseases

Ticks are small, slow-moving, eight-legged animals which attach themselves to larger hosts in order to dine on their blood. They are very widespread and remarkably adapted to an intermittent food supply; the American relapsing fever tick, for example, can live without feeding for 10 years. Unfed adult ticks are only 3–6mm long, like a sesame seed with legs, but after feeding distend to the size of a broad bean and become the colour of a kidney (chilli) bean. They are undesirable because:

● The sight of a slowly engorging tick firmly attached to one's warm and tender parts is unattractive

Table 3: Diseases Transmitted by Small Biters

Vector	Vector habits	Disease	Vaccine?	Treatment	Continent	Avoiding action
Anopheles mosquitoes	Evening and night biters	Malaria Elephantiasis Arboviruses Skin infections	no no no no	1% die yes none* yes	All* Tropics Tropics All	Tablets; bite avoidance: long clothes, bednets, repellents, insecticides
Aedes mosquitoes	Day biters	Dengue Yellow fever Skin infections	no yes no	none none yes	Asia, Africa, Americas, Africa, Americas All*	Long clothes, repellents; discard standing water near home
Culex mosquitoes (mainly)	Evening and night biters	Japanese encephalitis Elephantiasis	yes no	none* 30% die yes	Asia Tropics	Bite avoidance: long clothes, bed-nets, repellents, insecticides
Black-flies	Day biting swarms	River blindness Nuisance	no no	can be dangerous	Africa, tropical America Tundra etc.	Avoid rivers; long clothes; repellents
Sand-flies	Evening and night biters	Tropical sores Kala-azar Sand-fly fevers	no no no	difficult difficult none*	Tropical Americas, Mediterranean, Middle East, Asia	Repellents; long clothes; fans; sleep above ground (hammock or upstairs)
Tsetse-flies	Painful day biters	Sleeping sickness	no	difficult	Tropical lowland Africa	Avoid endemic areas (local advice); repellents; long clothes
Assassin bugs	Night biters	Chagas' disease	no	90 day course; can be dangerous	Lowland tropical Americas	Use hammock & net if sleeping in wattle & daub housing
Rat fleas	Hide in beds, etc.	Plague	yes	antibiotics	Poor housing, mainly tropical	Avoid rats & rodent habitats
Bed bugs	Night biters	Pain, skin infections	no	yes	All*	Better hotel; bed away from wall; light on
Mites	Day biters	Scrub typhus	no	antibiotics	S & SE Asia Australia	Repellents; long clothes tucked in
Ticks	Attach in daylight	Dozens	1	often difficult	All*	Repellents; long clothes tucked in
Leeches	Day biters	Skin infections	no	yes	S & SE Asia, Madagascar	Repellents; long clothes tucked in

none means that 'supportive therapy' will be given in hospital but that specific treatments which will clear the infection do not exist; all* means all continents except Antarctica; 1 means only for European tick-borne encephalitis*

- Some transmit serious infections
- All make a break in the skin which is often itchy and allows skin infections to establish themselves
- Some administer painful bites
- Some cause a transient but life-threatening paralysis

Most people are not aware of ticks crawling on them so the animals usually move considerable distances before they eat. They generally like to feed in some cosy corner near the genitals or another place where the clothing is tight.

Preventing Ticks Attacking

In tick country wear long clothes, tuck trousers into socks and tuck the shirt into trousers. Insect repellent repels ticks as well as insects.

Removing Ticks

It may take several days for a feasting tick to pass on disease, so removing any as soon as you find them will reduce the chance of disease transmission. If the tick is squeezed, crushed or damaged, though, the infection is more likely to be passed on. Since some tick-borne pathogens can get in through intact skin, the person attempting removal risks infection too. Also remember that if the mouthparts break off you will get a troublesome wound infection.

Ticks are tenacious: a barbed snout and a kind of cement holds the tick in place, so unless they are still in the process of settling down to feed, they are difficult to remove. The best method is to grasp the tick as close as possible to the skin with blunt curved tweezers and then pull the tick steadily away from the skin. If you do not have forceps, protect your hand with a plastic bag (or surgical gloves if you are that well equipped) and grasp the tick with finger and thumb tips as close to the skin as possible and pull steadily. Do not jerk or twist the tick. Once it has been removed, disinfect the skin with alcohol (whisky and gin at 40 per cent ethanol are good enough) and wash your hands with soap and water.

Very small tick larvae or 'seed ticks' can be scraped off with a knife, and again it would be sensible to sterilize the skin afterwards. You can remove these before they have had a chance to attach by stroking the skin with a finger wrapped in masking tape sticky side out. This is most easily done by a friend. If the ticks have not been damaged there is less need for skin sterilization which indeed may be impractical in the Central American jungle where they may crawl on you in enormous numbers. Where ticks or seed ticks are very numerous, it clearly makes good sense to take measures to prevent them getting on you, by wearing long clothes tucked in and repellents.

Tick-borne Infections

Ticks are efficient disease transmitters because of their longevity, because they like to feed on blood at each stage of their life cycle and because some diseases live in the tick from one generation to the next (e.g. tularaemia in America). It is perhaps not surprising to discover, then, that ticks carry an array of diseases affecting animals and man. At least nine infections acquired from tick-bites occur in the USA and Britain's only two surviving vector-borne illnesses (now that malaria has died out here) are louping ill, transmitted by sheep ticks of the Scottish borders, and the newly recognised Lyme disease which is described below. It is not worth describing the many various tick-borne diseases here. Most are geographically localized and physicians will recognize their local tick-borne diseases. Most start with rather non specific 'flu-like symptoms: fever, aches and pains and headache.

Lyme Disease

The first outbreak of Lyme disease was described in Old Lyme, Connecticut in 1975. It is now known to occur worldwide wherever the *Ixodes* tick is found; cases have recently been reported from tropical Africa and Ireland. In the UK, there is a problem where there are trees and bracken, especially in the New Forest, Welsh Uplands, the Highlands of Scotland and parts of East Anglia (particularly Thetford Chase). Sheep-dipping controls ticks over much of Britain, but there is still a risk where there are significant populations of deer.

A week to 10 days after being bitten by a tick (immature or adult), a slowly enlarging red patch, ring or weal usually appears (in 70 per cent of those infected); this does not usually itch. It may persist for months or may disappear after a few weeks. This is the hallmark of the disease. Other symptoms often accompany this, particularly aching joints (in 80 per cent of those infected), fever, aching muscles and headache. If not treated at this stage, the disease slowly progresses to a more serious illness which can affect the heart and the brain. Treatment within 4 weeks of the bite with *penicillin* or *oxytetracycline* for 7–10 days is highly effective. If the diagnosis is made later in the course of the illness, a stay in hospital will probably be necessary so that intravenous antibiotics can be given.

European Tick-borne Encephalitis

This is a virus disease of warm and low-lying forested areas in parts of central Europe and Scandinavia, particularly Austria, Czechoslovakia, West Germany and the former Yugoslavia. The ticks which transmit the disease live in the heavy undergrowth of deciduous forest so campers and orienteers are most at risk. There is a vaccine which gives good protection. An immunoglobulin injection is also available which will protect as long as it is given within 4 days of the tick bite. It is particularly advisable to have this injection if you develop a fever within 4 days of a tick attaching to you in these countries.

Rocky Mountain Spotted Fever

This is worth a special mention since its name is misleading. It is now mostly a problem of the USA **east** of the rockies although it occurs in all states except Maine, Alaska and Hawaii. Since pets bring ticks into homes it is an occasional problem in cities. In 1987, for example, four cases were reported from the Bronx in people who had not travelled outside New York city within the incubation period. It also occurs in Mexico where it is called *fiebre manchada*, Columbia (*fiebre petequial*) and Brazil (*fiebre maculosa* or Sao Paulo typhus).

Victims of the disease become unwell with fever, they may become delirious and usually develop the characteristic reddish–purple–black spots on the soles of the feet, palms, lower legs and forearms. It may later spread onto the trunk. The disease responds to treatment with antibiotics.

Tick Paralysis

This strange condition is most commonly described in people bitten by *Dermacentor* ticks in Pacific North West America (usually in Oregon or British Columbia) but it is known from all continents. It comes on 4–6 days after a tick has attached to a person (usually a toddler). Paralysis begins in the feet and hands. Loss of co-ordination follows, then paralysis of the face, slurring of the speech and uncontrolled eye movements. Finally, by about the eighth day, the breathing becomes irregular and then stops. Children under the age of 2 years are most usually affected.

Fortunately, though, as soon as the feeding tick has been found and removed, the symptoms usually disappear in the reverse order of their appearance. There are no long-term after effects. An antidote is available in Australia where the paralysis may continue after the tick has been detached.

The disease process seems to be due to a toxin secreted by the salivary glands of the tick only during a period of rapid egg development.

Other Tick-borne Diseases

Other tick-borne diseases occur in Africa, Asia, South America and there are even Siberian maladies transmitted by ticks and mites. Some are treatable with antibiotics, others are not.

The mites which transmit scrub typhus are described on p.137.

Summary

✛ Be **aware** of the malaria risk in the region in which you are travelling.

✛ Ensure you **avoid** mosquito bites, especially between dusk and dawn.

✛ Take your **antimalarial** tablets meticulously and for at least a month after returning home.

⚠ Seek medical attention promptly if you become ill within 3 months of returning home, tell the doctor where you have been and mention that you could have malaria, even if you have been meticulous in taking antimalarial tablets.

✛ Avoid tick and chigger bites wherever you are. If you discover any on you, get it off (without squeezing or damaging it) as soon as you can.

Heat and Dust, Sun and Sand

Strong tropical sun and intense heat cause a selection of health hazards: heat stroke can kill or permanently disable, sunburn can make life wretched and may lead later to skin cancer, and failing to adapt to the heat will make you plain miserable. The main ways of avoiding these problems are to make some changes in your behaviour. It is what you do rather than physiological adaptations which protect you—or not. This chapter also deals with the many hazards of the sea, freshwater bathing, deserts and forest environments.

The Hazards of Heat and Sun

The hottest place in the Indian subcontinent is in northern Sindh where summer shade temperatures reach 53°C. When the environment gets this hot, even local people die of heatstroke, albeit the poor who have to work and cannot afford to shelter from the midday sun. For Sindhis, the pace of life slows dramatically as temperatures rise: they realize that reducing the amount they expect to achieve is the only way to cope with extreme heat. It is interesting to experience the hot weather. People sit around and sup tea or bottled drinks and there is more time to chat. That is how locals cope with the heat. Foreigners who follow their lethargic example protect themselves from physical and mental burn-out. It is sad to see visitors unable to slow their pace and because of this having a thoroughly horrendous time.

The body adapts to the heat by increased sweating and by reducing the amount of salt lost in sweat; this change takes between 1 and 3 weeks. So, especially when you first arrive, do not try to do too much and avoid hard physical exercise in the middle of the day. Wear 100 per cent cotton clothes: as little as 30 per cent artificial fibre mixed with 70 per cent cotton feels very uncomfortable in hot climates.

You must greatly increase the amount of water you consume when the weather is hot so that you pass a good volume of urine at least three times a day. Passing small quantities of dark tea-coloured urine usually means that you are dehydrated. Increase your fluid intake by making a conscious effort to drink more because the body's thirst mechanisms are not good at encouraging enough drinking. Drink at least a large glass of water with every meal. And avoid the temptation to rehydrate with beer: top up with water or soft drinks before moving on to alcohol, which is dehydrating. If you allow yourself to become dry, you will feel awful and risk kidney stones (*see* p.118) as well as constipation.

Skin Care in the Sun

Tropical sunshine is surprisingly powerful so be very careful about exposing your skin, especially at first. Sunlight radiation not only ages the skin and makes it prematurely wrinkly, but it also stimulates unpleasant-looking warty growths called solar keratoses and increases the risk of skin cancer. Some would therefore say that sun-bathing at all in the tropics is daft. If you must sun-bathe, avoid being out in the midday sun (11am–3pm) and build up your exposure from 15 or 20 minutes a day. Untanned skin can burn in 15 minutes in tropical midday sun. A deep tan only gives as much protection as a factor 3 sun-screen. Sun-screens are by no means an absolute protection: factor 12 sun-screen will delay burning for about 3 hours. You will burn faster if the sun is reflected off water or other light surfaces (like a beach, the sea or snow). The processes which lead to skin cancer are not completely understood but it seems certain that although sun-screens protect the skin from burning they do not eliminate the risk of cancer.

The number of cases of skin cancer has been rising steadily since people from temperate climates started taking holidays in sunny places. In addition, those who are at special risk from skin cancer are fair-skinned people who spend much of their lives in the tropics; it is particularly important to make sure that white children are protected. The Australian campaign to protect people from skin cancer

has a useful ditty to help remember the sensible precautions to take: Slip Slap Slop.

Sun-screens

The ultraviolet (UV) radiation which reaches us on earth consists of UVA (wavelength 320–400 nanometres) and UVB (290–320nm). Shorter wavelengths (UVC at 100–290nm) are still intercepted by the ozone layer. UVB causes sunburn, but both UVB and UVA cause skin cancer and skin ageing. Even one episode of severe sunburn seems greatly to increase the risk of skin cancer.

Sun-screens either absorb UV energy or reflect it. Absorbent sun-screens only protect against UVB, although some also offer minimal reduction in UVA exposure. Reflectant sun-screens contain inert pigments (often zinc oxide or titanium dioxide) which protect against UVA as well as UVB. The disadvantage of these is that they can leave an unsightly white film on the skin, although most formulations now contain 'microfined' particles of titanium dioxide which are less visible.

The Sun Protection Factor (SPF) of a sun-screen is a measure of the difference between the dose of UV radiation which produces just measurable redness of protected skin, compared with unprotected skin. Manufacturers' SPFs refer mainly to UVB protection only. Unfortunately there is no standardization of the tests done by sun-screen makers to establish their SPF and so direct comparisons cannot be made between different brands. In addition, SPFs take no account of the sun-screen's actual performance which is limited by application technique, sweating, friction and bathing. Nevertheless the SPF provides a rough guide to the degree of protection from UVB. People with sensitive skins should choose a sun-screen with an SPF of 15–20 and others about 10. It is unnecessary (and even undesirable) to use preparations with very high SPFs (25 or more) since, even at the equator, the dose of UVB radiation received in a day is not 25 times the amount which will cause sunburn and very high SPF sun-screens allow extended periods of sunbathing and thus invite longer term damage from large doses of UVA.

Reduce sun damage by gradually acclimatizing to sunshine and never sunbathe in the middle of the day. The best sun-screen is shade and clothing (but remember that you can burn through thin material like cheesecloth).

Sensible Clothing and Other Skin Protection

Shirts with collars (rather than T-shirts) best protect the skin at the back of the neck. Wear trousers or long full skirts, not shorts. It is wise to keep the sun off your head when the weather is really hot and umbrellas are cooler than hats. Umbrellas are a cool means of keeping the sun off your head when walking or trekking; they are also a more comfortable way of keeping dry in monsoon rains than wearing a cagoule. Black umbrellas absorb sunlight radiation so are rather hot; while white umbrellas do not screen out enough sunlight so I have settled on a grey collapsible model. When I need my hands to be free, I wear a cotton bush hat which can be dunked in water when I am overheating: having cool water dribbling down the back of the neck is remarkably refreshing. A wet neckerchief draped around the neck is also very cooling and protects the back of the neck from sunburn. Cover up when riding on trucks, bus roofs or motor bikes; the cool breeze feels wonderful and disguises the fact that you are burning.

Skin cancer and sunburn are not the only reasons for keeping the skin covered in the tropics. Being reasonably well-dressed helps protect from stinging and biting organisms (see pp.54 and 130). It is also often more culturally sensitive and thus appreciated by local people: on several occasions I have been told, 'I knew you weren't a tourist because of the way you dress'.

Treatment of Sunburn

Calamine lotion or preparations containing calamine are soothing treatments for sunburn. They are often unavailable abroad so take some with you. Aspirin is a powerful anti-inflammatory medicine and so helps calm the heat of sunburn. *Silver sulphadiazine* (Flamazine) is also said to help if applied to sunburnt skin. Do not deliberately puncture blisters caused by sunburn. Oily substances trap in the heat and make sunburn more uncomfortable. Fluids and heat can be lost through badly sunburnt skin, so drink plenty. You may develop hypothermia (reduced body temperature) if you are in a climate with hot days and cold nights.

Medicines and Sun Sensitivity

A wide variety of medicines can sensitize the skin to the sun. If you are taking any medicines and develop a rash which seems to make your skin especially sun-sensitive, try stopping the medicine to see if the problem goes away. Common offenders are high dose (150 or 200mg daily) *doxycycline* (e.g. Vibramycin) and also *ciprofloxacin* and Bactrim which are all used to treat travellers' diarrhoea. The non-steroidal anti-inflammatory medicines such as *ibuprofen* (e.g. Brufen) and *diclofenac* (e.g. Voltarol) can also cause this, as can tablets to control diabetes and many other medicines.

Eye Protection

Remember that eyes as well as the skin suffer from too much sun. Wear sunglasses if there is a lot of glare, otherwise you will suffer from a soreness of the eyes like mild snow-blindness. Expensive glasses are not necessarily the best: seek sunglasses which claim UV protection and which carry the British Standard (or national equivalent) mark. A hat with a brim sometimes helps too, unless most of the glare is being reflected up at you from the sea or snow.

Cold Sores

If you are unfortunate enough to suffer from recurrent cold sores (due to the *Herpes simplex* virus), exposure to strong sunlight may reactivate them. *Acyclovir* cream (Zovirax in UK and US) which is available over the counter in the UK, is very effective in preventing cold sores erupting if it is applied early. Begin applying it when you first notice the sensation of an incipient sore, even before the sore appears. Pack some cream if you are a sufferer.

Heat Illnesses

Heat Exhaustion

Heat exhaustion is a particular risk in hot, high humidity environments especially following strenuous exercise in the sun. Over-weight people are more prone to it than the very fit, and new arrivals are far more likely to suffer than those who have been in the environment for 2 weeks or more. There is profuse sweating (which keeps the body relatively cool) but this loss of fluids causes weakness, exhaustion, muscle cramps, restlessness, rapid pulse and vomiting. The skin is very flushed with blood as the body attempts to increase heat loss, but this is at the expense of blood flow to the brain. The body temperature is below 40°C (104°F).

Take the sufferer to a cool shady place where they should drink plenty of water. People with heat exhaustion will probably be very fluid depleted and may need to drink as much as 2–4 litres in the first hour. If their temperature is 39°C (102°F) or above, they should be actively cooled by removing clothes, fanning and sponging with a cool (but not ice-cold) cloth. Cooling should be continued until the victim's temperature is below 39°C (102°F).

The sufferer should do no more physical exercise until at least the next day; some would say they should be evacuated to hospital. The point at which you decide to evacuate must depend on the level of competence of the first aider; if you have no experience of this problem, evacuate. Heat exhaustion, if not taken seriously can rapidly lead to heat stroke which is a medical emergency.

Heat Stroke (also called Sun Stroke)

Heat stroke can come on suddenly or can follow heat exhaustion. It is responsible for some deaths; permanent disability is quite common. The body temperature is usually above 40°C (104°F), but the most important sign of this problem is that the victim becomes confused or behaves irrationally. There is sometimes incoordination or delirium and eventually even convulsions or unconsciousness. Sweating is usually decreased, but the skin is not often dry. The pulse and respiratory rates are higher than normal. (Worrying pulse rates in adults would be over 100 beats/minute and a worrying respiratory rate over 30/minute. The respiratory rate is the number of the times the chest rises and people who know you are counting their breathing rate are unlikely to be able to breath normally).

The treatment is as for heat exhaustion:

- Place victim in the shade
- Remove clothing (his not yours, silly)
- Fan the victim
- Sponge with a cool wet cloth (but do not apply ice)
- Gently massage limb muscles to encourage heat dissipation
- Encourage drinking if possible
- Monitor the temperature; stop active cooling when it is below 39°C (102°F)
- Beware of the temperature rising again
- If the victim is unconscious, raise his legs above the level of his heart

Unconsciousness implies a very grave condition. If the victim has been unconscious for more than 2 minutes, evacuate him to a hospital while continuing to cool him.

Unconsciousness for longer than 2 hours is usually followed by permanent disability. Heat stroke is a very serious and dangerous condition.

Prickly heat and heat rash are covered on p.107.

Deserts

The risks of the heat and the sun are more obvious in deserts than in many other environments. If you are driving through desert consider the consequences of vehicle breakdown and carry plenty of water. Body fluid losses are huge, especially when you are receiving a good cooling breeze through an open window; make an effort to drink more. If you are stranded without water do not drink urine but consider other sources of water, such as the car radiator (as long as no anti-freeze has been added) or condensation which will collect under plastic at night. A big hazard of desert travel in vehicles is meeting unprepared travellers who scrounge water and leave you short. Carry plenty.

Avoid undue heat exposure and protect your skin from the sun by wearing a hat and long loose clothing. Avoid vigorous exercise when it is very hot: the *siesta* is a very sensible behavioural adaptation to the intense heat of the middle of the day.

Your appetite for salt will probably increase in a desert environment; shake more salt on your food to replace the lost salt that your body is requesting. Salt tablets are not recommended.

Dangerous Desert Animals

Snakes (*see* p.151) and scorpions (*see* p.143) are the major animal hazards of deserts, although some desert environments have some large species also capable of inflicting damage, like lions in the Kalahari.

Jungle, Tropical Forests and Scrub

Tropical and sub-tropical forests are hot humid places where you can lose a surprising amount of body fluids very quickly. Be sensible about the amount of exercise you take in these environments, particularly on first arriving. Build up the pace of activities over at least a week (even if you are fit) otherwise heat exhaustion may be the price you pay.

Wear long loose cotton clothes and insect repellent. They keep off biting insects (*see* p.138), ticks (*see* p.65) and also protect you from noxious plants (*see* below and p.108). Although most malaria-bearing mosquitoes bite at night, some forest-dwelling *Anopheles* are day-biters. Asian rain forests and deciduous forests during the monsoon are often crawling with leeches; insect repellents and long clothes keep them away (*see* p.140). Wear proper boots if you are planning to stray away from paths since you will have to be especially cautious about snakes, centipedes and, after dark in dry forests, scorpions. Never put your hands or feet anywhere you cannot see them. Shake out your boots before putting them on otherwise you may find yourself on the end of a scorpion's sting or centipede's jaws.

Noxious Plants and Wee Furry Animals

Tropical plants have evolved an impressive array of unpleasant ways of protecting themselves; some of these weapons may be used against you if you plunge into tropical undergrowth without the protection of suitable clothing. Some plants are covered in barbed thorns which you may not notice until you come into contact with them; they can be difficult to pull out. Be careful about what you handle. Furry-looking seed pods, for example are covered in little hairs which penetrate skin and cause discomfort which is only relieved by painstakingly removing each hair with a fine pair of tweezers. Prickly pears, young bamboo and a host of other plants have similar defence mechanisms. Cute little tenrecs (Madagascar's equivalent of a hedgehog) manage the same trick with their very fine spines and so can furry caterpillars.

Take care not to upset wasps for an angry swarm will make you feel bad for days at least (*see* p.145).

There are plants which secrete irritant oils, such as the New World poison ivy and poison oak. The giant hogweed, *Heracleum mantegazzianum*, causes a sunlight-sensitive blistering rash (*see* p.112). Avoid any plant which secretes a milky sap; some species cause blistering if you get it in your eyes. Others are extremely painful stingers. In Nepal, for example, nettles (called *sisnu* or *allo* which look like malignant mutants of the English stinger) are exceedingly unpleasant. There are a variety of antidotes which, like our European dock, grow with it. The most common is *Artemisia dubia* which looks like a straggly chrysanthemum and is called *titepati* locally.

Mosquitoes and larger predators love dense undergrowth; listen to what the locals say about their more unpleasant wildlife and do not go into the jungle scantily clad.

Man-eaters

Bears are probably the most dangerous animals of tropical, subtropical and even temperate forests (*see* p.156). Other large species generally prefer to leave you alone unless you appear suddenly, up close and they feel threatened. Do not amble through very long grass or dense scrub in wildlife habitats—or if you must, make lots of noise. Beware of snakes and chiggers too and make sure you wear boots and long trousers if in heavy undergrowth.

The salt concentration of sea water is not high enough for it to act as a disinfectant and a variety of disease organisms, including cholera, thrive in it. Swallowing sea water can be hazardous if you swim in heavily contaminated, land-locked or poorly flushed areas. The Mediterranean and many British beaches are particularly unhealthy. Faecal coliform counts (a measure of the amount of faeces present) are published at many UK bathing sites now. Skin problems are another consequence of bathing in heavily polluted waters.

A depressing number of tourists drown each year while bathing in idyllic, inviting tropical seas. Many have been drinking alcohol before they drown. People worry about sharks, sea snakes and scorpion fish (*see* p.147), but undertows and rip-tides are far more effective killers. Listen to what locals advise about swimming and if no-one else is bathing, pause to think why.

Even in the summer, temperate seas are rarely warmer than 15°C and at these temperatures swimmers easily get into trouble and drown. Beware of swimming too soon (less than 2 hours) after a heavy meal. Cramp can sink even the strongest swimmer. It comes on much more readily if your stomach is very full and if you have any alcohol in your system; the risk is greatest in cooler waters.

Water does not protect against sunburn, indeed drops of water act like lenses which magnify the burning power of the sun. Even waterproof sun-screens wash off or are sweated off quite quickly, so swim wearing a shirt as well as sun-screen. Being out all day in strong tropical sunshine—especially if it is reflected off water or other light surfaces—can give you soreness of the eyes rather like a mild snow blindness (*see* p.89). Protect your eyes with good sunglasses.

SCUBA Diving

A large number of 'diving centres' now exist all over the tropics: they offer aqua-lungs and all you need to be able to dive down deep. Many centres do not expect any previous training in the sport and offer only minimal tuition themselves. They have a vested interest in hiring equipment to you. Do not be tempted to 'have a go' unless you are trained to dive with this equipment or unless they offer training to a recognized standard (e.g. British Sub-aqua Club Sports Diver qualification). You can burst a lung and die of air embolism while ascending from a depth of perhaps 3 metres. Generally in tropical waters you can see a tremendous amount with only a mask and snorkel so stick to these unless you know what you are doing.

It is possible to suffer from decompression sickness if you fly soon after SCUBA diving. Unless you have been doing a great deal of intensive and deep decompression dives, allowing 24 hours between your last dive and your flight should avoid this problem.

Sunburn and Snorkelling

Sunburn acquired while snorkelling can be extremely severe. Wear a shirt (preferably one with a collar), long shorts and also use a water-resistant, high SPF sun-screen on the other exposed parts of your back, including the back of the neck and the backs of your legs.

Noxious Creatures

All marine animals should be assumed to be venomous and treated with great respect. Noxious creatures abound in tropical seas. The most dangerous species are described on p.145. Swimmers, bathers and paddlers are commonly stung by venomous fish—even in temperate regions. Fish toxins are inactivated by immersion in very hot water; prevention and treatment are described in detail on p.148.

Salt Water Crocodiles and Sea Snakes

Saltwater or estuarine crocodiles (*see* pp.149 and 151) are a significant hazard of sea-bathing in Southeast Asia, India, Sri Lanka and Australia. Sea snakes too (*see* p.150) are a potential threat, but deaths from these and from shark attacks (*see* p.149) are rare.

Coral

Coral causes problems in several ways. The small coral fragments which make up many palm-fringed beaches penetrate the soles of the feet and even a small piece is surprisingly painful and remarkably difficult to extract. Wearing shoes while paddling and swimming will prevent this annoying affliction and will give you some protection from the nastier stinging fishes and sea urchin spines too. Live coral looks soft, inviting and beautiful so that one is tempted to snorkel in close to admire its colours. However, it is highly abrasive and any scratches or scrapes you get by brushing against it will suppurate and be particularly uncomfortable, sometimes for weeks. Wash any abrasions thoroughly, remove any coral, sand or debris and apply antiseptic (*see* p.105). In addition to these hazards there are varieties of stinging corals, known as fire corals. They inflict extremely painful and persistent stings.

'Sea Lice' or Sea-bathers' Eruption

This problem has only recently been recognized and there are no accounts of it in reference books, so I will describe it in detail. Readers' observations on this would be especially welcome.

What Are 'Sea Lice'?

This problem has also been called Ocean itch, Caribe and Sea poisoning. Swimmers notice raised red wheals appearing a few hours after bathing in tropical seas and the symptoms persist for several days. The problem only affects some people so that when friends bathe together some may be afflicted and others not at all. The rash is most usually on skin which has been covered by bathing suits or other places where the skin is rubbed, such as armpits, the crooks of the arms, backs of the knees, inner thighs and in surfers wherever their skin has been in contact with the surfboard. In Florida, where there are most records of the problem, 'sea lice' seems to be caused by stings from larvae of the thimble jellyfish, *Linuche unguiculata*. These are tiny, almost invisible creatures just half a millimetre long which get caught between bathing costumes and the skin.

Where Are 'Sea Lice' a Problem?

The thimble jellyfish is a widespread tropical species which occurs off Central and South America as well as the Indo-Pacific including the Philippines and Singapore. Other jellyfish larvae are probably also capable of causing similar problems so 'sea lice' may afflict bathers wherever they swim in warm seas.

Who is Afflicted?

Not everyone encountering these creatures will be affected in the same way and those who have never met the larvae before will have no rash. The disease seems to be an immune hypersensitivity reaction to jellyfish venom. Those who have encountered the animals numerous times before will actually notice a mild stinging sensation as they swim. These individuals can provide an early warning for other swimmers.

In What Season is It a Problem?

Along the Florida coast the disease is only ever present between April and July (inclusive). Even then, it only occurs during certain years and usually—as with other jellyfish stings—when there are on-shore winds.

Treatment

'Sea lice' inject minute quantities of venom beneath the skin so that nothing that you put on the skin surface will go deep enough to counteract the venom. The only action which is really likely to help is to remove bathing suits and shower (preferably initially in salt water) after swimming. Showering in freshwater before the swimsuit has been removed will make the venomous cysts of the larvae discharge which will aggravate the situation. Anyone who has an attack of 'sea lice' will probably experience another when putting on the same swimsuit again. It is advisable, therefore, either to throw away the swimsuit or machine-wash it with detergent, and then tumble dry it.

Stinging Sea?

Interestingly I have noticed stinging sensations when bathing in Sri Lanka and Indonesia. Expatriates in Lombok blame the sensation (which unlike 'sea lice' seems to affect everyone in a similar way) on a stinging seaweed. The problem does indeed seem most apparent when there are a lot of broken pieces of weed in the water. What I guess happens, though, is that jellyfish larvae arrive at the beach with the same onshore winds which bring the weed debris. The good news about the Asian stinging sea, is that there are no after effects. There is only the slightly unnerving sensation of receiving stings—albeit mild stings—from some invisible force. It needs no treatment for it is a transient sensation.

Dangers of Bathing in Rivers and Lakes

The principal risk of freshwater bathing is drowning. A surprising number of river-side beauty spots and apparently tranquil, attractive pools have claimed the lives of careless revellers. Be wary, especially in limestone areas where rivers—or more dangerously parts of rivers—could suck you underground.

Drowning Inside a Vehicle

I was surprised to learn that in the UK more people drown inside vehicles than while swimming. Here is what to do if your vehicle ends up in deep water. When a car plunges into water it settles nose down since the heaviest part, the engine, is usually at the front and the boot (trunk) remains full of air. The car, once sub-merged, will begin to fill with water, but it is not until it is reasonably full that you will be able to open the doors and get out. If you are in the front of the car you may be submerged inside the car before sufficient water has entered to allow you to escape. The correct action, then, is to wind down the windows to allow the car to fill up quickly so that you can open the doors or exit through a window.

On Finding Yourself in a Rapid

If you fall out of a boat, find yourself swept into a rapid and are getting taken down-stream out of control there are several techniques which will help you survive. Ensure, firstly, that you are travelling feet first so that, if you hit any boulders or submerged obstacles, your feet will take the impact not your head. Even if you feel you can make headway by swimming against the current, resist the temptation to swim across the river. You will just get swept downstream faster. Swim heading upstream pointing just a few degrees towards the bank you wish to reach. That way you will slowly progress across in a 'ferry glide'. Ducks and other experienced river users use this technique.

Finally if you get caught up in a standing wave at the bottom of a small water shoot or waterfall you will be held in the water, unable to breath, just below the surface. The only way to escape is to swim **down**. The water at the bottom of the standing wave (or 'stopper' as canoeists call them) will flush you out and allow you to surface. This is one rare situation where a life jacket may reduce your chances of escape; consider jettisoning it if you are caught in a stopper and it prevents you from swimming downwards.

Bilharzia (Schistosomiasis)

Napoleon described Egypt as the land of the menstruating men. Bilharzia was so common that if Egyptian children did not pass blood with their urine, some parents wondered what was wrong. This is the major symptom of one of the three kinds of schistosomiasis or bilharzia.

The disease is caused by a minute worm which spends part of its life cycle in freshwater snails and the other part in people. The parasite causes 'swimmers' itch' as it burrows through the skin while you paddle or bathe in infected water. The species which occur in Africa and America (*Schistosoma haematobium* and *S. mansoni*) are slow penetrators. Since it takes at least 5 minutes to get through the skin, a quick splash across a suspect stream should do you no harm. Unfortunately oriental schistosomiasis (*Schistosoma japonicum*) can penetrate the skin in a few seconds.

From the skin, the worm rides along in the bloodstream, traverses the lungs where it often causes cough and wheeze 2–3 weeks after the swimmers itch and finally it sets up home in a favoured organ, where it will cause an illness with fever. Untreated, this will settle, then over the years with repeated reinfections it will cause increasingly debilitating disease which may kill after a couple of decades. Travellers will have the problem diagnosed within a couple of months at most, so the chronic disease is rarely a disease of travellers or expatriates. There is a good treatment, at present, so it can be cured with a single dose during the feverish stage of the illness. However, resistance is developing to this medicine so (as with all diseases) take care to avoid infection in the first place. A blood test will reveal whether you have been infected as long as it is done more than six weeks from the time of infection.

'Swimmers' itch' can even be a problem in Britain where schistosome parasites penetrate the skin, but are unable to complete their life cycle; an example is *Trichobilharzia* of Loch Lomond. This needs no treatment since the only symptom it causes is mild, short-lived itching.

Bilharzia Country

Bilharzia snails favour well oxygenated, still or slowly moving freshwater which has some plant life growing in it. The snails must first be infected by someone with the disease urinating or defecating into the water. The risk of infection is therefore greatest in water bodies close to human settlements. Bilharzia is a growing problem in some irrigated areas, mainly in Africa, but although it is trendy to criticize such irrigation projects for causing epidemics, few people realize that most projects which are properly built do not cause problems. Even where irrigation does encourage bilharzia, well-fed farmers are generally much better off than hungry people without bilharzia.

Where is Bilharzia a Problem?

The disease is prevalent in much of Africa including Egypt, Madagascar and Mauritius. It also occurs in the Middle East, Venezuela, Surinam, some Caribbean Islands and Brazil. The Indian subcontinent is clear except for a tiny area in Maharashtra State on the west coast of India. The focus which used to exist in southern Portugal has now been eradicated. The oriental form has a patchy distribution: it occurs in parts of China, Taiwan, Vietnam and the Philippines, but Indonesia is free except for two remote valleys in central Sulawesi.

It is relatively common for expatriates and travellers to be exposed to bilharzia in Africa. Try to avoid bathing or paddling in suspect waters and consider a blood test at least six weeks after leaving the area of risk.

River Blindness (Onchocerciasis)

River blindness is a problem in much of tropical sub-saharan Africa between 19°N and 17°S and also in central and tropical South America. This unpleasant worm is transmitted near to fast-flowing rivers where the small black-fly vectors breed. The Latin name of these little biting flies, *Simulium damnosum*, emphasizes their pestilential nature. The disease has a variety of manifestations, since it invades many parts of the body, but in expatriates and travellers the worms most commonly make the skin incredibly itchy and the itching is usually confined to a single limb or only the arms or only the legs. Generally people need to have had extremely heavy infestations for many years before the eyes are threatened.

Do not treat yourself, but get the problem properly diagnosed. Long trousers, socks and repellents protect the skin from bites in Africa, but in the Americas the arms also need to be covered with long sleeved garments. Black-flies are day biters.

Noxious Animals

Crocodiles

Freshwater crocodiles are dangerous in Africa including Madagascar; Asian muggers are not supposed to be dangerous but *see* p.151.

Piranhas

These fish, in contrast, are nothing to worry about (but *see* p.150); there are no reliable reports of human deaths from piranhas.

Stingrays

There are some very unpleasant freshwater stingrays in South America which are capable of inflicting severe and excruciating wounds. Prevention of attacks and treatment of wounds are as for salt water rays (*see* p.148).

Aquatic Leeches

Leeches are a hazard of bathing in freshwater in Southeast Asia and the Indonesian Archipelago. They very occasionally enter bodily orifices to produce bleeding from unusual places. Although thoughts of such infestations are horrifying, they are extremely rare in travellers and serious complications are unlikely (*see* p.140).

Infections

There are at least a couple of nasty bacterial illnesses—leptospirosis (Weil's disease) and shigella (bacillary dysentery) which may be acquired if bathers accidentally swallow water while they are swimming. Hepatitis A may also be acquired in this way. Many contaminated water bodies will be obviously polluted so the risk should be apparent. If in doubt, keep your mouth closed when swimming. Itching can also be a problem after bathing in polluted waters.

Summary

- ⊕ Whenever outdoors, wear shoes or some kind of foot protection, even when swimming.
- ⊕ Think about the risks before heading into an unfamiliar environment, make suitable preparations and take sensible precautions. Most accidents in hostile environments arise from poor planning and research or inadequate equipment and experience.
- ⊕ Heed warnings of local hazards.

⊕ Protect yourself from sunburn with a hat, suitable clothes and sun-screen.

⊕ Use a high protection factor (SPF 15–20), waterproof sun-screen especially when snorkelling or bathing.

⚠ Never sun-bathe in the middle of the day.

High, Cold and Dark

Hazards of Mountaineering

The hazards of trekking somewhere remote like the Andes or Himalayas are a combination of the problems of fell walking, plus special altitude risks compounded by illnesses of the developing world. It is crazy to assume that you will be able to, or will want to, complete a 3-week hike exactly on schedule. If illness or fatigue do not slow you down, local bureaucracy may well delay you before you start. Judgement is all important at altitude but can be impaired by even mild mountain sickness and exhaustion and these can rapidly lead to exposure, frostbite and death. Even minor injuries or blistered feet can mean the difference between reaching a safe haven and not. It is easy to over-stretch yourself and it is sensible to be able to recognize the early signs of these problems—especially if you are inexperienced in coping with mountain conditions. Take appropriate action to prevent minor problems becoming life-threatening crises.

More and more people are venturing high. About 50,000 trekkers a year visit Nepal alone and during the trekking season more than 50 people per day cross the Thorong La (a 5400m/17,700ft pass) on their trek around Annapurna. Most of these people have little or no mountaineering experience. This section comprises tips for people who are going to altitudes up to 6000m (20,000ft), but who are not experienced mountaineers and may not have done much mountain walking at lower altitudes. High altitude trips (above 6000m) need specialist advice.

It is easy to be misled by conditions in the mountains; the bright clear skies make foul weather seem an impossibility. One winter in Ladakh, I encountered a couple of intrepid French tourists who had wandered to the wrong side of a 5300m/17,500ft pass. When they set out, the sun was bright and warming and it was easy to forget that the ambient temperature was −11°C. They had no packs or spare clothes so that when the weather closed in unexpectedly, they narrowly escaped getting into serious trouble. In East Nepal, four tourists ventured high in good weather attired in sandals and summer clothes. There was an unseasonal snowstorm and had they not found a hut to spend the night in they would all have perished. In the morning, the least badly frostbitten member of the group struggled down for help and they all made it to safety—minus a few toes.

Sedentary individuals who decide to take up trekking should start slowly. Getting fit before a trip will enhance your enjoyment. Running, swimming and using stairs rather than lifts in buildings will all improve cardiovascular fitness. One woman who was evacuated by helicopter from Annapurna Base Camp recently was on her first ever trip into hill or mountain terrain. She had seriously underestimated how strenuous mountain walking can be and was lucky that a helicopter could be summoned by radio (her insurance covered this, otherwise—radio or not—this would not have been an option for her). Of 148,000 trekkers who visited Nepal over a three and a half year period, 23 died (mostly by falling off cliff paths) and there were 111 helicopter rescues.

Ensure that you allow enough time for the trip you have planned. Rushing makes the trip miserable and makes you more prone to mountain sickness, injury and accidents. Nor do you see as much. Only half of the trekkers who set out intending to walk to Everest base camp arrive. The others turn back, disappointed; they ran out of time and could not cover the distance they expected because of sickness and the strenuous nature of the walking. Particularly in Nepal, you do not need to rush up to great heights; lower altitudes are just as interesting, but different, and there are often fewer tourists.

Who Should Not Ascend?

Not many medical conditions put an absolute ban on high altitude mountaineering, but there are two: sickle cell disease and people prone to recurrent pneumothorax (burst lung). Do not climb above 3500m (12,000ft) when pregnant.

Walking Problems

Walk with a steady rhythm and pace yourself so that you do not need frequent rests; you should be able to keep going all day. If you are having to stop for breath or needing to pause because you are tired more often than for five minutes each hour you are trying to walk too fast. Soldiers use this technique of walking for an hour and pausing for five minutes, but you are not on a forced march, so walk at your own pace and enjoy the scenery. Do not be hassled into trying to keep up with macho show-offs. Adopt your own comfortable speed.

'Sahib's Knee'

Many people sustain knee injuries when they are trekking in the mountains. The reason for this is often poor walking technique on descent, combined with unfitness. It surprises people to discover that walking down is more strenuous than ascending. When tired, people step down onto a straight leg. This jolts the knee joint. To protect the knee and to develop a controlled walking rhythm you need to step down onto a slightly bent knee. The muscles and tendons of the thigh then absorb the repeated impacts. It is hard to walk downhill like this for long if you are unfit. To avoid injury, then, you need to rest when you are no longer able to take your weight on a slightly flexed knee. Plan your trek so that you can rest overnight if there is a very long descent on your route. Injuries sustained by walking on unflexed knees have been labelled Sahib's knee since this is how unfit British administrators suffered when visiting the hills during the days of the Raj.

The treatment of knee injuries and other strains and wrenches is rest. If you must continue walking, considerably reduce your daily distance and employ someone to carry your pack if possible. Tight strapping with a crêpe or ace bandage will help, although crêpe bandages need to be washed frequently to retain their stretchiness. The treatment of wrenches, sprains and sore joints is given on p.169.

Care of Feet

It is especially important to take good care of the feet when in the mountains. Change your socks whenever they get wet, especially in snow since it is very easy to get frostnip without realizing it. Any broken skin must be carefully cleaned and any incipient patches of infection treated (by soaking the feet in hot salty water) before bacteria have a chance to get a hold. Break your boots in before any big trip. Wearing brand new boots on a trek is asking for trouble, yet on a recent flight to Pokhara (the starting point for treks in the Annapurna region) I was amazed to see that most budding trekkers were wearing shiny new boots. The lightest possible footwear is most comfortable. Unless you are going high or expect to be walking in snow, trainers or tennis shoes suit most people and are less likely to cause blisters than new boots. Remove footwear when crossing rivers; wet boots are much more likely to rub and cause blisters. If a very stiff pair of boots are giving you a lot of trouble, try the old technique of wearing two pairs of socks (one thick and one thin) since this reduces friction and blisters. Take specialist advice on the kind of climbing boots you need for your particular trip and remember that the new kinds of waterproof boots need to be dried out every evening: they do not 'breathe' like leather boots. Do not puncture blisters but pad them with sticking plaster or mole-skin cut into a doughnut shape.

Nails of the big toes have a nasty habit of 'ingrowing' and becoming infected. This is avoided by cutting those toenails straight across, leaving sharp corners and *not* neatly rounding them off. Also keep these nails short. For advice on athlete's foot and cracked heels, *see* p.113.

Swelling of the Ankles (Oedema)

Some swelling of the feet and lower legs is common in mountain walkers even at low altitudes, especially if you are over-weight. As long as you continue to feel well this is no cause for concern. If the swelling becomes uncomfortable, rest with your feet above heart height. If the swelling is accompanied by pain or feeling unwell seek medical help if possible—certainly go no higher and evacuate at a gentle pace.

Cold and Wind Chill

At the low temperatures which prevail at altitude, it is easy to get seriously cold.

Chilling happens fastest if conditions are windy and/or you are wet. Carry a change of clothes packed in a plastic bag.

There have been a few deaths from mountaineers being poisoned with carbon monoxide from butane stoves left burning in badly ventilated tents all night in order to keep out the cold. Others have been burned alive. Beware.

Fluid Loss

More fluid is lost from the body at altitude and in windy conditions so you must make a conscious effort to drink more. The body's thirst mechanisms are poor at encouraging you to drink enough. If you have a fever or diarrhoea or have been badly sun-burnt you also need to drink lots more.

Dry Skin

The skin can become uncomfortably dry and scaly even at modest altitude, but particularly in the high cold deserts of the Andes or Transhimalaya. Pack some moisturizing cream, as well as creams and lip-screen (and possibly Body Shop jojoba moisture cream or lipsalve for dry lips) to protect you from the sun. If you have no moisturizer use butter or some other locally available grease.

Nose Bleeds

These can be a new problem for people staying in a high, dry climate. Anoint the inside of the nose with Vaseline or any greasy cream which is not highly perfumed. Butter or cooking oil will do if there is nothing else.

The Sun at Altitude

It is easy to get sun-burnt at altitude despite the cold; even dark-skinned people need to wear sun-screen and protect themselves with suitable clothing and a hat. The sun at altitude may provoke cold sores if you are prone to them (*see* p.73).

In Ladakh (where winter daytime temperatures may be −20°C) it is possible to get sun-stroke and frost bite simultaneously by lying with your feet in the shade and your head in the sun.

Snow Blindness

Nepalis describe snow blindness as like having your eyeballs rubbed in a mixture of chilli and sand. It is a very painful and debilitating inflammation of the eyes caused by too much sunlight radiation. This most usually occurs at altitude and in snow, but something akin to snow blindness can happen in any circumstance where there is a lot of glare. It is dangerous, because it temporarily blinds in a situation where you may need to see to stay alive. Treatment is to cover the eyes (tape them closed) and descend to recover. Cold compresses may help the pain.

Snow blindness is prevented by wearing goggles or sun-glasses. Poor porters in Nepal protect their eyes by tying a strip of cloth over their eyes which has slits cut for them to see out.

Mountain Sickness

Mountains kill a lot of people. One tenth of mountaineers who climb over 6000m (20,000ft) on serious expeditions die. Yet most deaths on mountains do not kill those who are on expeditions. Those who do not come back include many tourists and visitors to the Himalayan region, the Andes, Mount Kilimanjaro (at 5895m/19,340ft this is one of the highest mountains climbed by many ordinary tourists without technical mountaineering skills) and Mount Kenya. It is ignorance about mountain sickness which is often the reason for their demise.

People have known about mountain sickness for a long time. Chinese travellers in 35 BC described the Himalayas as the Headache Mountains. Yet the disease is complex and still not well understood. Acute mountain sickness (AMS) is caused by a failure of the body's biochemistry to maintain the correct balance of acid and alkali in the blood which in turn is necessary to control breathing and crucial fluid balance in the body. The acid/alkali balance is normally controlled by the concentration of carbon dioxide in blood, thus the body's drive to breathe is controlled by build up of carbon dioxide (rather than a deficit of oxygen). At sea level this ensures that you breath in enough oxygen, but at altitude, carbon dioxide is more soluble and the amount in blood needs to be higher before its concentration is high enough to stimulate a faster breathing rate. You need to breathe faster at altitude so that you take in enough oxygen from the thinner air. Despite this, the carbon dioxide drive to breathe initially lags behind the body's need for oxygen. When oxygen supplies to the brain are not maintained, headaches and confusion begin. The headache is a sign that the brain is swelling slightly.

After a few days at altitude, other longer term mechanisms switch in. These are enzyme and hormone changes which allow the breathing rate to settle to a slower rate again. This is acclimatization.

Symptoms of Mild Mountain Sickness

- Poor performance
- Slight headache
- Breathlessness on exertion
- Chest discomfort

- Insomnia
- Periodic (Cheyne–Stokes) sighing respiration when asleep
- Loss of appetite
- Nausea
- Vomiting
- Mood changes
- Fatigue

Action—watch out for increasingly severe symptoms. If you are planning to go higher consider stopping for a rest day and acclimatization. Descend to sleep lower down if possible or dramatically slow your ascent. Start *acetazolamide* treatment if possible (*see* below, p.95). Ascend no further if the headache is persistent.

Symptoms of Moderate to Severe Mountain Sickness

Severe mountain sickness may not necessarily lead on from mild AMS but can cause rapid deterioration over a couple of hours 'out of the blue'. Only some of the listed symptoms will be present.

- Severe headache*
- Disorientation
- Confusion* and memory loss
- Strange behaviour*
- Difficulty with balance, stumbling, etc.*
- Hallucinations*
- Drowsiness (person is difficult to wake up)*
- Severe nightmares
- Unwarranted breathlessness, perhaps even at rest (compared with colleagues)*
- Nausea and vomiting
- Severe fatigue
- Dry cough, frothy spit and even blood-stained spit*

Symptoms marked * are very worrying and should precipitate immediate descent, whatever the time of day or night. **Action**—descend immediately.

Bad headache, disorientation, breathlessness (especially if associated with coughing up frothy, blood-stained sputum) are signs that severe and dangerous problems are starting. These symptoms may lead very rapidly to death. The treatment is to descend immediately. In Nepal, trekkers who are too ill to walk are sometimes carried on up over high passes or go on up on horseback so that other members of the party are not inconvenienced. Some of these people die. Going down even as little as 500m can be sufficient to save someone's life, but descend as far as you can or until the victim is clearly well again. It is rare to be in a situation where you have to ascend before descent is possible so most deaths are unnecessary.

Mountain sickness is dangerous because it can come on rapidly. The early symptoms are non-specific and the victims are often too disorientated to recognize how sick they are; they even argue about descending. Over-ruling them can be difficult, but may save lives. This disorientation, and the reluctance of other members of the group to compromise their trip, is one reason why AMS kills so many people. **If in doubt, descend**. Do not wait until morning to see if the victim feels better.

Diagnosing Mountain Sickness

Assume illness at altitude is altitude sickness until proved otherwise. Various doctors have produced simple guidelines for diagnosing mountain sickness to help people decide when descent is necessary, but the symptoms of AMS so often overlap with other common illnesses of mountain walkers that none are foolproof. Lists of symptoms are also less useful than deciding whether someone looks ill or not. Headache is the most worrying symptom. There are no signs (except perhaps frothy or blood-stained spit) which are especially characteristic of AMS. It can be difficult to differentiate, say, dehydration and exhaustion from AMS: both cause headache, dizziness, confusion and nausea, but the wise action to take if there is any doubt is to descend. People suffering from mountain sickness should improve dramatically with descent. Few children ever complain of headache and often a child with mountain sickness will say that they have a headache for the first time in their life.

Periodic (Cheyne–Stokes) Respiration

When people first ascend to altitude their sleep patterns are often disturbed. Indeed some people are awakened by a feeling they are being suffocated. What is happening is that the body's drive to breathe has become sluggish and during sleep the breathing becomes progressively slower and shallower until it actually stops for a few seconds. Breathing restarts with a deep sigh and this deep inspiration is sometimes what wakes the sleeper. It is an alarming pattern to witness because as you lie in the darkness listening you begin to wonder whether your friend is ever going to start breathing again. You are just about to struggle out of your sleeping bag to shake them back to consciousness when the deep sighing inspiration starts them breathing again. This is normal in people newly arriving at altitude and is no cause for concern. *Acetazolamide* speeds up acclimatization and so reduces sleep disturbance due to this peculiar phenomenon.

Who is at Risk From Mountain Sickness?

The people at greatest risk are those who arrive at altitude by plane, train or bus and then ascend further without acclimatizing. Unfit people are flown in to a plush hotel at Syangboche (close to Everest) where mountain sickness is so common that oxygen is provided in all the rooms! Lhasa in Tibet (at 3350m), Cusco in Peru (at 3310m) and La Paz in Bolivia (3636m) are dangerous places because many tourists fly in for a short holiday and expect to ascend from there the day after arriving. Similarly in Peru you can ascend from Lima to nearly 5000m (16,400ft) by train in half a day. Sleeping at the lowest possible altitude helps protect from mountain sickness.

Being fit gives no protection. Indeed, the fitter you are, the faster you can ascend and so the more likely you are to suffer from mountain sickness. Men trying to prove themselves most often get into trouble and hearty middle-aged women seem best adapted.

Mount Kenya at just over 5000m (16,400ft) is not particularly high but it kills a lot of people. The first day's climbing takes you to 3000m and the second day there is a 1300m climb to the second refuge. From here it is an easy day to one of the mountain's three peaks. People feeling bad at the second refuge therefore tend to 'sit it out' rather than following the standard advice to descend to sleep low if they have symptoms of AMS.

It is difficult to give hard and fast rules about when a climb or mountain walk must be abandoned because of mountain sickness, but clearly not enough people pay attention to the early symptoms. If they did there would be fewer deaths.

Mountain sickness is unpredictable. If you have escaped it once, you may suffer the next time you ascend and if you suffered once it does not mean you will suffer every time, although you are probably more susceptible.

Children

Children are highly susceptible to mountain sickness but also acclimatize faster than adults. I would counsel against taking young children above 3500m (12,000ft) and even at this altitude you should be meticulously cautious, feel that you know what you are doing and be prepared to descend rapidly at short notice.

Avoiding Mountain Sickness

Mountain sickness is generally only a problem above 3000m (10,000ft), but some have died of it at this modest altitude. The only way to avoid it is to allow plenty of time for acclimatization and if you notice any symptoms, stop or at least slow down your ascent. A recommended safe rate of ascent is to take several days to reach 3500m (11,000ft), and then a further week to reach 5500m (18,000ft). This is an average ascent rate of about 300m per day, but take rest days and pace yourself according to the slowest member of the party. Even at this rate, not everyone will be able to go high. Many people are too impatient to ascend at this rate, or it may be that accommodation or terrain make it difficult to slow down; this is why Mount Kenya is such a dangerous mountain. If you exceed the recommended rate, watch carefully for danger signs. Be especially cautious if this is a first ascent or if you have had problems before. Even at recommended rates of ascent around the Annapurna Circuit, for example, half of trekkers suffer from symptoms of mild to moderate mountain sickness (headache, nausea and lack of appetite). Some people are inexplicably sensitive to even slow rates of ascent and die on relatively modest routes.

Local advice on mountain sickness may be misleading for two reasons. Some local guides and porters who live at intermediate altitude may not realize how much more susceptible foreigners who live at sea level are to mountain sickness and how easily they can succumb. Conversely, with increasing numbers of tourists visiting Nepal there are greater employment opportunities for inexperienced jobless lowlanders to work as porters; they may know even less about the hazards of the mountains than an inexperienced trekker. Indeed some die each year (e.g. recently on Larkya La) from mountain sickness or exposure. Any porters you use should be properly equipped (with shoes, jumpers, blankets, etc) and watched. Headaches should be treated with *acetazolamide* (*see* p.95), rather than simple pain killers. Allow time for them to rest if they are obviously flagging. Some trekking agencies in Kathmandu proudly announce that they can arrange Gamow Bag treatment (*see* p.96) for mountain sickness; does this mean that their clients often get into trouble with mountain sickness because of poor planning and slowness to descend when symptoms begin? Perhaps it would be wise to ask the trekking agency what they know about mountain sickness and what they might do in some hypothetical situations.

Prevention of Mountain Sickness with Medicines

There is some debate about whether taking *acetazolamide* tablets to speed up acclimatization is a good thing. I think it is. *Acetazolamide* alters the acidity of the blood and stimulates an increase in breathing rate. Thus it increases oxygen availability to the brain and tissues in the critical first few days at altitude; this tides the mountaineer over until other longer term mechanisms take over later.

This medicine certainly reduces the headache, nausea and insomnia that bother so many people above 3000m (9800ft); it is therefore excellent if you are ascending rapidly to altitudes of 3000–4500m by vehicle and cannot slow down your ascent if you feel unwell. Those who argue against its use suggest that it may suppress the early symptoms of AMS which act as warning signals and thus encourage people to go higher, faster. In practice this does not seem to be the case, especially when the medicine is used by adventurous travellers rather than mountaineers making major ascents to over 6000m (20,000ft). There is no firm evidence that it protects against the dangerous forms of mountain sickness so even if you are taking *acetazolamide* and you have symptoms of mountain sickness which seem to be getting worse, descend.

My colleague, Tony White, organized a research project during an expedition to the Andes. Some of us took *acetazolamide* and others took a look-alike placebo; Tony then tested mental function to assess the effects of altitude and the drug. Those of us taking *acetazolamide* not only felt better, slept better and had more stamina on caving trips, but our ability to perform complicated psychological tests was much better; we were as able to make rational judgements as we had been at sea level. In mountain situations clear thinking can be crucial, so I am a fan of *acetazolamide.*

Formulations of *acetazolamide* do not exist for children and there is no experience of the use of this drug in children (*acetazolamide* is only licenced in the UK for treating glaucoma in adults). So far, then, it cannot be used in the group of people most susceptible to mountain sickness. In future, other medicines (e.g. *benzo-lamide*), which protect against mountain sickness, may also become available.

Availability and Dosage of *Acetazolamide*

Acetazolamide is only available on prescription in the UK (and should strictly only be provided on a private prescription if it is to be used for foreign travel) and costs about £10 for 100 tablets of 250mg. It is also available over the counter in pharmacies in Lakeside Pokhara and Kathmandu in Nepal where it costs about one UK penny a tablet. Take two 250mg tablets or 'sustets' in the morning beginning 3 days before ascent and continue for at least 2 more days at altitude. Assuming that you wish to try the medicine before ascent (a 2-day trial several weeks before ascent may be wise to make sure you are not prone to intolerable side-effects), each traveller requires a minimum of 14 tablets. *Acetazolamide* is a diuretic so be prepared to produce more urine than usual while you are taking the drug.

The Treatment of Mountain Sickness

Descent is the only treatment for mountain sickness. If in doubt descend while the victim can still walk rather than waiting and having to evacuate an unconscious or uncooperative victim in the middle of the night. Even going down 500m may be enough to save someone's life, but go further down if possible. The newly developed Gamow repressurization bag (which weighs just 8kg/18lb) is no substitute for descent and if it delays going down it may actually do more harm than good. I have been horrified to hear of people suffering bad enough mountain sickness to be repressurized in the bag, then once supposedly 'cured', they continued to ascend. This is dangerous.

The very mildest end of mountain sickness, especially the altitude headache, can be treated with *acetazolamide* in adults (children should descend). It is best taken as a 'loading dose' of 750mg (three tablets) for small adults (less than 60kg/9st) or 1000mg (four tablets) for large people and then 500mg daily. AMS headache will respond in a few hours; do not ascend further if you still have the headache. However, *acetazolamide* may cause severe headache in well acclimatized people.

If you have to descend because of mountain sickess breathing out each breath through pursed lips is supposed to help. This apparently increases the air pressure in the lungs and is a kind of short-term do-it-yourself repressurization technique. It also gives someone who is feeling awful something to focus their attention on.

Side Effects of *Acetazolamide*

It is unusual for people to notice any dramatic side effects or reactions, but like all drugs *acetazolamide* has side effects. If you take it for a 2-day trial several weeks before ascent, you will be forewarned of any unpleasant reaction rather than suffering at altitude. The most common is tingling of the hands and feet which is occasionally sufficiently annoying to make people wish to stop the medicine; missing one or two doses should solve the problem.

Those who are allergic to sulphonamide antibiotics or other sulpha drugs are likely to be allergic to *acetazolamide* too and should not take it.

Other Hazards of Mountaineering

The Contraceptive Pill and Altitude

Women taking the combined contraceptive pill are theoretically at increased risk of pulmonary embolus, deep vein thrombosis and other blood clotting problems. Women climbing to extreme altitude (above 7000m) may therefore consider stopping the pill for any major ascents and for 6 weeks before ascent.

If you are contemplating this kind of climb seek specialist advice on this and other aspects of the medical risks.

Pregnancy and Altitude

Do not climb above 3500m (12,000ft) when pregnant and be extra careful about allowing time for acclimatization. If you are trekking during the first 3 months of pregnancy, consider the possibility of a miscarriage happening in some remote mountain village. The middle third of pregnancy is the best stage to be intrepid if you want to be. Travelling whilst pregnant is covered on p.124).

Exposure and Hypothermia

Exposure or hypothermia usually come on when you are exhausted, often wet, cold and hungry. As the body temperature continues to fall, exposure makes you feel inappropriately comfortable. You feel content and lose the drive to get somewhere safe. Sometimes the confusion of exposure makes people act in a bizarre manner: they take off their clothes or sit in puddles. That is why it is such a dangerous condition: people die of cold without ever realizing they were getting into trouble.

Heat is lost more rapidly when the body is wet or chilled by wind. Drinking alcohol also increases heat losses. Make sure that you are adequately equipped for your journey. Wear mittens not gloves and carry a spare pair since they are often lost. Carry a change of clothes in a plastic bag so that you can get warm and dry once you have reached a safe place. If you need to go on the next day, change back into the previous day's sweaty, damp clothes and keep one set dry for night-time. Rest for a day if you cannot face this.

Watch the people you are walking with and be forceful if you think they are getting into trouble. Stumbling is an early warning sign. People with early exposure shiver, but this ceases as the temperature continues to fall. Exposure and mountain sickness both cloud judgement so it is up to the unaffected to protect those who are affected. Exposure and mountain sickness on their own are dangerous enough, but they also make people prone to accidents, especially in combination with exhaustion. Plan carefully and be cautious in the mountains.

Chilly Children

Children have a higher surface to volume ratio than adults, so they cool much faster. They are at particular risk of hypothermia if you are carrying them; you keep warm through exercise while they freeze. Make sure they are warmly dressed and check often that they feel warm to the touch especially if it is windy.

Treatment of Exposure

The treatment of exposure is slow, gentle rewarming. One technique is to put the victim in a sleeping bag with someone else. Making the exposed climber too warm too soon can actually make things worse so hot baths are not sensible (even if they are available) and alcohol is also dangerous. The recommended rate of rewarming the body is only by about 1°C per hour but this rate may be doubled if shivering starts. Shivering is a good sign since is shows that the victim's survival processes are returning to normal. Even so, it will take many hours to rewarm someone thoroughly. Space blankets allow the body to rewarm slowly and steadily and are an appropriate treatment although they can be difficult to use since they do not work if the wearer is lying on the ground. Hot drinks also help the rewarming process.

Frostbite

Frostbite is rare in trekkers but is most likely on high passes in those with inadequate boots and little mountain experience. Frostbite means that living tissue has become frozen. In deep frostbite the toes (or other important members) look like a piece of chicken taken from the deep freeze. Frostbite is more likely at altitude (where tissues lack oxygen), where there are high winds to chill the body, at extremely low temperatures (below −10°C), if you are wet, if your boots are very constricting, in those with mountain sickness and in smokers. Contact with metal will make the skin more susceptible too since it conducts heat away. Beware of wearing metal glasses in extremely cold conditions. Earrings are not good mountain wear either. Frostbite is a reason for immediate evacuation and abandoning a climb.

Climbers will know times when their feet and hands have been numb for hours. Unfortunately, frostbite feels no worse than this; it is not painful until rewarming begins. The painlessness of frostbite makes it a dangerous condition. It is easy to injure a frostbitten limb and feel nothing, which is one reason why gangrene and infection can set in and amputation may be the final result. Superficial frostbite (frostnip) makes the skin look yellow-grey and leathery to the touch. In deep frostbite, the flesh is hard, white and obviously frozen.

Do not climb again for several months after suffering frostbite. If you know this beforehand, you may try harder to avoid the problem in the first place.

Treatment of Frostbite

The treatment is evacuation to a lower safer place (walk on the still frozen foot if necessary) and rewarm the affected part by immersion in a saucepan of fairly hot (40°C) water for periods of 20 minutes. Do not knock or even rub the limb.

After the limb has been defrosted, the skin must be kept clean and the limb used as little as possible. The greatest danger to frostbitten skin is infection which can enter through any small breaks in the skin. A few hours after the limb has been thawed, it swells and, over the next two days, huge blisters erupt. These should be left intact and will be reabsorbed over the next week. The frostbitten limb becomes horribly discoloured, even black and shrivelled if there is gangrene. If the frostbite has been superficial, new pink skin will form under the black dead shell. If there was deep frostbite the end of the toe or finger will gradually come away. This is painless, if revolting.

If surgery is required, there are usually considerable advantages in waiting at least a few weeks for this to be performed and it is best done by a surgeon experienced in frostbite damage. It is wise to return to a hospital in the developed world for this if possible. A frostbitten limb suffers permanent damage which makes it more likely to be frostbitten a second time, so **once frostbitten twice frost shy**.

Exposure and frostbite are conditions which occasionally afflict poorly equipped adventurous travellers. Certainly people venturing high with inadequate footwear are at high risk especially if they get caught in unexpected snowfall. Ask about local conditions before ascent and make preparations for the worst possible weather.

Further Information

Union International des Associations d'Alpinisme, Mountain Medicine Centre, St. Bartholomew's Hospital, London EC1A 7BE publish information sheets (mostly at £2 per copy) about the medical aspects of mountaineering. The majority are aimed at climbers; a few (e.g. on high altitude pulmonary oedema) are written principally for doctors.

Dr A.R. (Jo) Bradwell who is chairman of the Birmingham Medical Research Expeditionary Society (BMRES), Immunodiagnositic Laboratory, The Medical School, Birmingham University, Edgbaston, Birmingham B15 2TJ has a special interest in mountain sickness and is happy to give advice.

Caves: Curse of the Pharaohs and Other Hazards

Straying more than a few metres into most caves takes you into the realms of absolute darkness and it is foolish to enter unless you have reliable, specialist lights. Ordinary torches powered by dry batteries do not last long enough to be safe. A lot of non-cavers have to be rescued from caves because most people do not realize this. The fact that in Europe so few die is a compliment to the Cave Rescue Organizations.

If you get lost in a cave abroad, there is unlikely to be anyone to rescue you—except your friends. Make sure people know where you are going and for how long. The following notes are aimed at travellers who are carrying adequate lights (which are reliable for 10 hours) and also know about caving or pot-holing. Otherwise you should only visit 'show caves' with a local guide.

Those with experience of caving in Europe will know that exposure (*see* above) or hypothermia is a real risk, even in a reasonably warm climate, and that flash floods are a peril especially in high rainfall areas. In addition, there are three diseases that visitors to tropical caves need to be wary of: histoplasmosis, leptospirosis and rabies.

Histoplasmosis

This is a yeast-like fungus which is as happy growing on bat dung as in a pair of lungs. It is therefore a disease that people contract when exploring dark batty places like caves or Egyptian tombs. This may be the pathological explanation for the curse of the pharaohs which mysteriously killed some of the early egyptologists.

Those who suffer most from the disease are people from temperate regions who meet the fungus for the first time by entering a tropical cave. Usually they suffer an illness which at worst causes fever, headache, cough and chest pains that lasts for between 10 days and 3 weeks; the incubation period is 10–16 days. It needs no treatment except *aspirin* or *paracetamol*. Some people get a more serious pneumonia or an even more widespread illness which makes them extremely ill. Certain caves in some regions (especially Mexico and South Africa) are particularly dangerous. Cavers in South Africa have worked out which caves to enter first and so become 'immunized' against the serious disease they would otherwise get if they entered a 'malignant' cave first.

It is wise to contact local cavers—if any exist—before venturing underground, otherwise talk to people who live close to the caves. In Peru, for example, non-caving locals were very well aware of the risks of fungal infections and warned us against entering certain caves (rather confusingly they talked of the mushrooms that would grow in our lungs!).

Smog masks help to cut down the number of fungal spores you inhale and give some protection, although the high humidity of tropical caves makes them uncomfortable to wear.

Where is Histoplasmosis a Hazard?

The *Histoplasma* fungus grows best in soil contaminated with bird or bat dung or in accumulations of such offerings in barns, chicken houses and beneath bird roosts as well as in caves. It is principally a tropical organism although in America it has been found in the extreme southeast corner of Canada and also in Alaska and in subtropical Argentina. It has also be isolated in Italy, but is not known to have caused disease there. It occurs in Africa, in many parts of Asia and Australia so is a widespread fungus which may be suspected in any unsavoury-looking niche. Fortunately, the risk of serious disease from it is small unless you are entering a small confined space, particularly if a lot of excreta is being disturbed. Almost everyone who has lived in Tennessee, Kentucky and Ohio will have become immune to the fungus by inhaling spores lurking in the soil.

Leptospirosis

The second filth-related cave disease, is an illness which most often comes from rat wee. Bats also carry it and so the bug may infect anyone who scratches their skin on cave walls or boulders. It makes good sense to wear suitable clothing which protects the skin from scratches and abrasions as much as possible. Cavers who accidentally swallow when immersed in tropical cave waters may also catch leptospirosis. Non-cavers catch leptospirosis from ditches, drains and other contaminated surface water.

Rabies, Bats and Caves

The last of the three cave-related diseases is also transmitted via unpleasant media: bat urine and saliva. The more usual routes of rabies transmission are described on p.157. Rabies is an incurable disease usually caught when a rabid dog bites you or licks broken skin. However, any mammal can carry rabies and bats—particularly in the Americas—are quite frequently infected. Anyone handling wild animals therefore risks infection. There is an additional risk to cavers, however. Two people died of rabies despite not having come in direct contact with any suspect animals; they entered a cave in South America which was the roost of a large population of bats and it seems that they were infected when they inhaled infected bat excrement in the 100 per cent humidity environment of the cave. Anyone planning to explore tropical caves in the Americas would therefore be wise to be immunized against rabies beforehand (see p.11).

Other Animal Hazards in Caves

Caves, particularly cave entrances, are cool environments in which a lot of animals take shelter. It is common for hornets to build nests in cave entrances and you are likely to get stung if they decide you are a threat. Larger animals also shelter in caves, including large carnivores. I found fresh puma footprints in a cave in Peru which I intended to explore (but then thought better of it). In northern Madagascar, large hungry Nile crocodiles take refuge in the caves of Ankarana during the dry season. I have also had a couple of scares when I crawled into small cave entrances which were the homes of snakes. Even something as small as a badger can be quite formidable if you encounter it face to face in a low passage. Finally I have camped in a cave entrance in India where I discovered a great many ticks: fortunately I was sleeping on a camp bed and so none got their chelicerae into me. Consider the risks before entering any cave.

Summary

Make sure your clothes and foot-wear protect you in the environments you are exploring and remember sun-screens may be necessary even in cold conditions.

➕ Check possible threats from unseasonal weather from local sources.

➕ Consider taking *acetazolamide* if venturing above 3000m (10,000ft).

➕ If above 3000m (10,000ft), especially if you have ascended rapidly, be cautious about mountain sickness and descend immediately if anyone's medical condition seems to be deteriorating.

⚠ Exposure and frostbite occasionally afflict poorly equipped adventurous travellers.

➕ Make sensible preparations.

⚠ Do not enter caves unless they are very shallow or unless you know what you are doing.

⚠ Many accidents in hostile environments arise from poor planning or research.

Skin

The two most common skin problems in travellers are skin infections and sunburn; slip, slap, slop precautions for avoiding sunburn and its treatment are given on p.71. This chapter also includes advice on rashes, stings, itches, athlete's foot and bathing.

Skin Infection

Trivial Breaks in the Skin

The skin is very prone to infection in hot moist climates. Even the slightest cuts and abrasions allow bacteria to enter and cause problems which can be difficult to cure—especially during the monsoon. Mosquito bites—especially if you scratch them so much that you break the skin surface and allow dirt to enter—are one of the most common routes of infection; apply a cream to reduce the itching. Tiger balm or calamine-containing preparations both help; so does toothpaste if you have nothing else. Carefully clean and dress any wounds and keep them covered, especially oozing wounds, so that flies do not feed on them.

In many hot moist environments, tropical ulcers develop rapidly (within hours) and it is wise to have a good look at your legs before retiring for the night. Start treatment as soon as signs of infection appear. Clean the wound with a good antiseptic, rest with the infected part raised above heart height (e.g. raise the leg on a pillow in bed) and consider whether antibiotic treatment is needed (*see* p.105). Skin infections can spread rapidly so do not hesitate to seek medical help if any treatment you apply does not seem to be controlling it.

Dermatology Made Simple

If a rash is dry and scaly it should be moistened with greasy creams or ointments. If, as is more likely in the tropics, it is oozing and wet, the rash needs to be dried out with an antiseptic such as potassium permanganate or an iodine-based preparation.

Antiseptic creams are generally not the best thing to use in the tropics since they keep wounds moist and this encourages further infection. What is needed is a powerful antiseptic which also dries the area. I favour using a good old-fashioned remedy: *potassium permanganate crystals* dissolved in water (recipe on following page). Diluted *tincture of iodine* or any of the *povidone-iodine* preparations are excellent too. The most convenient is Videne powder (made by Riker Labs) but products marketed under the Betadine trade name are also good. Aerosol *povidone-iodine* is easy to use but may be too bulky for light-weight travellers. (Beware—both *potassium permanganate* and *iodine* stain clothes and skin and are disastrous if they spill in your luggage.)

You can also use antiseptic wipes (alcohol stings open wounds so choose non-alcohol ones), *hexachlorophane* (e.g. Phiso-hex or Hibiclens) antiseptic solutions or *mercurochrome* crystals.

If you have minor skin breaks or blisters from walking, soaking the feet in hot salty water will often prevent any more serious infection getting established; it is also very refreshing for tired feet. Bathing in sulphur springs also cures skin infections as long as they have not already become deep seated. I can vouch for the efficacy of the springs near Tingo Maria, Peru although they turn silver jewellery black.

Treating Minor Cuts, Abrasions and Insect Bites

Bathe any wound at least twice a day (more if you can) by dabbing with cotton wool dipped in a solution of half a teacup of boiled water with a few *potassium permanganate crystals* dissolved in it, to make very approximately a 0.01 per cent solution. *Potassium permanganate* does not sting much when applied to a wound, it is cheap (enough crystals to treat 100 people costs a few pence) and it is readily available in most developing countries. It will also prevent the infection getting a hold far better than Dettol or any cream. Diluted iodine or gentian violet are also good drying antiseptics and have similar advantages.

Skin Infection and What to Do About It

Signs of Bacterial Skin Infection

Some or all of:

- Itching
- Increasing pain
- Spreading redness
- Throbbing
- Pus discharge
- Painful lymph glands
- Fever

An early sign of infection is the skin feeling hot, looking red and perhaps throbbing. Lymph glands also often enlarge and become painful at 'junction points' in the body (e.g. neck, groin or armpits) and sometimes red tracks appear on the skin. If the redness and heat start to spread and particularly if you feel feverish (hot and cold) you probably have a more deep-seated infection which means you will need to take some antibiotics by mouth.

If medical advice is not to hand, take a week-long course of *flucloxacillin*, 250mg every 6 hours (or *cloxacillin* 500mg every 6 hours). If you are allergic to penicillin you should take *erythromycin* 500mg (or 250mg if you are of very small build) four times a day for 7 days. Taking *paracetamol* or *aspirin* regularly (every 4–6 hours) will help control the aches and pains which usually accompany fever. They will make you feel better even before the antibiotics start working (within 48 hours). It is also therapeutic to rest with the affected part raised to heart height to drain away any swelling.

Case History (Pakistan)

Jim was working in southern Pakistan; he had been feeling very unwell with fever, aches and pains which he had labelled 'flu. Prompted by questions about other aspects of his health, he volunteered that he had some uncomfortable lumps in his groin. Lumps in the groin are often active lymph glands fighting an infection in the leg and that was the cause in Jim's case. He had not noticed that red streaks were tracking up his leg above a tiny healing cut on the shin. When I asked him how he had acquired the little wound, he said 'I don't know— the dog bit me in the other leg! I suppose I should have done something about the bite, but it was over a month ago now, so I guess it is too late to do anything if the dog had rabies. It has healed up fine anyway.'

The dog bite had nothing to do with his immediate problem, but I stressed that it was still sensible to take precautions, so once he felt better he organized a course of anti-rabies injections. It is safest to have them as soon as you can after being bitten, but it is never too late, unless you are actually showing signs of 'hydrophobia' (*see* p.157).

The actual cause of Jim's illness was a skin infection which had sneaked in through a trivial break in the skin. Prompt disinfection would probably have prevented the problem. In the event, a course of *cloxacillin*, (500mg four times a day for 7 days) made him feel better in 36 hours. *Flu-cloxacillin* (250mg 4 times a day for 7 days) would have been my first choice of antibiotic but it is not available in many developing countries. If Jim had been allergic to penicillin, I would have suggested he take *erythromycin*. I also advised him to rest with his leg above the level of his heart (by lying in bed with his leg propped up on pillows) and this also aided healing. Three days later he was back to his normal energetic self.

Boils

Boils and abscesses do not need treatment with antibiotics unless you have lots of them. They are also hot and red, but the infection is confined to one small area with no 'streaking' or spreading of the redness. Never squeeze a boil: let it break by itself. Applying *magnesium sulphate paste* will make the boil or abscess come to a head faster and thus expel the poisons inside. Hot compresses are also soothing and helpful: apply a hot compress for 15–20 minutes every 4 hours. Antibiotics do not help.

Sometimes people are afflicted by crops of boils in different parts of the body. These will probably need to be cleared promptly with a course of antibiotics (*see* above), but again rather than self-prescribing, it would be wise to seek medical advice if possible. Occasionally things that look like boils turn out to be something very different (e.g. tumbu maggots, *see* p.130) and local doctors or paramedics will know the best treatment.

For notes on the treatment of cuts, wounds and abrasions, *see* p.167.

Rashes and Itches

A rash can be a sign of many diseases from harmless hand, foot and mouth disease, through syphilis to serious typhoid. It is probably worth consulting a doctor if you have a widespread rash to determine the nature of the problem. Generally if the disease causing the rash is serious you will feel terribly ill.

Itching without a rash can be due to many causes and you will probably need a doctor to make a diagnosis. Antihistamine tablets such as *chlorpheniramine* (e.g. Piriton in the UK or *diphenhydramine* (e.g. Benadryl in the US) and *calamine lotion* will help in the meantime. Be careful because both types of antihistamine tablet will cause drowsiness.

Itchy rashes become itchier when the skin is hot, so hot baths and a hot environment make them feel much worse; cooling the skin with tepid sponging or fans will help. If you itch, cut your finger nails very short and you will not do so much damage when you scratch. Some rashes indicate a particular illness; they are described below.

Prickly Heat

Many people are troubled by an itchy, prickly, heat rash when living in hot climates. Characteristically it is a fine, almost pimply rash, often over the chest. It is difficult to control. It is usually worst where clothing is tight or adherent, where clothing or bed-sheets rub the skin or where skin rubs skin.

Wearing loose, 100 per cent cotton clothes helps. Sleeping naked under a gentle ceiling fan is most comfortable for sufferers. Frequent cold showers (without soap) followed by careful drying (but avoiding friction of skin with towel) usually gives some relief. *Calamine lotion* can be very soothing for this condition too. Spending time in air conditioned rooms can also reduce the suffering caused by this surprisingly unpleasant affliction. If you are too poor to check into an air-conditioned hotel you may find some relief in the air conditioning of public buildings or the lobbies of international hotels.

Allergic Rashes

If the skin erupts in a series of raised red itchy weals, it may be a sign of an allergic reaction to something that you have consumed recently. Newly started medicines can cause this, or unusual foods. Antihistamine tablets will help to settle the symptoms, but will cause drowsiness; the best are *chlorpheniramine* (e.g. Piriton in the UK) or *diphenhydramine* (e.g. Benadryl in the US). Think about what might have caused this reaction and avoid it in future since the next allergic reaction will probably be worse. If the rash appears a few hours after bathing in the sea, it may be due to 'sea lice' (*see* p.78).

Poison Ivy

Brushing against poison ivy, poison oak and sumac plants commonly cause rashes in North America. The rash appears several days to a week after contact with the plant and usually begins as red streaks or patches. These develop into blisters which break down, ooze and crust over. There is often swelling of the underlying skin. The problem usually settles down in 4–7 days. There is no particularly good treatment, but cool compresses or calamine lotion can ease it.

Cashew Nut Dermatitis

The cashew tree is a close relative of poison oak, poison ivy and sumac and contact with the plant is a fairly common cause of allergic dermatitis in travellers.

Scabies

This is an intensely itchy rash caused by minuscule mites, *Sarcoptes scabiei*, burrowing beneath the skin. The itching tends to be worse at night and does not affect the head unless the sufferer is under 2 years old or is very debilitated. Scabies is acquired from prolonged and close contact with someone (often a child) who has an infection. It is therefore a risk if you sleep in communal accommodation or share a family bed. Symptoms can take up to 8 weeks to emerge, and in four-fifths of victims the infection is confined to the wrists and hands. There are a range of treatments, but the best are preparations containing the pesticides *malathion, permethrin* or *lindane* (*lindane* goes only under the chemical name *gamma benzene hexachloride* in many countries) since they need only be applied once. Even so they have to be painted all over the body, except for the face and scalp, but including under the nails. The solution is left on overnight and then washed off the next day. *Benzyl benzoate* is an older remedy which is readily available in many developing countries but usually needs to be applied three times. Expatriates need to treat all members of the household and wash all clothes and bedding in very hot water and dry them in the sun. *Lindane* should not be used in pregnancy, while breast feeding or in children; *benzyl benzoate* and *permethrin* should not be used in pregnancy. *Malathion* is safe for all.

Crotamiton (Eurax) cream has some anti-scabies action and is also an anti-itch preparation. Itching can actually increase for 24 hours after treatment and the itching can persist for as long as 2 weeks after successful treatment. Hot baths or other things which heat the skin make the itching even worse.

Itchy Heads

Itching of the head and/or body can be caused by head lice (*Pediculus humanus capitis*) or body lice (*Pediculus humanus humanus*) however clean you keep yourself. Lice of all kinds are generally caught by direct contact with someone with lice. Adult lice are difficult to spot because they are transparent but the egg cases (nits) which are firmly cemented to hair are white and easier to see. They appear, at first, to resemble dandruff, but, unlike dandruff, nits cannot be picked out of the hair. Fine tooth combs remove and reveal lice at all stages and so are a great diagnostic aid. Combing (with a fine tooth comb) nightly is also said to prevent colonization with head lice. Many villagers in the developing world are skilled at combing out lice and nits and crushing them between their finger nails. More high-tech treatment is two applications a week apart of one of the new insecticides (*permethrin* or *phenothrin*); *malathion* and *carbaryl* are also effective. Many treatments are available as shampoos. Wash brushes and combs as well and dry them in direct sunlight.

Body Lice

In very poor living conditions, lice can spread the very nasty louse-borne relapsing fever. This is a particular hazard of spending winters in primitive conditions in the Ethiopian highlands and of sleeping in crowded and very poor accommodation in a variety of places. There have been outbreaks recently in Sudan, West Africa, Vietnam, the Balkans, the Peruvian Andes and China. Preferably treat with *lindane*, *malathion* or *carbaryl* lotion (Kwell in US). There are plenty of louse treatments available in the tropics, but be careful of what you apply in pregnancy or to small children. *Malathion* is safe but can be difficult to find. Pubic lice are described on p.118.

The Geography Worm or Larva Migrans

This is yet another very itchy but localized rash. The disease affects people whose skin has been in contact with soil or sand polluted with dog faeces. Holiday-makers acquire it on the feet or buttocks after walking barefoot or sitting on contaminated beaches. The Caribbean and Sri Lanka are two places where tourists commonly catch it. The dog hookworm larva that causes the problem penetrates the skin then wanders in vain looking for some dog-flesh in which to set up home. It sadly roams the skin for many weeks, leaving a dry flaky red track which itches a great deal, until it finally dies unfulfilled. The head of the track advances a few millimetres each day; the map-like pattern it leaves explains the alternative name of geography worm.

The worm will do you no harm, but you will probably want to be rid of it because of the irritation it causes. The worm can be dispatched and the itching stopped by freezing the head of the parasite with an ethyl chloride spray or carbon dioxide 'snow' (the latter remedy may be available in clinics used by expatriates and other rich people, where it is used to dispatch warts). An alternative treatment (which is recommended in medical texts but seems too messy for self-treatment while travelling) is to crush up a few *thiabendazole* tablets, mix them with some bland skin cream and apply it to the area, keeping it in place for 12 hours using a waterproof dressing. Anthelmintics (e.g. *thiabendazole* or *albenazole*) taken by mouth for a few days are also effective and this method of treatment is useful if there are numerous worm tracks.

If the track is on the trunk (between the neck and the knees) and it progresses faster than a few millimetres a day, treatment with tablets will be needed, although with no great urgency (within a few weeks).

Fungal Infections

Fungal colonization of the skin is often a little itchy. The infected area usually has a well-defined, slightly raised edge which is redder than the paler centre. Infections in moist areas, for example under the breasts or within the vagina may not have this characteristic appearance. Fungal infections are common in sweaty corners, such as the armpits, groin, under the breasts and between the toes. Wash then apply *clotrimazole* (e.g. Canesten in UK and Asia; Mycelex or Lotrimin in US) cream or *miconazole* (e.g. Daktarin in UK; Monistat Derm in US) or *nystatin* 2–3 times a day. Also use antifungal powder if your feet are the problem (*see* p.113). Fungal problems can allow bacterial infections to get a hold, so if antifungals do not seem to be working, *see* p.105 to determine whether you have any of the signs of bacterial skin infection which may respond to antibiotic tablets.

Crutch Rash

If you have an itchy and red area with a well-defined border in the groin, or any other sweaty corner, smear on an antifungal cream (*see* previous paragraph) 2–3 times a day. Bacteria can colonize by way of a fungal infection so if the antifungal cream does not work, consult a doctor or if this is not possible consider a course of antibiotics (*see* p.105). Soreness and/or itching around the vaginal opening can be treated in the same way, although often it will need treatment with antifungal pessaries. Both problems are less likely if you wear 100 per cent cotton underwear and outer clothes. Underwear is best if loose, so men may be most comfortable in boxer shorts and women in French knickers. If you are an expatriate doing a lot of deskwork ensure that you use a cane chair which allows air to circulate (but beware: bed bugs like cane chairs too).

Impetigo

This is a very common superficial infection of the skin which often begins in a scratched mosquito bite or a crack at the corner of the mouth. It is an oozing, blistering, golden-coloured, crusting, slightly itchy sore which is highly contagious but is easily cured.

Remove crusts with a mild antiseptic such as *povidone-iodine* if you have it (salt water if you have not) and treat with a topical antibiotic cream or powder *chlortetracycline*, *fucidin*, *framycetin*, *polymyxin* or *neomycin* (e.g. Cicatrin in UK; Neosporin in US).

Other Skin Problems

Lyme Disease

This usually begins as a raised red non-itchy weal at the site of a tick bite. It needs antibiotic treatment and is described on p.66.

Painless Tropical Ulcers

A superficial painless ulcer which will not heal, particularly if it was acquired in Central or South America (where in its severe, advanced, untreatable form it is called *espundia*) is probably due to a protozoan disease, leishmania, transmitted by sand-fly bites. It requires expert treatment in a tropical disease hospital. Do not let anyone cut it out because drug treatments are difficult and the ulcer provides a useful monitor of whether treatment is succeeding. Precautions against sand-fly bites are given on p.61.

In other regions, especially the Pacific Islands (e.g. Papua New Guinea), rapidly growing tropical ulcers are often due to bacteria and again it would be wise to seek medical help. The treatment for these is usually antibiotic tablets and rest with the leg elevated above heart height. Both kinds of ulcers seem to arise from nothing.

Rove Beetle Blistering or 'Nairobi Eye'

Some species of small, slim, earwig-shaped staphylinid beetles (*Paederus* spp.) cause skin problems in many regions. If crushed or damaged they cause irritation and blistering on contact with the skin, but beginning after a one-day delay. If they fly into an eye and are damaged, inflammation, irritation and swelling starts after 12 hours or so and continues for several days. The delay makes this problem particularly difficult to recognize and avoid, until it is too late.

Most cases are reported from East Africa, but relatives in southern Spain also cause blistering if crushed or damaged and other species of rove beetles from elsewhere in the tropics and subtropics have similar effects. Outside lighting after dark can attract them in plagues.

Antihistamine tablets may help. Unless the affected skin is close to the eye apply *silver sulphadiazine* (Flamazine) or *calamine* to help control the burning sensation.

Even in temperate climates, small staphylinid beetles can fly in great numbers and may enter the eyes of cyclists and motor-cyclists, causing a burning sensation.

Blister beetles (of the Meloidae family) are another widespread family of insects which cause blistering, although without the one-day delay in symptoms. These medium-sized beetles are mostly black or brown, but can be bright metallic blue or green. Again, they only cause blistering if beetle body fluids come in contact with human skin. The coconut beetles (family Oedemeridae) of the Gilbert Islands also cause severe blistering.

Giant Hogweed *Heracleum Mantegazzianum*

Contact with the stem or seeds of the giant hogweed plant can, in some people, also cause blistering. This seems to be due to the plant toxin sensitizing the skin so that it becomes highly susceptible to sunburn and it can leave pigmented patches which may persist for 7 years. Wearing long clothing whenever you go into jungly areas should protect you from this and other noxious plants and animals.

Primroses in Europe also cause blistering in some allergic people not unlike the poison ivy rash. Nettles are discussed on p.76.

Moles

Moles are slightly raised, brown pigmented areas of skin. Sometimes skin cancer can appear to arise from a mole which changes or from a new mole. The nastiest form of skin cancer, malignant melanoma, causes 1200 deaths a year in Britain, but if diagnosed early, this form of cancer is curable. The signs which should make you worry and seek prompt medical treatment are:

- A mole that grows
- A mole which becomes irregularly shaped
- The brown pigment appears to start streaming out of the mole
- Development of different colour shades in the same mole
- A mole which itches, bleeds, oozes or develops a crust

Leprosy

Leprosy is a common problem in people living in poor overcrowded conditions. It slowly causes destruction of the extremities of the body so that people lose fingers, toes and noses. Lepromatous beggars in some developing countries deliberately touch foreigners, presumably in the hope you will be terrified into buying them off. Leprosy first appears as patches of depigmented skin which lacks sensation. Fortunately this disease is only caught after prolonged and quite intimate contact with an infected person so the risk of a traveller or expatriate catching the disease is minuscule. In South America a similar looking problem—which often destroys the nose— is caused by leishmania infection (*espundia*) spread by sand-fly bites (*see* p.61).

Foot Problems

Athlete's Foot

This is a dry scaly rash which causes soreness and sometimes itching between the toes; if the skin cracks, there is also some oozing. If you think you have athlete's foot get it treated before departure. Do not set out on a tropical trip with established athlete's foot since it will get much worse. It is cured by thorough washing and drying and then applying *clotrimazole* cream (e.g. Canesten) or *miconazole* (e.g. Daktarin) or *nystatin* 2–3 times a day. To prevent reinfection from your sweaty shoes and socks, sprinkle an antifungal powder (e.g. Mycota) into shoes every night and into your socks each morning. A colleague had the most appalling athlete's foot in Peru which cleared up quite quickly using antifungal powder alone. This treatment is fine unless you want some soothing cream for the soreness between the toes.

Using lots of antifungal powder protects against reinfection and the SAS think this is a sensible precaution during jungle exercises. Wearing sandals (and going bare foot indoors) as much as possible will also help. If you have to wear shoes ensure the socks are 100 per cent cotton or wool. Severe athlete's foot can become secondarily infected so if it becomes hot and throbbing or you feel feverish and unwell you may need antibiotics (*see* p.105).

One experienced expedition doctor recommends soaking the feet in a 4 per cent formalin footbath for 10–15 minutes three or four times before travelling to hot moist regions. I have not tried this myself but understand that this hardens the feet for 2–3 months and so may be worth considering if you are going on a very tough trip where your feet are likely to suffer (one example might be cavers going to Mulu, Sarawak). Too much Formalin treatment could possibly cause the skin to crack and thus allow infections to get in so if you are planning a long intrepid trip it might be worth experimenting with this long before departure.

Professor Shaoxi Wu of the Institute of Medical Mycology, Nanjing, China was seen at a recent medical symposium wearing a new invention: nylon socks which had been interwoven with Tu King bark, which has antifungal properties. These, and shoe inserts containing the same bark, apparently prevent athlete's foot. The Chinese are also incorporating the bark into underpants to keep fungal infections of the groin area at bay. The socks are cheap at about 25 pence, can be worn for three consecutive days (!) and retain their antifungal properties for 50 washes.

Cracked Heels

Some people who spend time in hot climates and wear sandals are greatly troubled by cracked heels which become extremely painful. The best treatment is to wear shoes and socks (the sweat softens the skin) until it improves. If this is a problem which troubles you a great deal the answer is to keep the offending area of skin fairly thin by abrading it away with pumice after soaking in a bath (but do not try this if the skin has already begun to crack). Alternatively apply some greasy lubricant: Body Shop peppermint foot lotion does the job and smells delicious.

Jiggers

Painful swellings between the toes may be due to these parasites. A description and treatment is given on p.131. Tips on care of the feet when walking are given on p.88.

To Bathe or Not To Bathe?

More medical problems are caused in Westerners by too much bathing rather than too little. If conditions make it difficult to bath or shower, be content to wash armpits, between the legs and under the breasts with soap and a wash cloth. However, being clean is a great morale booster; brave a cold shower if you are feeling demoralized.

You may find yourself living in a climate where you take two or more showers a day. If you use soap every time you bathe, your skin will be robbed of its protective oils. Cool water alone is good enough much of the time, although you should wash the areas which remain constantly moist (armpits, groins and between the toes) or you may suffer from fungal infections.

Squat Toilets and Anal Cleansing

In much of the tropical world people do not use toilet paper, but clean themselves with water after defecation. Think of it as a primitive bidet. The washing technique takes some practice (and is almost impossible on Western-style WCs), but in a warm climate it is a healthy practice, probably helps reduce fungal infections of the groin area and frees you from carrying toilet paper everywhere.

Always try to wash your hands with soap after visiting squalid toilets since it is possible to catch diarrhoea or dysentery if you put your hand to your mouth after touching a contaminated door handle for example. Your own faecal flora will not do you much harm, but other peoples' will. It is best to air-dry your hands rather than risk re-contaminating them on a dirty towel after washing.

Showers and Legionnaires' Disease

The first recognized outbreak of legionnaires' disease attacked 182 aged American legionnaires staying in a Philadelphia hotel; 29 of them died. Since that outbreak, effective antibiotic treatment has been established so that it now generally only causes grave problems in the infirm and in heavy smokers. Most people (more than 95 per cent) who are exposed to the bacteria do not suffer any illness at all. It is contracted mainly in first world or Western-style hotels and other large institutions (e.g. hospitals). In temperate regions it is most common in August and September. Direct sunshine kills the bacteria and they survive best in humidities above 65 per cent. Rainforests are occasionally a source of human infection and so it is by no means restricted to temperate climates.

Legionnaires' disease is not a risk for most travellers, unless they are immune deficient. Running a shower for a few minutes before bathing will flush out the *Legionnella* bacteria and so further reduce any chances of infection.

Summary

⊕ Pay meticulous attention to the care of your skin in the tropics and bathe even the smallest wounds in a good antiseptic.

⊕ Take precautions against being bitten by insects by using repellent and clothes which cover you; insect bites turn rapidly septic in hot moist climates.

⊕ In hot climates it is best to wear loose, 100% cotton underwear; men may be most comfortable in boxer shorts and women in French knickers.

⊕ Pack cool, loose-fitting, cotton clothes and a hat which will protect you from the sun.

+ Wear shoes, sandals or flip-flops as much as possible: bare feet are prone to injury, and offer parasites and fungal infections easy access.

+ A wash cloth/face flannel is an indispensable aid to washing the bare essentials (crutch, armpits and beneath the breasts) when the climate discourages cold showers.

Embarrassing Bits, Sex and AIDS

Not all genital disease is sexually transmitted. Fungal infections around the genitals are common in the tropics; they are not acquired by sexual contact (*see* p.110 for how to treat them). If you have an embarrassing problem, clinics specializing in venereal diseases will probably sort it out quickly for you. In many developing countries dermatologists double as venereologists. This chapter deals with sexually related problems, contraception, travel while pregnant and how to avoid HIV infection or AIDS.

Embarrassing Bits

Libido

Sexual appetite is reduced by many factors common in travellers. Fatigue, illness, anger, depression, alcohol consumption and being at altitudes above 3500m (12,000ft) temporarily and reversibly reduce libido.

Waterworks

Passing blood in the urine usually denotes a bladder infection and requires antibiotic treatment. Be aware, though, that bilharzia can cause bloody urine (*see* p.81). Some foods and medicines alter urine colour; eating beetroot colours the urine red, which can make it look as if you are bleeding. Very dark urine suggests dehydration or hepatitis infection. See whether drinking a great deal more lightens the urine colour before seeking medical advice. Men with pain on passing urine may have a sexually transmitted disease and must have a medical check-up at the appropriate clinic. Women who have pain on passing urine probably have cystitis (*see* p.120).

Kidney Stones

Kidney stones are hard deposits which build up in the urinary system. They are more likely to occur if you become dehydrated. They cause excruciating pain somewhere along a line drawn between either side of the small of the back, through the groin to the point where urine emerges from the body. The problem needs treatment in hospital with intravenous fluids and powerful pain-killers. If you have had kidney stones once you are more likely to get them again.

Crabs or Pubic Lice

These look like minuscule crabs. They feed on blood so cause a great deal of itching. They are usually acquired from direct (sexual) contact with someone who is infested. Crabs or pubic lice rarely leave the body unless damaged or dying so transmission via dirty bedding is unlikely. If you are hairy, crabs will not necessarily be confined to the pubic region: they can get as far as the eyelashes by way of chest hair and beard. Treatment is to apply an aqueous lotion of *malathion, lindane* or *carbaryl* to all hairy parts of the body and leave it on for 12 hours or overnight; it is best to apply a second treatment after a week. If you have crabs, you may have other sexually transmitted diseases and should attend a special clinic for a check-up.

Men's Health

A Painful Testicle

A testicle which becomes hot, red and painful needs medical attention. There are two likely diagnoses. If the problem has come on suddenly, it is most likely torsion of a testicle when the blood supply is cut off and the testicle dies within a matter of hours. Seek help from a surgeon urgently. Epididymitis is more common and is an infection which tends to come on more gradually and can be cleared with a course of antibiotics. The pain of both conditions will be helped by wearing underwear (or a jock strap) which gives some support.

Discharge or Sores

Discharge from the penis or an ulcer on the genitals may be due to infection with a sexually transmitted disease (STD) and even if you do not think you have exposed yourself to infection, a special clinic is the best place for a check-up. Self treatment is not wise until the true nature of the problem has been diagnosed. Seek help promptly; if the symptoms appear to get better without treatment, it does not necessarily mean that the problem has gone away, but just that it will be more difficult to diagnose when it causes problems later.

Useful Condoms and the British Standard Willy

It is sensible to pack a supply of condoms for several reasons. Firstly, penile sizes vary and Southeast Asian condoms may be rather small. Condoms bought in developing countries may not be made to the same stringent quality controls as they are in Europe. The shape of penises is also very diverse and surprisingly little research has been carried out by condom manufacturers, so even British condoms do not fit all comers. Men may therefore prefer to travel equipped with a brand of condoms that they know. There are a few specialist condom shops (e.g. Condomania in Covent Garden and Brighton) which may be able to help if the standard kite marked model does not fit. Carrying condoms in wallets, especially in hot climates, shortens their effective lifespan.

Condoms are useful items of travellers' equipment. Infantrymen and seasoned jungle travellers tell me that they use them to carry surprisingly large volumes of water, among other things. They are also good waterproof covers or containers. They can also be used as temporary fan-belts in cars, washing machines and vacuum cleaners and can be filled with ice and placed on swollen painful joints or piles to decrease inflammation and discomfort.

Women's Health

Thrush

Thrush which causes itching around the entrance of the vagina, is much more common in moist warm climates. One factor which can aggravate the problem is washing the genital area too often with soap: thrush can be a problem for women who keep themselves too clean. Treatments are as for crutch rash (*see* p.110) although antifungal pessaries such as *clotrimazole* (e.g. Canesten) are often necessary. Women should also wear skirts and not wear knickers at home, when social circumstances allow it. Air circulation helps to clear the infection.

Cystitis

Women commonly suffer from cystitis which is an infection of the urinary tract and bladder. Such attacks can become dramatically more frequent in the tropics. This may be because most people do not drink enough when they are living in hot climates. Cystitis makes women feel they want to pass urine very frequently, but only small volumes are produced and there is usually great pain at the end of the act of urination. If the only symptom is pain and frequency of urination try drinking a glass of water containing a teaspoonful of bicarbonate of soda (baking powder), then drink a glass of plain water every 20 minutes. This has the effect of flushing out the bacteria. The first couple of times you pass urine you will notice stinging but the more you pass the less it will sting. The pain should be subsiding after 3 hours using this routine. Antibiotics will probably be needed if it does not get better with this treatment, or there is blood in the urine, or you have a fever.

Take a 3-day course of *trimethoprim* 200mg twice a day (not safe in pregnancy) or *co-amoxiclav* (Augmentin) 500mg every 8 hours (but not for those allergic to penicillin). People who are allergic to penicillin and are pregnant should take *cephalexin* 500mg (unless allergic to cephalosporins) or *nitrofurantoin* 100mg every 6 hours (unless close to the baby's due date). And drink plenty.

Cystitis is not a sexually transmitted disease but, like thrush, it is common in women who are sexually active. A design fault in the female has positioned the opening of bowel and bladder too close together so that infection passes from the back passage. Wiping from front to back after using the toilet can thus help reduce the frequency of attacks and so does passing urine after intercourse. Also, avoid using antiseptics or perfumed cosmetics in the genital region or cosmetics in the bath water. Tight-fitting garments, especially jeans and leotards can aggravate the problem too.

Cystitis in men or children needs a proper medical assessment.

Contraception

Although the pill is available in most developing countries, your regular brand may not be. The progestogen only 'mini-pill' is certainly hard to come by in many Asian countries. 'Normal' steroid hormones, although available in Japan, have never been licensed there as oral contraceptives. This means that travellers have a hard time acquiring supplies there. The International Clinic in downtown Tokyo might be a place which will understand the problem. Ensure you have enough supplies for your entire time away. If you are planning an extended trip it may be worth considering using a Norplant implant or an intrauterine contraceptive device (IUD); both give 5 years' cover. Injectable 'depo' contraceptives have come in for a great deal of bad press, more for political than medical reasons. Their advantage is that they give contraceptive cover for 3 months (in the case of Depo-Provera) or 8 weeks (Noristerat) and they usually have the pleasant side effect of reducing bleeding during menstruation. Injectable contraceptives, then, could be a useful method for women planning trips up to 3 months long. As with all medicines, they have their disadvantages which need to be discussed well in advance. The best advice on depo injections, implants and IUDs would probably come from a family planning clinic rather than your GP. Whatever method you decide to use, plan well ahead to ensure that any new contraceptive method suits you several months before departure.

Women should carry condoms to protect themselves from acquiring sexually transmitted diseases and as a contraceptive back-up in case of missed pills or a major stomach upset.

Morning After Pills

So-called 'morning after' emergency contraception is an option for up to 72 hours after unplanned, unprotected intercourse. In the UK it is available from GPs, family planning clinics and hospital casualty departments, under the brand name Schering PC4. High-dose Ovran contraceptive pills are identical; both are taken as two tablets as soon as possible (but within 72 hours of intercourse) and two more 12 hours later. They often cause nausea and even vomiting and are probably ineffective if vomiting occurs within 2 hours of taking the pills.

There is a new pill, RU486 or *mifepristone*, which will prevent an unwanted pregnancy only in the first 9 weeks. This is strictly an abortifacient and so although it is available in France and Sweden and is soon to be licensed in the USA, it is under stricter legal restrictions than the 'morning after pill' and it has some ethical problems. In the UK it is only available in some hospitals and cannot be obtained from GPs or family planning clinics.

Problems of Pill-taking While Travelling

Contraceptive pills may not be absorbed properly if you vomit within 3 hours of taking the pill or if you have very profuse diarrhoea. A slightly upset stomach with a couple of loose bowel motions should not be a cause for concern. Taking antibiotics and certain other medicines can also reduce the efficiency of pill absorbtion. In these cases you should take alternative contraceptive precautions (condoms, a cap or femidoms) for the rest of the cycle or as described below. It is worth carrying condoms with you for this reason and also as a back up in case you need to stop taking the pill. You will need to stop taking the pill if you develop jaundice (when the whites of the eyes and then the skin goes yellow). You may also like to consider stopping the pill if you experience a great deal of swelling of the ankles. This happens to some people in hot climates and the pill tends to increase swelling. Finally, there are some theoretical additional risks to taking the pill when ascending to very high altitudes (over 7000m/23,000ft); *see* p.96.

Rules for Taking Missed Pills

If you forget a pill, or are late taking the pill, or vomit within 3 hours of taking it the following guidelines will ensure your contraceptive safety.

For the mini-pill (progestogen only pill):

If less than 4 hours late there is no problem; if more than 4 hours late

- take the forgotten pill
- take the next pill on time
- take extra precautions or do not have sex for 7 days
- keep taking the pill

For the combined oral contraceptive pill:

If less than 12 hours late, there is no problem; if more than 12 hours late

- take the forgotten pill
- take the next pill on time
- take extra precautions or do not have sex for 7 days
- keep taking the pill

The time women on the pill are most likely to conceive is around the pill-free break, and so a break of longer than 7 days is risky. If, at the time of the forgotten pill, more than seven pills remain in the packet, take the usual pill-free 7 days. If, however, there are less than seven pills left, begin the next packet immediately without a pill-free break. Take additional contraceptive precautions for 7 pill days after the missed pill (or the end of diarrhoea or the end of the antibiotic course).

Delayed Menstruation

If you are taking a combined contraceptive pill which is monophasic (i.e. the pills are all the same colour) you can continue one packet straight after finishing the previous one, without the normal 7 pill-free days break. This usually delays menstruation which may be convenient when travelling and is safe. It is not really an option if you are using a biphasic or triphasic pill (with two or three pill colours), but you can discuss missing one period with your GP before travelling.

Menstruation and Tampons

Tampons can be difficult to find abroad so take a supply, unless you are prepared to make do with local sanitary towels. When travelling be especially careful about washing your hands before putting tampons in, since infection is more likely in the tropics.

Periods may become erratic when abroad and period pains may become more of a problem. Reducing the quantity you drink for a day or two before the period is due and for the first day of bleeding often helps reduce pain, particularly if there is some bloating during this time. *Ibuprofen* (e.g. Brufen in UK or Motrin in US), other *non-steroidal anti-inflammatory medicines* (*see* p.189) or *paracetamol* (*acetaminophen* in the US) also help. Otherwise the contraceptive pill can reduce such symptoms.

Some women stop menstruating when travelling which seems a very convenient adaptation. This is nothing to worry about unless you fear an unwanted pregnancy. Finally, note that menstruating women are considered unclean in many religions and it would be blasphemy to enter a temple or mosque while you are bleeding.

Disposing of Sanitary Towels

Proper disposal of sanitary towels is difficult. If they are put into the ordinary rubbish disposal system, they may end up being scattered by wind and dogs. There is no more revolting sight than to see used dressings littering the streets. The only sensible option is to burn them. Otherwise washable sanitary towels can be purchased from The Green Catalogue (UK ✆ 01249 444665; 📠 01934 732748).

Travelling While Pregnant

If you feel well during pregnancy, and feel like travelling, do it! One woman managed a successful ascent of the north face of the Eiger when 6 months pregnant. There are some special considerations if your trip is long or the destination without reasonable medical facilities.

Miscarriages are very common and perhaps one fifth of pregnancies end in miscarriage. Having a miscarriage in a remote place could be a horrendous experience. Sometimes women also need a surgical dilatation and curettage under general anaesthetic to remove retained products of conception following a miscarriage. There are many developing countries where I would not wish such a procedure to be carried out on me. If planning a shortish trip (less than 4 months), it would make good sense to delay departure until after the most likely time for a miscarriage. Most miscarriages happen at the eighth or the twelfth weeks of pregnancy (counting the first day of the last period as the first day of the pregnancy). Usually if the pregnancy goes beyond the twelfth week it will go on to term and a healthy baby will be the result.

The safest time to travel is during the second 3 months of pregnancy. The risk of miscarriage is small and there is little chance of early labour or other complications. Whether travelling or not, there are dietary precautions that pregnant women should take. Ensure that milk and dairy products are pasteurised or boiled and avoid unpasteurized soft cheeses and raw eggs; dried egg is safe.

Most airlines will not allow pregnant women to fly after the 32nd week on long-haul flights and many demand a doctor's letter to confirm the stage of pregnancy. Airlines vary on their rules and requirements (and insurance companies are most stringent). Discouraging flying in late pregnancy is not because it is unsafe, but because the airlines does not want women delivering babies in the cramped conditions of an airliner. Having attended to someone who had merely fainted in a jumbo jet while people climbed over us to get to the toilets, I find it hard to imagine a more unpleasant place to give birth.

There is one very real risk throughout pregnancy and that is malaria. If you contract malaria during pregnancy it will affect you in a much more severe way than if you had not been pregnant. Pregnant women and small children are the ones most likely to die of malaria. Many doctors (myself included) counsel against travel to high risk malarious regions (especially sub-saharan Africa, the Pacific Islands and Indo China) when pregnant. Antimalarial tablets give some protection against the disease; these must be taken rigorously and measures to avoid mosquito bites between 5.30pm and 6am are essential. During pregnancy, *folic acid* needs to be taken with some malaria tablets. Hepatitis E which is a filth-to-mouth acquired disease is also very serious during pregnancy and women must be extra careful about eating safe food (*see* p.22).

It is wise to avoid as many drugs as possible during pregnancy, especially in the first 3 months. Precautions on taking medicines during pregnancy are outlined on p.192.

Sex

There is often the opportunity for pleasant romantic encounters while travelling but the risks of acquiring AIDS are now considerable (as well as hepatitis B and a selection of more than 25 other sexually transmitted diseases). It is foolhardy to enter into casual sex. Even using a latex condom or femidom only reduces and does not eliminate the risks. Using spermicidal pessaries or creams in addition to condoms further reduces the likelihood of acquiring infection since these are powerful viricides as well as sperm-killers. A general physician practising in a port in Madagascar told me that 10 per cent of his consultations were for gonorrhoea. This figure is not untypical of communities where many people are passing through. So if you too are passing through, think about the consequences of casual sex, especially with people you meet at nightclubs, with prostitutes or bar-girls.

Sexually Transmitted Disease (STD) in Women

Women should carry condoms or femidoms when they travel so that they can protect themselves from infection (and pregnancy) in case of unplanned romance. They are also a useful contraceptive back-up when diarrhoea stops absorption of the contraceptive pill. STD in women usually causes an unpleasant vaginal discharge. It may compromise future fertility and certainly make you more vulnerable to acquiring AIDS. If you suspect you have STD get it treated promptly; most big towns have special clinics.

AIDS and Other Risks of Medical Treatment

AIDS cannot be acquired from mosquito bites. It is almost exclusively spread through sexual contact and it is important to remember that AIDS is a disease of heterosexuals, as well as of homosexual men. It is very common in Africa, in major cities and among prostitutes and it is increasing in Asia and in most other parts of the world. Some countries deny its existence, but it is unlikely that any are free from the disease. About 100 British travellers a year are infected with HIV and the rate is rising rapidly.

Latex condoms offer some protection. Although spermicides destroy the AIDS virus and therefore should help reduce transmission, frequent use of spermicides increases the chances of ulcers forming and any such broken skin allows easy access for the virus. Ulcers due to STDs or any areas of broken skin make infection much more likely. Get any genital infection treated promptly by consulting a doctor in a special clinic.

Medical treatment, including blood transfusions after serious accidents or transfusions of blood products for other serious illnesses, are routes of infection which are difficult to avoid. The best advice I can give is to try to select expensive hospitals and clinics where staff say that blood is screened (you can only take their word) and try to ensure intravenous equipment and syringes are new. In Asia, people are very clever at replacing or resealing packets so that the contents look new: it is wise to carry your own.

MASTA (see **Useful Addresses**, p.211) sell 'AIDS kits' comprising needles, syringes and a small amount of intravenous fluid which could be used in case of an emergency admission to hospital. The largest AIDS kit is bulky because it contains 500ml of intravenous fluid along with the 'giving set' and other useful items.

Although it would seem reassuring to carry intravenous fluids, the volume required in a real emergency is large and it would be impractical to carry enough plasma expander to be really useful. I know of situations where an AIDS kit has been produced but it was not used by the local medical staff. A serious motor cycle accident befell a member of a small expatriate community (in an area where hepatitis B was prevalent). Not only was the AIDS kit not used but people offering to donate blood were turned away. In the event, the patient survived without being infected, although he nearly died because he was given blood of the wrong group. Be safety conscious, avoid accidents and realize that riding a motor cycle abroad may be the death of you.

Many doctors regard a comprehensive AIDS kit as a useful precaution, and clearly if you are travelling with someone with at least paramedical skills it could be life-saving. I never carry intravenous fluids, but it is undoubtedly good sense to carry a few needles, syringes and sutures and insist on local doctors using them if you need to go to hospital.

Some third world doctors give unnecessary injections so be wary.

Blood Transfusions

The dangers of transfusing unscreened blood and blood products are now well known, but many developing countries do not have the resources to carry out this screening. Nor, unfortunately, is sending safe, screened blood by courier from home a real solution. In most emergency situations it is unlikely to get to you quickly enough. All you can do is ask local advice on the safest hospitals.

The situation in Bolivia is not untypical of many developing nations. At present, only 30 per cent of hospitals in the country screen blood and a recent survey found that 54 per cent of blood was contaminated with Chagas parasites, hepatitis B, syphilis or HIV. Most (47 per cent) contaminated blood bags carried the Chagas parasite. This disease is curable in the early stages, but may not be recognized until a stage when treatment is difficult or ineffective.

The good news is that the Red Cross are presently working to introduce a system of accreditation which will monitor hospitals claiming to screen blood, and they will only be passed if the screening is effective. This means that it will be possible to pick a clinic or hospital where reliable screening is taking place. These kinds of projects are functioning or are starting up in many developing countries. Indeed, screened blood is available in almost every capital city throughout the world. The downside is that in areas where HIV is highly prevalent, even properly screened blood is not absolutely safe; there is a lag time between infection and the production of detectable antibodies.

Many safety-conscious people become quite reckless when travelling. They do not wear helmets when riding motor cycles or seat belts when driving cars and they often drive when drunk. Why take the risk? Even if you survive the accident and manage to get to hospital, the risks of emergency medical care abroad are still appreciable.

Ear-piercing and Dentistry

Travellers sometimes have their ears or noses pierced or get tattooed. In many tropical countries there is a remarkably high prevalence of hepatitis B and so there is a substantial risk of catching this, or AIDS, if the needles have been used before. Similarly, dental treatment and acupuncture can be risky if sterilization techniques are poor. Avoid these procedures and any unnecessary injections.

Summary

○ Have a dental check before your trip so that you avoid dental treatment abroad as far as possible.

○ Avoid all unnecessary medical treatment which involves injections and also do all you can to avoid situations which make medical treatment necessary.

⚠ Take care to reduce the chances of road accidents; motor cycles are the most hazardous form of transport.

⚠ Consider the dire consequences of casual sex anywhere. Both men and women would be wise to carry a supply of condoms.

⚠ Remember that alcohol and other drugs affect your judgement.

- ⊕ Get a check-up in a special clinic promptly if you have any symptoms of sexually transmitted diseases: discharge, pain on urinating or genital ulcers.

- ⚠ Avoid acupuncture, tattooing and ear-piercing unless it is with sterile equipment.

- ⊕ Drink plenty of water to avoid cystitis and kidney stones.

- ⚠ Injecting drugs carries the risk of acquiring AIDS and hepatitis B.

- ⚠ Carrying illicit drugs in many countries is a very serious crime. Intoxication and addiction in itself kills a fair number of travellers each year.

Many of the animals described in this chapter are venomous, but the actual danger they present to the traveller is usually out of all proportion to the fear they engender. The beasts which most people fear are, numerically, unimportant and the risk to the health of the average traveller is slight. Most hazards from tropical animals are vastly over-stated and it makes much more sense to worry about road accidents than snake bites. Most injuries from animals, both in travellers and people at home, are from domestic dog bites. In the US, where disease and causes of death are accurately recorded, and where many dangerous animals reside, most deaths due to venomous animals are from honey-bee stings. Worldwide, most deaths from animal bites are caused by diseases spread by mosquitoes. This chapter, then, mainly covers the varieties of animals which interest us because they are revolting or scary rather than those which are truly harmful.

Many noxious animals advertise their unpleasant nature with warning coloration and markings, so do not handle any beasts which are very strikingly marked unless you know they are harmless. Avoid patting stray dogs, however cute they seem.

Skin Invaders

Some creatures lay their eggs on human skin so that when their young hatch they can eat the living tissue. Accounts of such horrors are just what some travellers like to dine out on—or write books about. The good news, though, is that only two animals commonly invade human skin and when they do, they dine on a small discrete area: you will never be eaten alive. These two are insects called tumbu flies and jiggers (not to be confused with chigger-mites). If they colonize you in numbers, though, they can be very unpleasant. Botflies in South and Central America also invade skin. Old and new world screw-worms will feed on living tissue in wounds and the Congo floor maggot sucks blood from skin. Many other fly maggots can cause benign (if revolting) infestation of dead tissue and so they have been used medically for centuries to clean up (debride) sloughy wounds.

Tumbu Flies

Tumbu flies or *putsi* (*Cordylobia anthropophaga*), are related to our blue-bottles or blow-flies. The maggots of this African species develop in human skin, causing an area of inflammation like a boil. These 'boils' usually come in crops, most often over the back, arms, waist and scrotum (if you have one). The adult fly lays her eggs on clothes which have been left drying in the shade so that maggots usually get to their victims by way of clothes, or directly from the soil. Eggs or young maggots also contaminate laundry which is left to dry on the ground. When the clothes come into contact with someone, the maggots invade the skin. They grow to a maximum size of 15mm in about 8 days. Then the mature grub, which is club-shaped, will fall out through a small hole in the centre of the boil and the inflammation will settle down.

The maggot can be encouraged to leave before its 8-day feast is over, although the eviction is not a pleasant spectacle. The maggot first has to be suffocated by placing a drop of mineral oil over the openings of its two breathing tubes; these appear as a pair of black dots on the surface of the boil. If gentle pressure is then applied, the maggot should pop out. Otherwise as it suffocates, it will wriggle violently and when it emerges, it can be grabbed with tweezers and removed. Too much force at this stage will damage the maggot and if any part of it is left in the skin there will be an unpleasant inflammation reaction. Be firm but gentle. You will come to no harm by leaving the maggot alone, although you probably will not want to.

The way to avoid infestation is to be careful about where you dry your clothes. Hang them on a line in the sun or inside where flies cannot reach them. Only take the washing in when it is so dry that it is 'crisp', for the maggot is unlikely to survive a thorough baking in the sun. Otherwise iron clothes inside and out. The waste-bands of underclothes, bed-sheets and babies' nappies must also be ironed. Tumbu flies are a problem in the hot and high humidity regions of East, West and South Africa.

Removing Unwanted Lodgers

When removing or evicting any unwanted guests, be they jiggers, fly maggots, ticks or leeches, they must always leave intact. If any part of the beast is left behind in your skin, it will cause inflammation and infection which will be difficult to clear and will be far worse than anything that the parasite would have done to you if you had left it in peace.

Jiggers

Jiggers, which are also known as chigoes or sand-fleas, are degenerate fleas. They are picked up by walking barefoot in endemic areas, usually where soils are fairly dry and sandy; it is even possible to acquire them indoors. The most troublesome species, *Tunga penetrans*, occurs in tropical Africa, Central and South America. Eight to ten days after a pregnant jigger has set up home in you, she will have swollen to the size of a small pea which causes a painful swelling at the side of a toenail, between the toes or on the soles of the feet. Left unmolested she will shed

Table 4: Animal Hazards and Where They Occur

ANIMAL HAZARD	ASIA				AFRICA
Note: This table should only be used as a rough guide since accurate information on animal hazards is difficult to obtain. Small biting animals which transmit disease are listed on p.64.	**East** Japan China etc.	**South East** Indonesia, Thailand, Malaysia	**South** Pakistan, India, Nepal, Bangladesh, Sri Lanka	**Middle East**	**Sub-saharan**
Skin-invading maggots				•	•
Jigger fleas					•
Ticks	•	•	•	•	•
Fleas, lice & bed bugs	•	•	•	•	•
Chiggers & scrub itch mites	•	•	•		
Dangerous spiders	•	•	•	•	•
Nasty centipedes	•	•	•	•	•
Leeches	•	•	•		•
Venomous caterpillars		•	•		
Itch-inducing (furry) caterpillars	•	•	•	•	•
Dangerous scorpions			•	•	•
Venomous sea creatures	•	•	•		•
Stingrays	•	•	•		•
Nile crocodiles					•
Saltwater crocodiles		•	•		
Potentially lethal snakes	•	•	•		•
Big game (including bears)	•	•	•	•	•
Rabid dogs	•	•	•	•	•

AFRICA	AMERICA		PACIFIC		HABITAT
North	Caribbean	South & Central	Australasia Australia, New Zealand	Islands Fiji, Solomons, Papua New Guinea etc.	
		●		●	rural lowlands
		●			dry, sandy
●	●	●	●	●	rural
●	●	●	●	●	poor housing
	●	●	●	●	scrub & forest, especially secondary forest
●	●	●	●	●	warm regions
●	●	●	●	●	most tropical & sub-tropical rural areas
					moist forest
	●	●	●		forest, scrub, plantations
●	●	●	●	●	rural areas
●	●	●	●		dry forests, scrub, desert
	●	●	●	●	tropical seas
●	●	●	●	●	shallow coastal waters; also tropical S.American rivers
●					rivers & lakes
			●	●	estuaries, mangrove swamps, coastal
	●	●	●	●	scrub & forest
		●			scrub & forest
●	●	●		●	villages and towns

133

several thousand eggs, then die and her body will then stimulate an inflammatory reaction; her remains will eventually be rejected with a load of pus.

Treatment is to pick away at the site with a safety pin or needle until you can remove the whole, very pregnant, egg-filled body of the lady jigger (*see* p.131). After she has been removed, the hole must be doused with antiseptic and a dressing applied to stop any secondary infection. If the animal bursts during removal the eggs will go everywhere and will probably re-infest you. Douse with spirit, alcohol or kerosene to kill the remaining eggs. Do not smoke while you are doing this or you may catch fire.

Bot-flies

Bot-flies (*Dermatobia hominis*) lay their eggs on mosquitoes. When the mosquito takes her blood meal, the hitch-hiking fly eggs hatch and the maggots penetrate the victim's skin via the bite hole or a follicle. Once in the skin they grow until after 2 or 3 months they measure 2cm. They are unpleasant and unnerving parasites because they move about so that you can feel, and sometimes hear them, fidgeting.

Nicotine is toxic to most animals and one removal technique is to poison the maggot with the base of a used non-filter cigarette then squeeze the beast out; this is probably best done by a local who has practised the technique. The disadvantage of this method is the convulsions it throws the beast into before it gives in. Barb McLeod, an independent traveller who has spent a lot of time in bot-fly country in Belize (*see* **Bibliography**, p.219) has developed a technique which she claims is completely effective and does not throw the beast into disturbing paroxysms. Cover the bot-fly's breathing hole with a generous quantity of non-water-based glue. There is no need to wait for this to dry before placing a circular patch of adhesive tape on top. The tape should be 1–2cm in diameter, the size depending upon the size of the 'boil' and its location. Apply a second seal of glue along the edge of the tape and allow this to dry well. The bot-fly may try to force a new breathing passage by secreting lymph under the edge of the tape. Leave the tape on over night and by morning the larva should be thoroughly asphyxiated and can easily be squeezed out or removed with tweezers. This is a good method since any attempt to grab the live animal risks pulling it apart which will set up a nasty inflammation reaction and infection.

Medical texts say that the only way to extract bot-flies is surgically. However, a recent paper published in a prestigious American medical journal (JAMA 1993; **270**:2087–8) suggests that the best treatment is to apply strips of bacon over the 'boils' which encourage the maggots to emerge far enough to be caught and removed with tweezers. The McLeod method sounds best to me.

Wearing long clothes and repellents will protect you against being attacked.

Small Biters

Mosquitoes, ticks, sand-flies and the little beasts which transmit malaria and other common vector-borne disease are described on pp.49–68. Details are given there on how to remove ticks, too.

Six-legged Biters

Insects are small animals with six jointed legs; many have wings. There are more insect species on earth than all other animals put together. Most make useful contributions to the earth's ecological balance; a very few make themselves unpopular with mankind.

Fleas

Fleas are dynamic jumpers. They may be acquired in cheap hotels. They tend to leave a line of bites across the abdomen, then settle down in your sleeping bag. Turning your bedding inside-out and leaving it out in direct sunlight usually makes them go elsewhere. If this does not get rid of them, insecticides may be necessary. Fleas are difficult to see and even more difficult to catch for they are small and fast-moving; they are flattened side to side, dark nut-brown and look as if made from polished leather. In a very few regions rat (and rarely human) fleas transmit plague; this is a rare disease in travellers and responds to prompt antibiotic treatment.

Lice and 'Crabs'

These are sluggish movers which are usually acquired by direct contact with someone who is infested or, in the case of headlice, also via a shared comb or brush. Like scabies (*see* p.108), it would be unusual to acquire lice from dirty bedding—unless the bed was still warm! The best over-the-counter remedies are *malathion* or *carbaryl* (*see* p.109).

Red-flies, Mangrove-flies or Gad-flies (*Chrysops*)

These horse-flies are found in West African forests east of the Dahomey Gap and in the Central African equatorial forests. They transmit the loa worm (*Loa loa*) which causes most problems in people who have not encountered the worm before (e.g. travellers and expatriates). Local people with life-long exposure are not often troubled by it. A single mangrove-fly can inoculate 100 worm larvae into the skin. They cause terrific itching. Later, prickling and itching sensations, swelling, aches and pains occur as the worm wanders beneath the skin surface.

They sometimes cause 'Calabar swellings' which persist for about 3 days. Occasionally an adult worm (which is up to 7cm long) in the eye becomes visible to the person infested and takes up to 30 minutes to meander across the conjunctiva: an alarming spectacle. These can be removed if a surgeon is immediately to hand. Untreated infestations die out in about 15 years. Avoid bites by covering your skin with long clothes on forest jaunts; repellents are not very effective against these flies. Expatriates in endemic areas should ensure that their houses are screened to keep out the flies. Loa loa is treatable.

In the US, related gad-flies (also called deer-flies) transmit tularaemia, a serious plague-like disease. Tularaemia also occasionally occurs in Europe (mainly Scandinavia and eastern Europe) where ticks (*see* p.63) or mosquitoes usually transmit it.

Stable-flies (*Stomoxys*)

These look like ordinary house-flies but they have a painful bite. They do not transmit any diseases, although they have been known to lay eggs in available body orifices (*see* dung beetles on p.142).

Assassin Bugs and Chagas' Disease (American Trypanosomiasis)

Chagas' disease is a debilitating affliction spread by the painful bites of barber or assassin bugs in some parts of tropical lowland South America; precautions and further information are given on p.62. Assassin bugs are flat-backed insects often shield-shaped and brown in colour. The assassin bugs of South America are nocturnal and infest wattle-and-daub type housing; if you are planning to use simple local accommodation, sleeping in a hammock with a mosquito net will reduce the likelihood of bites (*see* p.53).

Some true bugs live in freshwater in temperate as well as tropical regions (backswimmers and water scorpions). They have a surprisingly painful bite for their size, but they do not usually bite unprovoked. There is an exception: the aggressive giant water bugs of the family Belostomatidae can reach lengths of 10cm and are capable of inflicting a deep painful wound. They sometimes attack swimmers and so have been given the common name of toe-biters. Cayenne is one place where they are encountered.

Bed Bugs

Bed bugs (*Cimex lectularius*) are true bugs, and thus related to assassins; they have a painful bite too. They are a hazard of seedy hotels where there are cracks and holes in the plaster or brickwork since this is often where they skulk during the day; they also lurk in bed frames and corners of mosquito nets. The best way to avoid them is to find a more upmarket hotel. If you are unfortunate enough to discover bed bugs after setting down for the night, move the bed away from the wall and keep a light on if possible. One bed bug takes between 10 and 20 minutes to drink its fill of blood and if interrupted will bite repeatedly until it has had enough, or you kill it. Bites are painful enough to keep you awake and are often very inflamed and itchy after the bug has departed. There are seldom any long-term problems after bed bug bites and they spread no disease (except insomnia).

Eight-legged Biters

Chiggers and Mites

Chiggers or red bugs are little red mites of the family Trombiculidae known in Britain as harvest mites. They do not enter the skin nor do they suck blood, but their name leads to confusion with the jigger-flea. These are quite different. There are about 700 species; of which 20 are important as they cause scrub itch (also called trombidiasis). In Asia and the Pacific Islands, they transmit scrub typhus (*see* below). Chiggers are well known to people who walk through long grass, particularly in the tropical Americas, for although they are only 1mm long they really make their presence felt. Keep them off by applying repellent and tucking trousers into socks, otherwise they will latch on to ankles, the groin, armpits and wherever clothing is tight. They stay on for 4 days but the welts and severe itching that these little red mites cause lasts for 10 days. The reason that they cause such trouble so long after they have left is that they leave behind a stylosome (drinking straw) created partly as the body's reaction to their saliva and this continues to irritate and inflame the skin. If you scratch as vigorously as you would like, you are bound to get a nasty secondary skin infection.

Australian Whirligig Mite

These red mites (*Anystis* spp.) are large as mites go—up to 1.35mm long. They are fast moving predators producing painful bites with a small area of inflammation which may persist for several days.

Scrub Typhus Mites

The small Asian mites that transmit scrub typhus (a rickettsial disease that responds to antibiotics) look like chiggers but do not cause itching and therefore often go unnoticed. As the name implies, these mites are common in scrub and secondary forest. Scrub typhus mites occur within a large but defined region of East Asia and the Pacific Islands, down to Queensland, Australia and Sri Lanka in the south and as far west as Pakistan.

Mauritian Red Poison Mite

One mite that is worth mentioning as a curiosity is the red poison mite of Mauritius. Its toxic secretions if conveyed to the mouth by way of the hands are sufficiently potent to cause unpleasant and sometimes dangerous swelling of the mouth and throat. Wash your hands if you come into contact with red crawlies in Mauritius.

Preventing Mite Bites

To avoid mites, chiggers, ticks and the diseases that they carry, put on insect repellent; the best are DEET-based (diethyltoluamide). Tuck trousers into socks and avoid high grass. These precautions will protect you from leeches and biting insects too.

Spiders

Almost all spiders are venomous, but most are unable to bite into human skin. As a general rule, those which spin elaborate webs are less in need of venoms to immobilize their prey and so these species are less likely to be dangerous. Dangerous species either dispense nerve poisons (*Lactrodectus, Phoneutria, Atrax*) or toxins which destroy an area of living tissue (*Loxosceles, Lycosa*). These five medically important genera are described below. Most spiders harm by biting. However, some of the very large hairy spiders flick off their body hairs towards the source of their annoyance and these cause marked itching and inflammation; the hairs are particularly unpleasant if they go into the eyes.

Brown Recluses or Fiddle Spiders (*Loxosceles*)

These are long-legged brownish spiders which are widely distributed throughout the Americas and they have also bitten people in the Mediterranean, North Africa and Israel. The name fiddle spider comes from the violin-like mark visible on the back of many species. Bites cause localized death of skin tissue and underlying structures. There are occasional fatalities; there have been about six deaths this century from these spiders in the US. Men have been bitten on the genitals while sitting on outdoor toilets, so check before you sit. Antivenom is made in Peru, Brazil and Argentina.

South American Wolf Spiders (*Lycosa rartoria* and *L. pampeana*)

Wolf spider bites can cause tissue death resulting in a scar up to 20cm long. There is an antivenom in Brazil. *Lycosa tarentula*, a European wolf spider was blamed for epidemics of bites which could only be cured by dancing the tarantella. It is feared, but rarely kills anyone except the infirm.

Black and Brown Widows (*Lactrodectus*)

The widows have a very bad reputation but again deaths are unusual. These are small black or blackish-brown spiders with a red hour-glass shaped design on their backs. They are very widespread and occur in much of the Americas, Africa, southern Europe, warm parts of Asia and Australia. Bites are usually on an extremity and, if venom is dispensed, pain at that site spreads up the limb to the lymph nodes in the groin or armpit, then to muscles which suffer cramps and spasms. The victim can then become exhausted and dehydrated. Pain is difficult to control even with pain-killers, but hot baths may help. Recovery usually takes 1–2 days, or half an hour if antivenom is given. Deaths are rare but occur occasionally in small children, the elderly or those with long-standing heart or respiratory disease. Antivenom is made in Australia, the USA, Russia, the former Yugoslavia, Italy, South Africa and South America.

Huntsman Spiders (*Phoneutria*)

These are also called wandering spiders or banana spiders and they are found in South America. They are large, with 4cm bodies and 13cm leg-spans. Their bites cause intense pain, sweating and cramps, but recovery is usually complete in 12 hours. Deaths are unusual and occur in children and weak adults. Antivenom is made in Brazil.

Funnel-webs (*Atrax*)

The nastiest funnel-web spiders fortunately have a very restricted range and only occur in an area immediately surrounding Sydney in Australia. Because antivenom treatment is available, deaths from funnel-web bites are now rare. They are medium-sized, heavily built 'tarantula'-like spiders which either give a series of superficial bites or grasp firmly with their legs and drive their chelicerae in with sufficient force to pierce the skull of a chicken.

Many-legged Biters

Centipedes

Centipedes are fast-moving animals. Most of their many segments have a single pair of legs. This distinguishes them from millipedes which do not bite, have a sedate lifestyle and two pairs of legs per segment. Bites by large tropical centipedes are very painful but not life-threatening. The standard medical advice for treating such bites is to inject local anaesthetic, but its pain-killing properties are short lived. More powerful injections of morphine or pethidine may be required.

Leeches

The good news about leeches is that they do not transmit disease; they only harm you if the bite becomes infected. Apparently British troops serving in the Malayan jungle wore condoms at night because they were so worried about leeches crawling into their urethras. While aquatic leeches (*see* below) occasionally manage this unpleasant trick, it is only in people bathing in infested waters.

Leeches are common in rain forests and in other scrubby or forested habitats during the wet season, particularly in Asia, but also in Madagascar. Usually they climb on to you from the ground. They can squeeze through small holes and get at you between the fibres of socks and through shoelace holes. They also hitch a ride as you brush through wet undergrowth and sometimes drop down from trees. Their bite is usually painless (they have concocted their own brand of local anaesthetic). Often you are unaware of their presence until you notice a squelching sensation in the boots which turns out to be very bloody socks. The leeches responsible for the bleeding may well have left by the time you make this discovery. The small wounds will continue to bleed for some hours because of the anticoagulant that the leech has injected to help it feed quickly.

Avoid all this by applying diethyltoluamide (DEET) insect repellent to the outside of boots (but beware since DEET dissolves plastics), put DEET on your ankles and tuck trousers into socks. Leech country is usually hot and steamy so if you only apply repellent to the skin you will sweat it off in an hour. Get leeches off with a dab of salt (as little as a grain will do) or tobacco and then clean and cover (if possible) any broken skin.

Aquatic Leeches

Aquatic leeches inhabit mountain streams and stagnant water and the species which bother people most occur in Southeast Asia. They are acquired when swimming or drinking from infested streams or pools. Avoid attack by drinking only boiled or filtered water and taking care where you bathe. Unlike their terrestrial cousins, some aquatic leeches are slow feeders and stay attached for days or even weeks. If one has invaded some body orifice (this problem is enormously rare in travellers) you will need to have it removed in hospital. If it is attached inside the mouth, throat or nose try gargling with (or sniffing in) a strong salt solution (if you swallow any it will make you vomit).

Other Small Animals with Bad Habits

What is Dangerous?

Local information about dangerous animals is not always accurate. I was told in Sulawesi, for example, that I would be dead in 24 hours after handling a very large, rather attractive millipede. While centipedes have extremely nasty stings, the only noxious property that millipedes have is that the juice they secrete when upset will cause conjunctivitis if rubbed into the eyes. So will snail and slug slime. The secretions of a few tropical millipedes and contact with damaged rove beetles (Staphylinidae) or blister beetles (Meloidae) in many parts of the world (including as close to home as southern Spain) may blister skin (*see* p.112).

Squirters

Tailless whip-scorpions, cicadas and a range of other creatures squirt or spit irritant juice when annoyed. If any goes close to your eyes wash it out with plenty of water. In North America there are a couple of hundred insects known as walking sticks; some are known as musk phasmids since they exude a white liquid with a pleasant musky smell. These are insects to be wary of, however. One species, *Anisomorpha buprestoides*, a 7–12cm long yellow and brown striped stick insect can spray its 'musk' a distance of about 40cm. When inhaled this stuff causes pain and if it gets into the eyes the severe burning sensation it provokes takes 36 hours to go away.

Caterpillars

Many moth caterpillars can cause dermatitis or other unpleasant effects on contact with the skin. Some induce blood blisters if you brush past them. They are usually buff-cloured but some have large eye-like markings and spiny-looking appendages to warn you that they are unpleasant. There are very spiny and nasty-looking Brazilian caterpillars. The most notable is *Lonomia achelous* (family Saturniidae) which has poison spines that deliver a toxin which interferes with blood clotting and can make people very ill. Similarly armed caterpillars are also known from Venezuela. Stings by the 'long-haired' caterpillar *Premolis semirufa* (Arctiidae) can cause such deep inflammation around the joints that it can leave the victim permanently disabled. The caterpillar feeds on leaves of the rubber tree so is a hazard to South American rubber tappers.

Furry caterpillars can also cause great irritation and discomfort if you lean on them or they get caught up in your clothes and their hairs are forced into your skin. In rural areas there can be veritable plagues of these attractive-looking insects: they enter houses in such numbers that it is easy to lean on one, get them caught up in clothes or pick something up on which one is perched. The fine 'hairs' inject irritant chemicals akin to histamines which can leave the skin irritated for a month or more. In Nepal, locals say that many of the 'hairs' can be removed immediately after they have entered the skin by rubbing the hand in someone's hair (although if you try this make sure there is no risk of the hairs entering the eyes). When a friend squashed a caterpillar under her hand, though, they said that her fine Western hair would not do. She did not feel that she could rub her hand in her Nepali colleague's hair unfortunately! Furry caterpillars occur all over the world and are a particular hazard of the wet season in sub-saharan Africa.

In Peru there are rufous funnel moth caterpillars (*Megalopyle superba*, family Megalopygidae) which are so large and 'furry' they are known as the *cuy rojizo* or reddish guinea pig. They are notorious for the severity of the skin reactions contact with them causes. Related caterpillars occur in the southern US, West Indies and South America. There are also similarly unpleasant species in the old world tropics and subtropics. Keep away from any furry-looking or spiky caterpillars; the more strikingly they are marked, the more likely they are to be venomous.

Moths with Unusual Habits

In Southeast Asia and the Southwest Pacific there are a range of moths which drink tears from the eyes and also enjoy saliva and other body secretions if they are handy. I do not know what the medical significance of these weird habits is, but presumably they could introduce infection, particularly conjunctivitis. The *Calyptera* genus of moths which live in the mountains of Southeast Asia and Papua New Guinea have developed a taste for blood and occasionally attack people, at night, usually at or above an altitude of 1000m (3000ft) and during the rainy season. Using an action like that of an electric carving knife, the moth saws into the skin with its serrated proboscis and sucks up the blood. The initial wound is painless, but it does hurt when the moth starts emptying saliva into the wound and later there is transitory inflammation around the site. The only likely problem arising from this is infection, since these moths also like to dine on cattle dung.

Small Spiny Creatures

The smallest tenrecs (Madagascar's equivalent of the hedgehog) will deposit their very fine spines in your skin if you handle them. Each spine then has to be painstakingly removed with a fine pair of tweezers. It takes hours to do this.

Dung Beetles and Flesh-Flies

Dung beetles have unpleasant egg-laying habits and mothers attending my roving clinics in Sri Lanka commonly complained that insects flew out of their toddlers' faeces as they were deposited on the ground! This bewildering but harmless affliction needs no treatment and it is most unlikely to befall even the sleepiest of travellers. House-flies, bot-flies, blow-flies, flesh-flies and hover-flies occasionally deposit eggs in open wounds and in body orifices so that their maggots can infest the ears, nostrils, eyes and genitals almost invariably of children or very debilitated people.

Stingers

Scorpions

Many scorpions are able to inflict extremely painful stings but those which are dangerous to adults are exceptional. If scorpions worry you, as they worry me (I was stung in Madagascar), be thankful that the metre-long *Brontoscorpio* species became extinct 300 million years ago. Some of the largest survivors, *Heterometrus* spp. of South-east Asia and *Pandinus imperator* of West Africa, look terrifying enough but their poison only causes intense pain and they do not have the powerful cardiac and nerve poisons of some of the smaller species.

Where are Scorpions a Hazard?

There are species capable of lethal stings, mainly in children, in North Africa and the Middle East, South Africa, India and in North, Central and Southern America and Trinidad. Scorpions are most common in dry arid regions, but they do not tolerate extreme heat. They seem to be most in evidence after rain. They are nocturnal so most stings happen at night or when a slumbering scorpion is disturbed after it has settled down in your shoe or rucksack. As a general rule, scorpions which have big claws and slim 'tails' rely on their claws as their principle weapon so they are less poisonous. Those with small claws and a more substantial 'tail' and stinger are more likely to be seriously venomous. Unfortunately, there are exceptions to this rule. One is the Middle Eastern *Hemiscorpius lepturus* which is common in Iran and has an exceptionally long slender stinger but is very dangerous.

Mexico has the worst statistics for deaths from scorpion stings anywhere in the world. There are well over 1000 deaths per year: most in children under 5 years of age. Many scorpions can cause serious problems in infants and children and medical help should be sought promptly when a child is stung. Even in Mexico, though, most stings are painful for a maximum of 4 hours and only eight of the 25 local species pose a serious threat to humans. Antivenom is available for the dangerous species, such as the 5–8cm long, elongated, narrow bodied *Centruroides* 'bark scorpions'. These dangerous species also occur in Arizona but they rarely kill there, since antivenom is readily available. Administration of antivenom carries its own risks and should not be done by amateurs.

The red scorpion of South India is exceptional in causing numerous deaths **in adults** each year; its venom poisons the heart and circulatory system.

Some scorpion toxins also contain nerve poisons so that my finger which received a sting 8 years ago in Madagascar still has abnormal sensation.

Scorpion Antivenoms and Other Treatments

Scorpion antivenoms are manufactured by various institutions in the US, Germany, Mexico, Brazil, Turkey, Algiers, South Africa, Egypt and Iran. The Lister Institute of Preventative Medicine, Elstree, Herts WD6 3AX, UK, stocks some. Scorpion haemolymph (the scorpion equivalent of blood) neutralizes scorpion venom. A child was saved in Israel by a haemolymph injection when antivenom was unavailable.

Injecting local anaesthetic in or around a stung finger will only give temporary relief from the pain so an injection of one of the powerful morphine like analgesics may be required. Some doctors believe that this treatment is risky when there are respiratory complications after the sting. Red scorpion envenoming, for example, can cause flooding of fluids into the lungs (pulmonary oedema). Clearly, if the sting happens in one of the regions where dangerous species occur, it would be wise to seek medical help to allow the situation to be properly monitored.

Applying ice packs, immersion in water or cooling by hanging the affected limb out of a car window increases the pain. Avoid rubbing or other kinds of friction and keep the stung part warm and cushioned.

Hymenoptera (Thin-waisted Insects: Bees, Wasps, Hornets, Ants)

No insect repellent is effective against stinging insects such as bees, ants, wasps and hornets. Back off calmly if you encounter a swarm and they should not attack you; never thrash or flail about. Wasps and their kin are attracted by sweet things, brightly coloured floral patterns and perfumes.

Honey-bees

Bee stings should be scraped or flicked out with a knife, fingernail or pin; grasping stings with tweezers will inject the remaining venom left in the stinger. Treatment is then to apply ice, elevate the part that has been stung and take antihistamine tablets and/or aspirin. Most people in Britain who are allergic to bee stings are bee-keepers or their relatives. Allergy is less likely in children than in adults.

A severe allergic reaction to stings can compromise breathing and this can be fatal in minutes. Those who know they are allergic would be wise to carry *adrenaline* (*epinephrine* in the US) for injection (*see* p.13). Such a severe reaction is unlikely unless there have been previous stings. A hypersensitive individual will usually notice that with each previous sting they suffered increasingly extensive and persistent local swelling. Be warned.

Wasps and Hornets

Wasps are not always yellow and black and stripy. The common Asian field wasp is plain orange and there are other species which are navy blue. Wasps do not leave their stingers behind, but otherwise their stings require similar treatment to bee stings.

Fire Ants (*Solenopsis richteri* and *S. invicta*)

These originated in South America but they have now spread into the US where huge numbers of people are stung every month. Victims suffer pain, itching, swelling and redness around a central weal which lasts for a few hours, later little blisters or pustules occur. As with stings from their cousins (wasps and bees), fire ant stings can cause dramatic allergic reactions in people stung previously.

Sweat Bees

Sweat bees are small (3–4mm long) black bees which are attracted, often in tens, to sweaty skin, mouths and nostrils. They are annoying, slow moving, easy to kill and their stings trivial. However, if one is crushed, it will release pheromones which stimulate its mates to attack. They then become intolerable. They live in many parts of the tropics and sub-tropics and have pestered me in dry deciduous forests in both Madagascar and lowland Nepal.

Nasty Marine Creatures

It is best to assume that everything that lives in tropical seas is venomous. Touch nothing unless you are sure it is harmless and wear stout gloves if you are collecting anything or generally rummaging around in crevices. Collecting living creatures is not only bad news for them, but could be for you too.

Cone Shells

The very attractive cone molluscs (*Conus* spp.) of the Indo-Pacific seas are equipped with a venomous tongue-like harpoon tooth. They range up to about 23cm in length, the majority being much smaller. They have been known to sting collectors through the trouser pocket. Stings can cause unpleasant tingling and numbness and sometimes even paralysis and death from respiratory arrest. Resuscitation can be life-saving; there is no antivenom. Do not collect live specimens.

Octopuses

Octopus saliva contains a vicious toxin which can be introduced into the skin by a bite from the animal's powerful beak, which is situated between the tentacles. Bites are painful and bleed, swell and become inflamed. Blue-ringed octopuses, *Hapalochlaena maculosa* and *H. lunulata* of Australia, Indonesia and the Philippines possess such toxic nerve poisons that they can cause fatal generalized paralysis within 15 minutes of a bite. They are only 10cm long and occur in shallow waters.

The flying squid, *Onychoteuthis banksi*, is also dangerous, but since it only comes up to shallow waters after dark, it rarely comes into contact with people. Those who get bitten are almost entirely fishermen. These squid are sold as food throughout their range and it may be worth exercising care when preparing them for the table in case they are still alive.

Jellyfish and Their Kin

Jellyfish, sea wasps, Portuguese man-of-war, fire coral, sea anemones and sea nettles all have venomous stinging capsules called nematocysts. Jellyfish stings are most common when there are onshore winds. At worst, jellyfish envenomation causes paralysis of the muscles of respiration. Although this paralysis is transient, it lasts long enough to kill, unless someone is on hand to carry out resuscitation.

Five jellyfish species are known to have killed humans. Three of them are box jellyfish, *Chironex* spp. or 'sea wasps'. They are box-shaped with tentacles hanging from the four corners of the box-shaped 'bell'. The largest and most venomous sea wasp, *Chironex fleckeri*, inhabits the tropical coasts of Australia and Southeast Asia. These fast-swimming jellyfish have bodies as big as basketballs (20cm diameter) and tentacles which trail out for 3m behind them. The tentacles (which carry the sting-cells) are translucent, so they are difficult to see and thus easy to brush against by mistake. Those stung experience incredible pain and often collapse and die, sometimes within 4 minutes. Flooding stung skin with vinegar helps inactivate any undischarged stingers. There is a specific antivenom in Australia.

Chiropsalmas quadrigatus kills many people in the Indo-China seas: from the Maldives in the west to the Philippines in the east, with one victim in Texas. It also occurs in the Atlantic from Brazil to North Carolina. The fifth lethal species is the Portuguese man-of-war (*Physalia physalis*). It is common in the warm waters of the Atlantic, Pacific and Indian Oceans. Finally there has been one reported death from stings of *Stomolophus nomurai* in southeast China, which has a 1.5m diameter bell. Stay away from big jellyfish wherever you are.

Treatment of Jellyfish Stings

Try to remove any fragments of tentacles, remembering that the tentacles can still sting after they have broken off the jellyfish. Vinegar (4–6 per cent *acetic acid*) inactivates the stingers of the dangerous Indo-Pacific and Australian box jellyfish, but do not use this on other species. A 50/50 solution of baking soda in water inactivates the stingers of the unpleasant *Chrysaora* jellyfish of the Atlantic. Massive discharge of stingers is **caused** by applying alcoholic solutions, such as methylated spirits and suntan lotion, and this exacerbates poisoning: never 'treat' jellyfish stings with them. Superficial pain usually responds to cold packs or ice applied for 15 minutes.

Giving mouth-to-mouth resuscitation and, if necessary, cardiac massage to a victim who is not breathing is very worthwhile. The effects of the venom are often remarkably short-lived so that if the victim can be kept alive for a few minutes, (s)he will survive and recover completely, albeit permanently scarred.

Sea Anemones

Anemones sting their prey, so wherever they are encountered they should be treated with respect. One species, *Anemonia sulcata*, as close to home as the Adriatic coast, can inflict painful stings.

Starfish and Sea Urchins

These have venomous spines and grapples which can also produce dangerous poisoning. Spines embedded in skin are at best a painful nuisance. Remove them after softening the skin with 2 per cent salicylic acid ointment or acetone or magnesium sulphate paste (readily available in pharmacies). This technique may also be useful for extracting deeply embedded pieces of coral. The dangers of coral, fire coral and 'sea lice' are described on p.78.

Dangerous Sea Fish

About 100 species of fish can administer dangerous stings and a selection (barracuda, moray and conger eels, garfish, groupers and sharks) are able to inflict severe bites. Fish stings are common and it is estimated that there may be as many as 1500 stingray stings and about 300 scorpion fish stings a year in the US alone. Fatalities from fish stings are rare; so are deaths from shark attacks.

Stonefish and Their Friends and Relations

Stonefish often lurk in shallow water, well camouflaged, half buried and looking like stones. A bare foot impaled on venomous fins or spines is an excruciating experience. There is a stonefish antivenom. Scorpion fish make themselves more conspicuous, but are just as venomous.

Weever Fish

Venomous fish are not peculiar to tropical waters. Weever fish are common around British coasts especially in Cornwall, where they are responsible for many excruciating stings during July and August. Like scorpion fish they are also armed with venomous dorsal fins and lie partially buried often in sand in shallow water so that people paddling on beaches frequently tread on them. The sting is so painful that a Welsh trawlerman cut off his toes to get relief.

Stingrays

Stingrays are aggressive and very common. They are equipped with up to 30cm-long venomous spines on their tails which are used to lash out against legs or bodies. They inflict many injuries in North America each year. It is not unusual for victims to receive lacerations 13–17cm long as well as the excruciating venom. There are nasty freshwater species in South America and they are very widespread in all tropical, sub-tropical and most temperate seas. In Australian coastal waters there is a species which reaches a length of about 5m and a weight of 350kg. Stingrays occur as far north as Scandinavia and are found in the Mediterranean. Fish stings cause awful pain and swelling which is at its worst 30–60 minutes after being stung. Sometimes stings cause collapse and even death.

The Stingray Shuffle

Few animals choose to attack unprovoked, but stings are their defence when surprised by someone. Wearing shoes will give you little protection from stingrays (although you will avoid other venomous fish) but adopting a shuffling walk (the stingray shuffle) when paddling in shallow water will advertise your presence and the fish will swim away before you tread on it.

Treatment of Fish Stings

Fish venom is inactivated by heat so the treatment (whether the sting is from a tropical or temperate species) is to immerse the affected limb in water that is uncomfortably hot but not scalding (45°C). Relief from the pain is usually immediate but may return. Continued soaking will probably be needed by topping up with hot water for 30–90 minutes; by this time most of the pain will have gone. Repeat the hot soaks if the pain returns. Antivenoms do exist for some species, and doctors can also inject local anaesthetic which gives some relief too. Morphine and pethidine do not really help the pain. Even in regions where modern medical facilities are available, the hot water treatment will bring the quickest relief. Any pieces of your assailant which remain in the wound or skin must be removed otherwise infection is bound to set in. Foreign bodies, be they fish spines, pieces of coral or rusty nails will all lead to infection if left in a wound. Some debris will also tattoo the skin.

Sharks

Being eaten alive by a shark is the kind of image that nightmares are made of, yet the risk of shark attack seems to be extremely small. There are perhaps 50–100 deaths a year **worldwide** due to sharks. Compare with about 400 deaths annually from drowning in chilly UK waters. You are more likely to be struck by lightning than end up inside a shark's belly.

I have also been told that the nearer you are to the equator, the less dangerous sharks are likely to be. Equatorial waters are so overstocked with fish that sharks do not trouble to attack something as large and indigestible as a snorkler or swimmer. I have friends who have snorkled unscathed among sharks in Indonesia. The problem with sharks, though, is that they are unpredictable creatures. Most attacks seem to be either from 'rogue' individuals or if someone is unfortunate enough to precipitate or get caught up in a 'feeding frenzy'. This is described in horrendous detail in Caras's *Dangerous to Man*. Sharks then become so mad that injured individuals turn to eat their own entrails. Hungry sharks can smell blood and damaged flesh (especially fish oil) from half a kilometre. Spear-fishermen who carry their catches on their belts may be more liable to attack. Menstruating women may also attract sharks.

A common prelude to a shark attack is the shark circling its victim: if you are being circled, it is time to get out of the water. Try to keep calm and swim away steadily since thrashing will excite the shark. Keep it in view and if it comes close try banging it on the nose, poking it in the eye and shouting under water: these techniques sometimes work. Shark skin is highly abrasive and will tear your skin if the shark brushes past you; this could precipitate a feeding frenzy which would definitely be bad news.

Most shark attacks occur between the latitudes of 30°N and 30°S. It would certainly be sensible to take local advice before swimming. If there have been shark attacks, or if there are nasty currents or other dangers, locals will know about them.

Saltwater Crocodiles

Some authorities think that the saltwater crocodile is the most vicious animal in the world, since it is fearless, bloodthirsty and huge. It is the biggest of the crocodiles with reliable records of beasts 7m long and many claims of others in excess of 10m.

They are found in the sea, mangrove swamps, tidal parts of rivers and estuaries in Southeast Asia, India, Sri Lanka and Australia. Ask local advice before you bathe.

Sea Snakes

Sea snakes are highly venomous, but fortunately they rarely bite. They are sluggish creatures which loll around in warm sea, rocking gently with the swell and they are easy to see because they are strikingly marked. They are air-breathing reptiles and it is said that they may get cross enough to bite if you happen to be snorkelling above them when they have decided to surface for a breath. The only time that they are commonly provoked into biting people is if they are caught up in a fishing net or are otherwise put at a disadvantage. Sea snakes go in for orgies and gather together in numbers when they are mating; apparently if disturbed at this time they can be aggressive but perhaps it is understandable that they object to interruptions. If you encounter a group of sea snakes, keep well clear of them. Treat even individual sea snakes with respect and they will leave you alone.

Of those few people whose skin has been penetrated by sea snake fangs, about 80 per cent receive no venom and suffer no ill effects.

Nasty Freshwater Fish

Candiru

If you urinate while swimming in South American rivers, there is a fish (so it is said) which follows the stream of urine to its source, then climbs inside, sticks out its barbed fins and stays there. It can then only be removed surgically, perhaps by means of a penile amputation. The minute candiru fish does indeed imbed itself inside others, but usually within the gills of fish. The myth of candiru parasitizing man is a frequently repeated travellers' tale which seems to be complete fiction.

Stingrays are a hazard of South American rivers (see p.148).

Piranhas

Piranhas do not seem to be such a hazard to freshwater bathing in South America that their reputation makes them out to be. Indeed most species are almost exclusively vegetarian, while others daintily nibble the ends off fins or scales of other fish. Reliable reports of human deaths seem to be lacking, although the occasional aquarist has been injured by a pet piranha. Their teeth are sufficiently sharp that Indians use piranha jaws as razor blades. Larger members of the *Serrasalmus* genus may occasionally be a hazard to someone who is injured or otherwise weakened but this is only likely if the piranhas' natural food is scarce or if they have been provoked (perhaps in a shark-like feeding frenzy, see p.149) by slaughter-house waste being dumped into their river. Most piranhas are about 20cm (8ins) long, but the largest reach 60cm (2ft) in length.

Venomous Snakes and Other Dangerous Reptiles

Crocodiles

Crocodiles are highly dangerous and merciless killers which take about 1000 lives a year. The new world crocodilians do not seem to be dangerous. Most deaths are due to the Nile crocodile (*Crocodilus niloticus*) in Africa (including Madagascar) and the saltwater crocodile (*Crocodilus porosus*) in Southeast Asia, India, Sri Lanka and Australia. Africans are supposed to be so frightened of Nile crocodiles (for good reason!) that South African doctors suggested that introducing them into bilharzia-infected canals would stop people bathing in them and thus cut down bilharzia transmission. Like other crocodilians, Nile crocodiles continue to grow throughout their lives and so old specimens can be very big. In the Ankarana Caves in Madagascar there was what seemed to be a reliable report of an individual 7m long. The mugger crocodile (*Crocodilus palustris*) of the Indian sub-continent is said not to be aggressive but while I was working in Sri Lanka the remains of a man were recovered from one particularly large mugger which lived in a freshwater reservoir. This species grows to a length of over 5.5m.

Crocodiles usually hunt victims who are drinking (or washing) at the waters edge. The reptile speeds towards the river bank and just as it is about to run aground, it launches itself at its lunch, exploding out of the water unexpectedly. If this happens, the only hope for escape is to attack the eyes of the creature; these are its only vulnerable spot. Even if you did have a Crocodile-Dundee knife to hand you would not be able to sink it through its thick skull. Cheetah and leopard remains have been found inside Nile crocodiles so even a well-armed victim may succumb.

Venomous Land Snakes

Most snakes are not dangerous. Out of a possible 2400 species worldwide, 500 are venomous, but less than 200 are responsible for causing severe envenoming resulting in death or permanent disability. A good proportion of those snakes which are venomous do not have the capability or temperament to be harmful. Even those which are venomous give a harmless bite more often than not. However, since the division between harmful and harmless species is far from clear, anyone bitten by a snake should be assessed by an expert. There are still about 40,000 deaths per year (mainly in India due to cobra bites), but it is exceptional for travellers to be envenomed. Those at high risk are agricultural labourers, who disturb happily basking snakes. Peninsular Malaysia boasts a particularly rich array of venomous species but even here only about one in a thousand people bitten by snakes dies.

They carried the farm labourer in on a board; the sweat poured off him and his eyes showed that he was scared to death. He had been cutting sugar cane and had been bitten on his bare leg by a snake that he had disturbed. The old man who gave advice in all crises cut into the wound and applied the anus of a beheaded chicken to it. The decapitated corpse was said to provide suction to draw out the poison. The suction effect only lasts a couple of minutes after decapitation so in the labourer's case 12 chickens were sacrificed before the old man was satisfied that the victim would recover, which indeed he did.

Most authorities now condemn cutting into a snake bite but other aspects of this traditional Nepali treatment are based on a kind of perverse good sense which helped the victim. Most people who are bitten by snakes are scared almost literally to death, but if they start thrashing around in a blind panic any venom that has been dispensed will be distributed more quickly and effectively.

An important part of the labourer's treatment, then, was a complicated ritual which occupied everyone and made him feel that something was being done. Keeping calm is an important part of snake bite treatment but it is the most difficult to achieve. Those managing the situation must appear confident and cool even if they are panicking inside.

What to Do if a Snake Bites

Travellers are rarely unlucky enough to receive a dangerous bite, but everyone wants to know what to do if they are on the wrong end of a pair of fangs. Snake venom is a kind of meat tenderizer produced by modified salivary glands; it partially digests the prey before it is eaten, so it has some very unpleasant effects.

The victim should be encouraged to keep still. The bitten part should be washed with clean water and soap and wiped gently with a clean cloth. This removes any venom from the skin surface. If venom has entered the body, that part will swell so any rings, watches and jewellery must be removed. Even in expert hands tourniquets are dangerous and there are more limbs lost through tourniquets applied after a harmless bite than lives saved by them. Splinting the bitten limb slows absorbtion of the venom and reduces pain.

Prompt evacuation to a doctor or hospital is the next priority. If the victim begins to show signs of envenomation, antivenom will be administered in the safe environment of the clinic or hospital. Administration of antivenom carries its own risks and should not be done by amateurs. It can be dangerous to give antivenom if no venom has entered the body. Finally, if the offending snake can be captured without risk of someone else being bitten, take it to show the doctor, but beware since even a decapitated head is able to envenomate in a reflex bite.

While evacuation is being organized, the following rules will help protect the victim. Many 'first aid' measures that some people think should be taken will actually make things much worse:

- **Do not** give aspirin, but offer paracetamol which is safe
- **Do not** incise or suck the wound
- **Do not** apply ice packs
- **Do not** apply potassium permanganate
- **Discourage** movement of the bitten limb by applying a splint
- **Keep** the bitten limb **below** heart height to slow spread of the venom
- **Don't** panic—it is likely that no venom has been dispensed

Tourniquets

Tourniquets may be appropriate occasionally, but only under these circumstances:

- The delay in getting to competent medical help is going to be more than 30 minutes but less than 3 hours
- The biter was an elapid snake (cobra, krait, mamba or coral snake), or a sea snake or an Australian snake
- You are sure of the species which has done the biting and it is one of the above
- You know what you are doing and feel competent, and also calm enough, to take charge of the situation
- The tourniquet is released for 15 seconds every 30 minutes
- The tourniquet is removed after 2 hours
- You have a watch and can write down what you are doing

A great many limbs are lost through incompetently applied tourniquets. Too often they are applied after a bite by a harmless snake or a bite by a venomous snake which has dispensed no venom. Home-made tourniquets often do little to stop the venom dispersing throughout the body, yet they can still cut off circulation sufficiently to lose the limb.

Applying a broad, firm crêpe bandage around the bitten limb and splinting it is a safer option than using a true arterial tourniquet. Even this must be released every 30 minutes so that blood gets to body tissues.

Electric shock or stun guns do not inactivate venom, nor do 'snake stones' used in the Indian subcontinent, but these may be useful in the same way as the decapitated chickens; they would be seen to be doing something and thus may help keep everyone calm.

Habits of Snakes

It is worth repeating that not all venomous snakes are dangerous. Many of the beautiful and brightly coloured coral snakes have such small mouths that they are only really capable of getting their teeth into an ear lobe or finger web. In a comprehensive review of snake bites in Peninsular Malaysia the only record of coral snake envenomation was a single case in 1937 and the victim survived. Some South American species are large enough to bite a finger.

Other species, like the back-fanged snakes of Madagascar, can only inject venom as their victim is being swallowed so that they can only poison those that stick a finger down their throats! Yet others do not have the temperament to attack. Sea snakes, for example have a very powerful venom but attacks by them are virtually unknown. The highly venomous krait and also the much feared bushmaster are similarly unlikely to bite even if provoked, but don't try it: kraits certainly still claim a few lives.

Most deaths from snake bites are in the highly populated Indian subcontinent (especially Myanmar, India and Sri Lanka) because snakes are most often forced into contact with man. Perhaps the most feared snake of this region is the huge king cobra or hamadryad (*Ophiophagus hannah*) which can be 4.8m long and when in threatening mode can stand 2m off the ground, at eye level. When they attack they do so with enthusiasm and are efficient dispensers of venom. However, they are a scarce day-active species and an encounter with one is most unlikely. They are fast movers, but contrary to folklore, they cannot outrun a fleeing man. The Indian cobra (*Naja naja*) which claims most victims worldwide is usually not aggressive, and often extremely timid, but it is occasionally fierce and attacks when disturbed. The young can be real delinquents and are much more dangerous than the adults, being much more easily excited and ready to strike repeatedly and with determination. Indian cobras are usually more active at night although they hunt for food during the late afternoon and evening.

Other Health Hazards from Snakes

The most common health problem caused by snakes is infection. Even the non-venomous British grass snake inflicts a deep dirty wound which is impossible to clean properly so there is a risk of sepsis, tetanus and gangrene. It is wise, therefore, to seek medical attention following any snake bite.

Pythons and other non-venomous constrictors should be treated with respect. They can reach a length of 10m and the largest individuals occasionally kill people. A colleague has a gruesome portrait of a python (*Python reticularis*) killed in Sulawesi; it is sliced open to reveal the body of a man inside who had been consumed on his wedding night. Pythons have also swallowed people in Africa (*P. sebae*) and South America (*Eunectes eunectes*).

Poisonous and Dangerous Lizards

In Madagascar, I have been assured by local people that chameleons are deadly. In Thailand, geckoes and in Nepal, cute little skinks are believed to be poisonous. All these reptiles are entirely harmless, indeed there are only two types of venomous lizard: the Gila monsters and the beaded lizard. Both are large (45–80cm) and live in the Southwest USA and Mexico. There is no antivenom, but humans are rarely bitten and there are no reliable reports of deaths from venomous lizard bites. The komodo dragon of Indonesia, which is a large flesh-eating monitor lizard, has killed at least one careless tourist, however.

Hazards of Meeting Mammals

Man-eaters

Wildlife documentaries allow us to watch predators dispatching prey from the comfort of our sitting rooms and it is easy to forget that these wild animals are capable of injuring us too. Few animals will pick a fight, but they may feel that they are protecting young or defending themselves. Large primates, especially chimpanzees and baboons, are very dangerous. Any large female animal is likely to attack if you go too close when she has young with her. Other species may attack if you surprise them so do not go walking through dense scrub or long grass which could hide a rhinoceros or buffalo. Big carnivores are probably best faced. Running away will do you no good since they can easily outrun you and this is exactly what prey species do. Do something that a prey species would not do, like throwing rocks or running at the animal shouting and brandishing a big stick. The predator will then be so surprised and confused that it will probably retreat.

Dangerous African Animals

If venturing into wildlife country on foot, be sure to take a guide who understands animals. Many 'old Africa hands' consider buffalo, hippopotamus and large primates (chimps and baboons) amongst the most dangerous species. Buffaloes are very aggressive and hippos are particularly likely to attack if you are between them and the river, their refuge.

Large Asian Species

In Africa there is (as a sweeping generalization) plenty of space both for wildlife and man. In Asia where the pressure on land is so much greater, large wild animals are frequently in conflict with farmers. Elephants in particular can be very disgruntled and ill-tempered and seem to be much more likely to attack than their African cousins. In Sri Lanka where elephants have been ousted from some favoured spot, they get their own back by killing people—several a year—who have set up home on what they consider their territory. Large cats in the Indian subcontinent seem to become man-eaters more frequently, perhaps because they are so often in close contact with farmers and their protected areas are relatively small. Of course if there is a man-eater about, everyone will be talking about it, so talk to people before camping alone in big cat country.

The great Indian rhinoceros is dangerous if you encounter it at close quarters on foot. This is likely to happen if you go walking through elephant-high grass in reserves where they are common. Find a tree to climb if you encounter one; no doubt adrenaline will rapidly improve your climbing skills!

Bears

Bears are a hazard in places as far distant as the Rockies and the Himalayas. There have been, for example, eight fatal bear maulings in Alberta in the last 15 years (but compare this with 38 horse-riding deaths in the province over the same period). Nepalis living close to forested areas are rightly wary of their local bears. Sloth bears of the lowlands are short sighted and tend to attack without provocation if they smell someone. They commonly lash away at the face with their powerful claws.

A Bear Story (Nepal)

A guide who had worked at the Chitwan forest reserve in Nepal told me that he had an especially frightening encounter with sloth bears there. He had heard a pair foraging in some tall vegetation and, being scared of them, beat a hasty retreat hoping that he had not disturbed them. They came after him and, when he realized they were gaining on him, he climbed a rather thin spindly tree. They are particularly good tree climbers but the guide hoped they would be reluctant to chase him up a sapling. The bears growled angrily up at him at him, but did not try to climb. He made a lot of noise, shouting and banging on the tree with a stick. Finally, in desperation, he threw the stick he'd been carrying and it hit one of the bears; they sloped off.

I asked what made him so frightened since he had escaped. 'Bears attacked my grandfather. They tore away his eyes, his nose, his bottom lip and chin; he did not live long after that—only a few months.' Heed local advice about large wildlife, then, and pay due respect to any species which make a living from killing.

Dog Bites and Rabies

The most common injury inflicted by any largish animal, whether in people at home or abroad, is dog bites. In England and Wales 209,000 people per year attend hospital for dog bites and there are about 10 deaths a year from bites alone. This is despite the fact that Britain is rabies-free, a large proportion of people are immunized against tetanus and good medical care is readily available almost everywhere.

Dog bites abroad are bad news because of the nasty injuries they inflict, because wounds frequently become badly infected and because there is a substantial risk of tetanus and, in many countries, rabies too. Even with both rabies and tetanus cover, bites can (and often do) become infected so they must be carefully cleaned and dressed and medical help sought (or antibiotics started) if signs of infection manifest themselves (see p.105).

Rabies is a huge problem in much of the developing world, particularly the Indian subcontinent, Africa and Latin America. More than 25,000 people die from rabies each year in India alone and most are infected by stray dogs. Only three people are known ever to have survived rabies—despite treatment. Never handle wild animals which seem inexplicably tame; this can be a sign that they are dying of rabies.

First Aid for Bites

Clean bites by scrubbing with soap under running water for 5 minutes then liberally apply *povidone iodine* or alcohol (at least 40 per cent—gin and whisky will do) or 0.01 per cent *aqueous iodine*. Then seek medical help for further wound care (but do not allow anyone to suture the bite). If you are in an area where there is a great deal of rabies, **even if you have had pre-trip rabies immunization**, you should have a booster, or a course if you are not immune (see p.11).

Tetanus cover is also necessary if you have not been immunized within the previous 10 years (if in doubt get boosted). If the usual tetanus injection which protects you long term is given at the time of the bite, this may not become effective fast enough to protect you. A special post-bite immunoglobulin needs to be given if you are not immune, and a course of immunization started for future protection.

The WHO recommends that dogs which have bitten people should be tied up; if the dog survives for 10 days it is said to be free from rabies and therefore there is no risk to the bitten person. The WHO guidelines are really a hang-over from the days when the only treatment for suspect bites was the dangerous and painful series of 'Semple' nervous tissue vaccines given into the abdomen on 21 consecutive days followed by booster doses. Now the logical treatment is to vaccinate all people with suspect bites using the new safe vaccines.

Serious reactions to the crude Semple vaccine (which is a 5 per cent suspension of mouse or monkey brain) can happen as frequently as 1 in 76 courses (with 41 per cent of those affected dying), although the overall incidence is more like 1:2000. The risk is greatest in Japanese people for reasons which are not well understood. In many developing countries this Semple vaccine is all that may be available, although some embassies can arrange supplies of the safe human tissue culture vaccine for travellers who have been bitten. Try to obtain cover with the Merieux inactivated rabies vaccine (which protects for 3 years) or other tissue culture product, otherwise fly home for treatment; the Semple vaccine is not worth the risk.

Are You an Ostrich?

I have encountered a surprising number of people who have been bitten by dogs or other animals that they feared might be rabid. At the time they were far from medical help and so hoped for the best and took no treatment whatsoever. Yet once the symptoms of rabies become apparent it is an incurable and invariably fatal disease and the mode of death from rabies is horrible to witness—even for case-hardened doctors. The incubation period between the bite and the onset of symptoms depends upon the distance of the bite from the brain. The virus travels along the nerves and only causes the awful encephalitis and hydrophobia when it arrives at the brain. At this point there is no treatment which will save the victim. Most adults are bitten on the leg and so the incubation period for the disease—and thus the time they have to be vaccinated—may be as much as a year. It is pure madness, then, not to seek medical help, even if this is weeks or even months after the bite. The days of the painful series of injections into the abdomen are long gone and the post-bite treatment is a series of ordinary intramuscular injections which generally have fewer side effects than your pre-trip immunizations.

Act as soon as possible. Thoroughly clean the wound and do not delay seeking medical treatment. Those with the ostrich-like head-in-the-sand approach to protecting their health should realize that it is never too late to have post-bite injections. Bites closer to the brain certainly need urgent action. Small children are often bitten on the face by dogs and the incubation interval is then only about 10 days.

Case History **(USA)**

On 13 April 1990, a man in Texas noticed a bat on the ground that seemed to be ailing; he picked it up and it bit him on the finger. He thought little about the incident, for the bat was small and it had only just broken his skin; he did not wash the bite and he did not seek medical attention since it did not seem to be infected. He remained well until 30 May. He died on the 5th June despite all that the American health services tried to do for him.

Dangerous Domestic Animals

Because humans have so much contact with domestic animals, they are much more likely to injure us than wild animals. There have been reports of deaths or severe injuries after attacks by camels, cattle, water buffalo, elephants, pigs, cats and even sheep and ferrets. Be wary of domestic animals that you do not know. Domestic animals and even pets can also act as disease reservoirs; parrots with runny noses harbour nasty pneumonia-causing bugs for example.

Cats

Cats can be quite vicious and even trivial scratches or bites carry a risk of cat scratch disease. This is usually a mild illness where the lymph nodes enlarge 2–3 weeks after a cat bite, scratch or a cat flea bite. A study has suggested that one third of American cats are infected with *Rochalimaea henselae* bacteria which cause the disease. It is unlikely to cause significant problems except in the elderly or debilitated. Occasionally pus needs to be aspirated from a lymph gland if the swelling does not settle. It also responds to antibiotics. Americans have also been catching bubonic plague from their cats recently.

Rats and Other Rodents

Many people regard rats and other rodents with fear and loathing. They also carry health risks. They are a reservoir of bubonic plague, leptospirosis (Weil's disease), tularaemia and carry the dangerous hantavirus in Europe, the Far East and in the USA. Zoologists planning to handle wild rodents might like to think about these health risks (as well as that of rabies) in planning any fieldwork and should certainly wear leather gloves.

Summary

✚ Insect repellents not only deter six-legged assailants, but also repel leeches, ticks and chiggers. The best repellents are based on DEET (diethyltoluamide).

⚠ DEET is an excellent repellent but beware it dissolves plastic (including some watch-'glasses').

- ✚ Stop leeches climbing up onto your ankles by applying repellent to shoes.

- ✚ A dab of salt will get leeches off; when in leech country carry some salt in a film canister.

- ✚ Wearing long baggy cotton clothing (preferably with trousers tucked into socks and shirt tucked into trousers) will also help protect you from leeches, chiggers, ticks, mosquitoes, snakes and other biters.

- ✚ Wearing shoes will protect you from jiggers as well as hookworm, an assortment of venomous animals and also injuries to the feet.

- ✚ When walking around in the open at night wear proper shoes and carry a torch with you so that you do not stumble upon a snake or scorpion and provoke it to defend itself.

- ⚠ If bitten by a snake, splint the limb, keep it low and get to hospital; never incise the wound and do not apply a tourniquet.

- ⚠ When removing jiggers, fly maggots, ticks or leeches, make sure that they leave in one piece. Any bits of the beast which are left behind will cause infection which will be difficult to clear. Rove beetles will do you no harm (even if they fly into your eye) as long as you can evict them without damaging them.

- ✚ Wear shoes whenever bathing, strolling along the beach, swimming or paddling.

- ⚠ Do not bathe in places which locals say are dangerous.

- ⚠ If a dog bites you in an unprovoked attack, assume that it is rabid and seek medical advice promptly after thoroughly cleaning the wound.

- ✚ Consider rabies immunization before travelling to remote places.

- ⚠ Never handle wild animals which are inexplicably tame and do not pet unknown tame animals.

Accidents and Common Diseases

Anyone planning a trip to a remote place where there is no chance of calling an ambulance should be familiar with simple first aid measures and should go on a first aid course before the trip.

This chapter does not attempt to be a comprehensive first aid course, but rather aims to remind those with some knowledge of first aid of the basic principles and to offer some tips to complement well-known procedures. It also covers the relatively trivial health problems which afflict travellers but which are not true tropical diseases.

A programme of teaching simple resuscitation in Brighton proved to be so effective that whenever anyone collapsed with a heart attack in a public place there was someone close by who could perform artificial respiration and cardiac massage. This improved survival from heart attacks in the city more effectively than money spent on improving high tech equipment in coronary care units. Usually, if the body can be kept alive through the initial major shock of the heart stopping, then there is a very good chance of survival and recovery. You cannot learn these skills from a book so go on a Red Cross, St. John's Ambulance or similar course and learn what to do in a crisis.

Among the rather younger and fitter population of people who travel independently, the most common cause of death and serious health problems is accidents, mainly car accidents and drowning. In the developing world road accidents are common, vehicles are poorly maintained, safety has a low priority and people often drive crazily. Electrical equipment can be particularly dangerous and electrocution is frequent. Poisoning from badly maintained kerosene or gas fires also happens quite frequently among people living in mountainous regions. So even if you are not safety conscious at home become so when you are travelling.

Information and precautions relating to the medicines suggested in this chapter (as elsewhere) are to be found on p.189 together with a discussion of the pros and cons of taking drugs. Only prescribe medicines for yourself if medical advice is not available and always check the precautions on the packet inserts.

If there is a serious accident, drowning or a major medical crisis (like a heart attack) people die through one of two causes:

- Failure to get air into the lungs
- Failure to get blood to the brain

This makes resuscitation a simple process, but you must also give thought to your own safety and ensure you do not make the situation worse in any way.

Safety

Take time to assess the situation. Check whether you might put yourself in danger by trying to help. See whether the casualty is in any immediate danger of further injury. Is he still connected to an electricity supply? Is the foul air at the bottom of the well which overcame him also going to poison you? Remember that if there is a chance of a spine or neck injury movement might be harmful. If someone else is immediately to hand get them to help you since it is difficult to resuscitate someone single-handed. Use techniques learned on your first aid course and the ABC mnemonic to remind you what to do. Keep in mind that if you have any broken skin, you could acquire hepatitis B or HIV infection through contact with blood, so use surgical gloves if you have them.

Send for help, then:

A is for Airway—check that the mouth and throat are clear: people often vomit in a crisis, or inhale teeth or debris, or the accident can crush part of the face. Clear the airway with your fingers as far as possible. If there is damage to the face which seems to be interfering with breathing pull the jaw forward (away from the face), hook the tongue forward with your fingers if necessary and tip the head up and back.

B is for Breathing—check that the victim is breathing by placing your cheek close to their nose and mouth. If they are not breathing give mouth to mouth artificial respiration, or another method of assisted ventilation if this is more familiar.

C is for Circulation—check that the heart is beating by feeling the chest, or (if you are used to finding them) pulses in the neck or groin; wrist pulses are difficult or impossible to feel if someone has lost a lot of blood or is otherwise in shock. If there is no pulse give cardiac massage. If there is a great deal of bleeding, this must also be staunched or your cardiac massage will soon be to no avail.

Miraculous recoveries have happened after apparent drowning through people continuing resuscitation for a long time; do not give up after a few minutes.

It is dangerous to move an unconscious patient who may have a spine or neck injury and moving a fractured limb is undesirable as well as agonizing. Someone who is conscious but has a back injury will generally be in such pain he will realize he must not be moved. If a casualty is experiencing a great deal of pain through your efforts to move him, stop and reconsider what you are doing and realize you may be making things worse by your actions.

Severe Bleeding

Establish where the blood is coming from (gently clear away the blood with a clean cloth) and press on the bleeding point. Blood loss always looks more dramatic than it is and cleaning up a bit will often reveal only a modest wound. If it is safe to move the victim, raise the part that is bleeding above the height of their heart.

If bright red blood is spurting out with each heart-beat, an artery has been severed and you should press hard on the bleeding point until it has stopped (more than 10 minutes). Fortunately in most accidental injuries, crushing and tearing of arteries puts them into spasm so they often stop bleeding spontaneously. 'Clean' wounds, like those from glass or stab-wounds, often bleed more because the incision is neat.

Stop the bleeding by applying a clean cloth if you have one and pressing on the bleeding point; pressure with two thumbs (one on top of the other) often works well. Bleeding from a long cut can be reduced be pressing the sides of the wound together with your thumbs, then holding the wound together with Steri-Strips (although these do not stick on wet skin). If a lot of blood is coming out of a large fleshy area (buttock or thigh) you may need to put your hand into the wound to try to get hold of the source of the bleeding.

Press hard for a long time (10 minutes or more may be necessary), then put on some kind of dressing and tie or strap it firmly in place; crêpe (ace) bandages are useful strapping, or use an ambulance or military field dressing pack. If all this gets soaked with blood, put on more cloth and apply firm direct pressure again. Do not remove the blood-soaked cloth and do not peek to see if the bleeding has stopped. Get to medical help, but discourage the medical attendant from stitching the wound if possible (see p.167).

When there is a lot of bleeding (for example from a cut on the scalp or face) the wound always looks horrendous and you may think that the victim is close to death. Cleaning away the blood will often reveal only a tiny nick in the skin.

Steri-Strips or butterfly closures can be a very useful and easy way of closing a wound, but it can be difficult to get them to stick if the skin is wet or there is a lot of blood. Use direct pressure to staunch the flow and pull the wound together later with Steri-Strips.

If something is sticking out of the wound, do not remove it unless it is small and superficial like a splinter. Pad the area and apply pressure around the object to staunch the blood flow. Get to competent medical help as soon as you can.

In case of bleeding—press where the blood is coming from and elevate the bleeding part. Never use a tourniquet.

Fits, Faints and Unconsciousness

Head Injury and Concussion

Any period of unconsciousness after a fall or accident implies some trauma to the brain (called concussion) and the longer the period of unconsciousness, the stronger is the possibility of serious damage: unconsciousness for more than a couple of minutes is worrying. Nausea and vomiting are common after a head injury. Confusion or a change in the victim's normal behaviour can be the first sign of bleeding within the skull. Sleepiness or long-lasting headache after head injury need urgent medical assessment too.

Convulsions or Fits

Adults

If someone is having fits or convulsions, take the following action:

1. Clear the area of hard objects (chairs, tables, etc.) so that the person does not injure themselves by thrashing against them. Pull the victim away from any danger. Do not force anything into his mouth.

2. Loosen any tight clothing (if this is easy to do) and wait for the fit to subside.

3. Place the victim in the recovery position (*see* p.166).

People who are fitting may bite their tongue but this will probably happen in the first moments of the attack so trying to force something between the teeth will probably do more harm than good; it is not recommended. The victim will usually be incontinent and will be sleepy and disorientated after the fit. Gently reassure them but realize that they may not really be aware of what is going on and will just want somewhere to rest and sleep for a while. It is very rare for people to experience a fit for the first time in adulthood; it could be a sign of cerebral malaria, meningitis (which can both be rapidly fatal) or some other serious disease so the victim should be taken to see a doctor urgently.

Children

Fits are common in children under the age of 5 years. If a child has a convulsion, turn him onto his side so that he is less likely to choke. Do not force anything into his mouth. Wait for the fit to subside, then if the child is hot, give a dose of *paracetamol* syrup and strip off his clothes and cool him by sponging with tepid water.

The most likely cause of the fit is a rapidly rising temperature due to some kind of infection. Seek medical help promptly to determine the cause of the fever, since it could be meningitis or cerebral malaria, or simple tonsillitis. Do not worry, children grow out of fits induced by fevers and they do not lead on to epilepsy later.

The Recovery Position

Someone who is breathing but unconscious is at risk of vomiting. Vomit may enter the lungs and choke or drown the victim. Drunks are particularly vulnerable to death in this way. It is important not to leave an unconscious person on his back, unless injuries make moving him difficult. Place the arms by the victim's sides and cross the leg furthest away from you over the nearer leg. Then, grasping the shoulder and hip, roll the victim onto his front. Tip back the head by pulling up the chin to help ensure the casualty can breath (remember the ABC above) and swing the top arm up so that it rests on the floor with the casualty's elbow in line with the shoulder; this slightly raises the chest off the ground and makes breathing easier. Bend up the uppermost leg and flex it at the knee so that it slightly supports the pelvis.

Fainting

Lie the victim down and elevate the legs to above heart height; if you have nothing to prop the legs up on, simply bend them at the knee. Check for the heartbeat by feeling the chest or find a pulse in the neck or groin if you know how to do this; pulses at the wrist are difficult to feel especially in someone who has fainted. If there is no pulse, start resuscitation. If the victim has simply fainted get him to lie flat for a few minutes after recovery.

People are often embarrassed by fainting or feeling faint and it is sometimes difficult to get people to lie down to prevent a faint or stay down for a few minutes once they have fainted and are recovering.

Feeling Faint or Dizzy

Feeling as if you are about to faint is a common symptom if you are unwell. Feeling dizzy on standing up or getting out of bed is known as postural hypotension which implies that you have insufficient body fluids circulating to get enough blood to your brain. A serious but rare cause of this symptom is blood loss. If you think that you may have lost blood after an injury or from internal bleeding (have you vomited 'coffee grounds' or passed blood?), get medical attention urgently.

The most common cause of postural hypotension in the tropics is dehydration, so try drinking a litre of water (or oral rehydration solution, *see* p.29) and continue drinking until you need to pass water. Until you are topped up with fluids again cope with the problem by sitting with your legs over the side of the bed for a minute or so before standing up. You will have plenty of practice of this technique if you have profuse diarrhoea.

Occasionally women with very heavy periods become anaemic and also suffer the same dizziness on getting up; a doctor may be able to sort this out, but is not an urgent matter.

Does it Need Stitches?

In the sterile high-tech West we are used to cuts being stitched promptly in hospital casualty departments. In hot steamy unhygienic environments this can cause a great deal of trouble, especially if the wound is very deep or very dirty. Sometimes stitches are required to stop massive bleeding, but otherwise, in tropical environments it is often safer to allow even quite big wounds to heal naturally or delay stitching for a week. Animal bites, in particular, should not be sutured.

Case History (Indonesia)

Ray had slipped in some remote moist jungle on the island of Sumbawa. As he fell he impaled his arm on a cut bamboo shoot which was left sticking out of the ground. The stake went clean through the muscles of his forearm. He presented himself to a local clinic, and the paramedic who was on duty sutured the entry and exit wounds.

A few days later he consulted me because his arm was becoming increasingly painful and swollen and he was feverish.

When I removed the stitches, which were by now under tension, it allowed much of the pus that was building up inside to drain away. The wounds were left open, cleaned three times a day and antibiotics started. His tetanus immunizations were up to date. The whole thing settled down over the course of the following week.

The injury that Ray had sustained was impossible to clean because it was so very deep. Suturing the wound was therefore asking for trouble because it was stitching in the dirt. Leaving a wound like this open allows it to expel any unrequired material naturally, the healing process is faster and infection less likely to set in.

Cuts, Wounds, Bites and Abrasions

Deep or very dirty wounds should be washed under a running tap or by pouring on water from a bowl or jug. There is no need at this point to worry about water sterility—just use lots of it. Make sure there is no mud, gravel or glass inside the wound since these will guarantee an infection and delay healing. Pick out any bits with clean fingers.

If there is a lot of bleeding, do not apply a tourniquet. Stop the bleeding by elevation and firm direct pressure (*see* p.164). You will be unable to assess the extent of the damage while everything is covered in blood, but do not be too enthusiastic about clearing away blood clots because bleeding will restart.

Wash wounds thoroughly but do not worry about sterility or applying antiseptic initially. Bathe the wound in dilute *potassium permanganate* solution or another antiseptic (*see* p.104) and change dressings at least once a day—more frequently at first.

All wounds (especially deep dirty wounds and animal bites) carry a risk of tetanus infection. You should be immunized against this every 10 years; if you are not, make sure you are protected by both active and passive immunization as soon as possible after the injury. Animal bites also carry the risk of rabies. Both rabies and tetanus are extremely serious infections which continue to cause deaths because people do not take sensible precautions against them. Bites should not be sutured; this will seal in the infection.

Burns and Scalds

Remove the victim from the source of the injury. If it is an electrical burn beware of being electrocuted yourself: turn off the electricity supply, or kick the victim free, or use a broom handle or similar non-conductor to disconnect the victim from the supply. Electrical burns are often very deep and will readily become infected so seek medical help if you can. To treat minor burns pour cold water on them for at least 20 minutes and continue bathing them until the burn or scald no longer feels hot to the victim. Do not apply creams, lotions or any other substance. If clothes are fused into the burn, as commonly happens with man-made fabrics, trim away any loose pieces; do not pull away adhered cloth. Cover the burn with a clean, dry, non-fluffy dressing. Aspirin will help reduce the pain and burning and so will elevation of the burnt area above heart height.

In superficial burns, skin sensation remains and the skin appears red and mottled. Deep, severe burns are generally less painful because the nerve endings have been destroyed. The skin looks white or charred. In case of severe, full-thickness burns the immediate threat to survival is loss of fluids through the burn site. If the victim is able to drink, offer sips of water (or oral rehydration solution). Encourage him to drink a cup an hour. A remarkable amount of heat and water can be lost through badly burnt skin, so drink plenty. Drink in sips if in distress. Beware, there is a risk of hypothermia if the victim is not kept warm.

The next serious problem in severe burns is infection and evacuation home is advisable. Signs of infection include: increasing pain, spreading redness, pus dripping from the wound, itching or a bad smell. Infection will set in very rapidly in tropical environments.

Muscle Strains, Sprains, Bruises and Wrenches

Twisted ankles improve with gentle exercise. Badly strained muscles and wrenched joints are best treated with RICE:

- ✚ **R**est
- ✚ **I**ce (or cold water) compresses
- ✚ **C**ompression
- ✚ **E**levation

The best cold compress is ice cubes in a plastic bag wrapped in a pillowcase, but if this is not possible, bathing in cool water while gently moving the limb will help. Compression means strapping. Elevation means supporting the damaged part above heart height; use pillows to chock it up if you are resting in bed. Giving an injured limb firm support by strapping with a crêpe (or ace) bandage provides comfort and often allows you to walk. Rest and aspirin (or another *non-steroidal anti-inflammatory* medicine) relieve the pain in the short term and then gentle movements will help disperse the bruise and aid healing. Gentle movements do not mean continuing on a strenuous mountain walk carrying a heavy backpack. Remember that crêpe bandages need to be washed frequently to retain their stretchiness. As the part heals, reduce the amount of strapping or the limb will remain weak. It is difficult to balance the treatment of giving enough support to avoid further injury, but allowing enough mobility to stimulate the return of full power.

The *non-steroidal anti-inflammatory* group of medicines are all good at reducing pain and aiding healing in all kinds of wrenches, sprains, strains and even breaks. Aspirin is the best known of these medicines; three others in ascending order of potency are *ibuprofen* (e.g. Nurofen or Brufen in UK; Motrin in US), *naproxen* (e.g. Naprosyn in UK and US), and *diclofenac* (e.g. Voltarol). Medicines in this group should not be taken together, but if you wish to take an additional painkiller, *paracetamol* or *codeine* can be taken with any of these.

Bruising

Severe bruising is helped by cold compresses immediately and then after 12 hours or so by hot compresses or hot baths and elevation, followed by gentle mobilization with a crêpe bandage for support at first. As the bruise begins to disperse, it often changes colour, through lurid red, purple, black, brown, green to yellow. If there has been internal bruising or bleeding, these colours may only appear a week or so after the initial injury and so can be quite alarming. The bruising and discolouration may also appear a long way below the original injury.

Bruising, when there has been little to provoke it, may be a sign of serious illness, if this is a new symptom for you. Easy bruising that is associated with a fever is sometimes a sign of some very serious, but rare, tropical infections. Seek a medical opinion in this case.

Backache and Muscle Strain

Backaches and muscle strains are more common in the unfit and the overweight so prepare for your journey by doing some fitness training and trying to shed some weight if you are heavy. To protect the back from injury, always lift heavy items from the legs and with a straight back. Never stoop down to pick things up.

Pain is a useful sensation; it tells that something is wrong and that something needs to be done. The action that is usually required is rest. If you do wrench something, try to arrange to stop travelling for a while; car travel is particularly bad for backache. Strapping the affected area and taking *non-steroidal anti-inflammatory* medicine will help joint pains (*see* p.169). However, try to avoid taking pills in order to carry on; there is no need to carry on.

Muscle-cramp

Cramp can be due to poor fitness, over-doing unaccustomed exercise especially in the heat, or lack of salt. Stretch the cramped muscle gently but firmly and stimulate the circulation by massage. Drink a couple of glasses of water containing a teaspoonful of salt (if this does not taste salty, drink more). In the longer term, shake more salt on your food. Increasing your salt intake is generally necessary in hot climates. Health educators discourage salt consumption in temperate climates, but it is a necessary part of the tropical diet. Salt tablets are not a useful way of taking in salt.

Fractures and Dislocations

Often the victim will have heard or felt a bone break. There will be swelling, an unnatural shape or position, and a reluctance or inability to move the fractured limb because of pain. It is movement of one end of the fractured bone on the other which causes pain so try to immobilize the limb with whatever you can improvise. Bandaging a broken leg against the good one with plenty of padding in between, or one finger against another are useful technique. Cushion the broken limb as much as possible as any movement is excruciatingly painful. Remember that broken limbs swell, so check that any bandaging is not reducing the blood supply. Third world paramedics are often very competent bone-setters, but evacuate to hospital if you can.

Broken Nose

If you break your nose it will probably be obviously crooked. Take some pain-killers. It will not be all that painful at first so apply a thumb to either side of the nose and straighten it as best you can. All you need to do is to get it reasonably straight. You will get no better treatment in hospital. Cold compresses will help to reduce bleeding from the nose and will soothe the pain somewhat.

Dislocations

Dislocations are usually difficult to treat unless they happen frequently to an individual: some people frequently dislocate knee caps or shoulders. It may be possible to relocate dislocated fingers or toes without anaesthetic. The principle is to pull the digit slowly, but steadily and firmly back out straight until it jumps into place. Any rough grinding sensations imply a fracture is present, which is best splinted and treated by a professional.

Eye Problems

Ultraviolet sunlight radiation is harmful to the eyes as well as to the skin so ensure you protect them with good sun-glasses in the tropics and at altitude.

Something in the Eye

If something is protruding from the eye, you need to find a doctor. If evacuation is going to take some time you need to protect the eye. Large objects which have penetrated the eye tend to fall out. Small objects can generally be wiped out gently using wet cotton wool twisted into a point or the corner of a clean handkerchief.

Usually the victim's own instincts will protect the eye sufficiently, but if a long and difficult evacuation is foreseen, it may be sensible to protect the eye from further damage. One way of doing this is to make a cone-shaped shield out of a piece of cardboard, stiff paper or thin plastic. Cut a circle which is larger than the eye socket and cut a radius (like the first cut when slicing a cake). Then overlap and stick the edges of the cut to form a flattish cone. Many first aid books suggest gently packing around the eye with bandages so that the injured eye is covered **without** any pressure on it. This can be very difficult to do in practice and may do more harm than good. Note that even if the other eye is undamaged, the victim is unlikely to want to open the good eye and so will need a great deal of help and support during evacuation.

If there is something small in the eye, like a grain of sand or even an eyelash, first ensure that the outside of the eye is clean by wiping with a damp cloth and then while looking up, grasp the eyelashes of the top lid and pull the upper lid over the lower one. Blink. If this does not work, get an assistant to pour water into the eye while blinking as much as possible. Use tepid water and pour from close to the eye, or gently trickle water into the eye from a syringe without a needle. The coloured part of the eye is very sensitive so pour gently onto the white part. Looking away from the water will make the procedure more comfortable. If these attempts do not work, the assistant should grasp the top eyelashes, roll the upper lid back over a cotton bud and inspect under the upper lid where grit often lodges. The surface of the eyeball should be checked too and any particles gently brushed away with another cotton bud. Even the tiniest of foreign bodies can be very painful and a magnifying glass will aid the search if you have one.

Black Eye

This is simple bruising around the eye so the treatment is cold compresses, as for bruising anywhere else. If there seems to be any injury to the eye or headaches begin after sustaining the black eye, seek medical help immediately. Double vision on looking up after an eye injury is a symptom which needs medical assessment reasonably promptly.

Yellow Eyes

If the whites of your eyes turn yellow you have jaundice, probably due to infectious hepatitis (hepatitis A); there is no specific treatment (but *see* p.180).

Red Eye

Conjunctivitis

Superficial eye infections or pink-eye are very common, especially in the tropics. The infection usually starts in one eye, but rapidly spreads to the other and makes the eyes feel sticky, gritty, red and painful. Often the first thing you notice is the eyelids stuck together with green gunk in the morning. Conjunctivitis like this is usually caused by bacterial infection and requires treatment with antibiotic drops into both eyes every 2–3 hours at first. *Chloramphenicol* or *neomycin* are fine, as are the newer, fancier antibiotics which cost more, but are probably no better at treating eye infection. If the symptoms do not start to improve after 36 hours, try *tetracycline* drops or ointment. If this does not work seek medical help. Avoid eye preparations which contain any extras especially *hydrocortisone*, *betamethasone* or other steroids. If you notice a change in your ability to see or if there is great pain in the eyeball or behind the eye you should see a doctor—preferably an eye specialist, general physician or specialist in internal medicine. If the problem remains confined to one eye only and especially if the visual acuity (vision) seems to be failing in that eye, seek medical help quickly.

Conjunctivitis can be caused by viruses. In that case the inflammation and irritation will be less, there will be less discharge and green gunk and there will usually be an associated cold and/or sore throat. This will get better without treatment (although antibiotic drops will do no harm if in doubt). In both bacterial and viral conjunctivitis, bathing the eye in warm, slightly salty water will aid removal of any discharge.

Getting noxious chemicals in the eye including slug slime, cicada spit, whip-scorpion squirt or centipede ooze can also cause conjunctivitis. Bathe the eye in warm, slightly salty water. If the inflammation is very bad, tape or pad the eye closed and go to see a doctor.

Sore Gritty Burning Eyes

This can be caused by insufficient tears. It is a common problem in all climates, but even more frequent in hot and dry regions. Hypomellose or artificial tear drops are useful and safe and can be applied as often as necessary—even half-hourly if you wish.

Subconjunctival Haemorrhage

This is bleeding which turns the white part of the eye blood-red; blood does not cover the coloured part of the eye. It looks horrendous but is harmless (unless it appeared after a bad head injury, see p.165) and needs no treatment. Very rarely it can be a sign of widespread disease (e.g. louse-borne relapsing fever or one of the viral haemorrhagic fevers) but, if this is the case, other symptoms will be present and it will be obvious that you are very ill.

Redness and Swelling Around the Eye (Periorbital Cellulitis)

If the eye becomes very painful, red and puffy and there is also fever, urgent medical attention is required. If you are somewhere remote start taking *flucloxacillin* 500mg four times a day (or erythromycin if you are allergic to penicillin) and seek medical help immediately.

Insects and Irritation of the Eye

A burning sensation or swelling around the eye can be caused by insects flying into the eye and being damaged as the victim tries to extract them. Sometimes the inflammation begins a whole day after the insect flew in. This problem is dealt with on p.112.

Styes

Styes are small boils on the eyelid; they are best treated by applying a hot compress (use a face cloth) or a teaspoon which has been dipped into hot (but not uncomfortably hot) water to warm it. Gentle pressure (but do not squeeze) with some source of heat over the stye will help the stye come to a head and discharge the pus it contains. Pluck out the eyelash which is at the centre of the stye with tweezers if possible since this will also aid draining of the pus.

Antibiotic creams or drops are unlikely to be helpful in a simple stye. If the infection starts to spread elsewhere on the face take antibiotic tablets as for skin infections (see p.105).

Glasses and Contact Lenses

If you wear glasses (or contact lenses) carry a copy of your lens prescription with you. Replacements are usually available and cheap in the tropics but eye tests can be unreliable. If your prescription is wrong, you may not be able to see as well, but you will do your eyes no harm.

Contact lenses can introduce infection into the eye and this is more likely to happen in a hot climate, especially when people are travelling rough and hygiene standards are difficult to maintain. There are a selection of bugs which may cause eye problems, the most worrying being *Acanthamoeba*. Consider wearing glasses instead of contact lenses, or at least carry a pair of glasses with you so that as soon as any hint of irritation or infection begins, you can remove the lenses. Note also that at altitude contact lenses can deprive the eye of oxygen, although this only seems to be a problem above 8000m (26,000ft).

Something in the Ear

Inexpert attempts to remove objects or insects from the ear canal usually push the offending object further in, which may damage the ear drum. Lie on your side with the problem ear uppermost and fill the ear with water; the object should float out. Soaking in a bath with ears under water may also help. If this does not work you will need medical help. A medical worker with an ear syringe may be able to flush out the object, but many foreign bodies need to be removed in a hospital Ear, Nose and Throat Department.

Something Stuck in the Throat

If you swallow a fish or meat bone, you may feel as if the bone has stuck, but this is rare: more often the throat has only been scratched in which case no treatment is necessary. If a foreign body has stuck in the throat it will be almost impossible even to swallow saliva and the large quantities of additional saliva that are secreted in this case will be spat out. The neck will often also feel very tender on prodding from the outside.

The definite test of whether it is a scratch or whether there is something stuck is to wait for 12–24 hours while taking a cool soft diet (but not ice cream unless you are somewhere hygienic please!). People with a scratch will improve while those with something stuck will feel worse. The treatment for something stuck in the throat is its removal in hospital under general anaesthetic.

Inhaled Object and Choking

If someone is choking on an inhaled object or piece of food, stand behind him, place your fist in the middle of his upper abdomen just under the rib cage, your other hand on top of the fist and pull both hands towards you and upwards sharply. The idea is to force air out of the lungs and with it the object the victim is choking on. A small child can be held upside-down and smartly slapped on the back.

If you are the victim you can achieve a similar effect by slumping forward onto a chair back so that this forces air out of the lungs.

Bleeding Under a Finger- or Toe-nail

Injuries to fingers or toes can cause bleeding under the nail. Even a tiny amount of blood trapped in such a confined space is intensely painful. Heat the end of an uncurled paper clip to red heat in a flame and place it firmly on the black nail, at right angles to the nail, so that it burns through the nail but not to the nail bed. You do not need to apply much pressure; the paper clip should just burn through. Do not use a pin or needle; they are too sharp and you will push through to the sensitive nail bed (ouch!) before making a hole big enough to let the blood out.

The paper clip technique is a very satisfying piece of first aid because as soon as the blood is released through the hole made by the paper clip, there is immediate relief of pain and you have a very grateful patient. The nail may later come off, but this will be weeks afterwards and a new one will grow in its place.

Common Ailments

Few of the illnesses people catch abroad are serious. Although people die while travelling, less than 1 per cent of deaths are from infectious tropical diseases. This section is not comprehensive but covers the illnesses which commonly trouble people whether in the tropics or at home. Sore throats and colds are common in the tropics and coughs and chest infections are probably even more common than at home.

Fever

Fever is a common symptom of many diseases; it makes most people feel intermittently uncomfortably hot, then chilled to the marrow. Fever in itself causes feelings of lethargy, aches and pains and headache. Taking *aspirin* or *paracetamol* (*acetaminophen* or Tylenol in the US) regularly (4–6 hourly) and drinking plenty will help these symptoms. Children and those with ulcers or stomach problems should not take aspirin. It is easy to become dehydrated when you have a fever, especially in a warm climate, and dehydration will make you feel even worse.

If drinking plenty and taking *aspirin* or *paracetamol* does not make you feel considerably better, think about the cause of the fever and consider further treatment. Common infections which cause fevers are colds, 'flu, chest infections and skin infections. In women, urine infections are common, and in children ear or throat infections are common. In many cases you will know what is causing the fever and you can refer to the appropriate section of this book for treatment. Whatever illness you have is probably common and treatable, but bear in mind that malaria (*see* p.54) and some other serious infections are a risk in many regions. If you are in any doubt about what is wrong, and simple rehydration and *aspirin* do not make you feel much better, seek a medical opinion. Seek help as soon as possible if a child is ill. Children should be given paracetamol not aspirin.

Case History (Peru)

When my sister and I were second year medical students, we organized a scientific expedition to Peru and, being keen and ignorant, we carefully read up about all the nasty tropical diseases we might catch. About 10 days after arriving at the first study site near Palcamayo in the Andes, my sister started feeling ill, then one morning awoke with spots. She thought these were flea bites and furiously hurled her sleeping bag into the river. I looked at the rash and thought she had not been attacked by fleas (the pustules were not in the usual breakfast-elevenses-lunch-tea-supper trail), but my mind started sifting through the tropical diseases she might have. We were most worried about verruga or Oroya fever—a rapidly fatal incurable disease (we vaguely remembered) which was infamous in an area only a couple of hours from where we were camping.

Then Mandy, who being non-medical was capable of more rational assessment, said 'Ooh that rash looks just like the one my little sister had when she had chickenpox!' And chickenpox it was. Later we discovered that oroya fever is not only exceedingly rare but it responds to antibiotics and so is not all that dangerous after all.

Malaria

A fever with no obvious source may be due to malaria, even if you are taking anti-malarial tablets. Malaria can be difficult to diagnose since it can mimic other conditions and it can even be a cause of diarrhoea. If there is any suspicion that you may have malaria, seek medical help quickly if you can, particularly if you are in Africa or the Pacific Islands, otherwise take the emergency treatment you are carrying (*see* p.58).

Case History (Out of Africa)

I was called to see a 5-year-old girl; she had returned to England from Kenya one month previously and had just stopped taking her malaria tablets. She was very unwell with a high fever. Her parents were sure that she had malaria because they had friends who had developed malaria on stopping their antimalarial tablets a month after leaving Africa. When I examined her I found that she had huge inflamed tonsils and swollen tender lymph glands in her neck. She proved to have bacterial tonsillitis which responded to a 10-day course of penicillin.

The girl's parents were right to consult a doctor. East Africa is a high risk area for malaria, but their care with taking malaria tablets, using mosquito nets and repellents had paid off and the child was merely suffering from a common treatable childhood illness.

Coughs and Sneezes and Chest Problems

Coughs and colds are, perhaps, the last thing you might expect to catch while travelling in hot countries, yet they are as common there as anywhere. Moist warm atmospheres in the tropics allow germs to survive for longer between victims. The fever which these infections cause can largely be controlled by taking *paracetamol* or *aspirin* every 4–6 hours. If you carry soluble forms of these tablets you can gargle and swallow them to help relieve sore throats.

Sore throats and colds are usually caused by viruses and so antibiotics are of no help. If you are feverish, be sure to increase the amount you are drinking since even mild dehydration will make you feel considerably worse. If you have a cold and a drippy nose, use cloth rather than paper handkerchiefs or your nose will get very sore. The common cold lasts about a week. If it goes on longer, suspect allergy and try antihistamine tablets (e.g. Piriton or Benadryl) or seek medical help.

Breathing Problems

The rate at which someone breathes can be a helpful guide to disease in the chest. Unfortunately, though, it is almost impossible to record accurately your own breathing rate or the respiratory rate of someone who knows you are timing it. The normal respiratory rate of an adult is about 12–20 breaths a minute. A rate of 40 a minute implies something may need treating or that the person is hyperventilating through anxiety. If the person is asthmatic, remind them to use their inhaler. Normal respiratory rates in children are below 30 and in babies below 40.

If there are breathing difficulties and/or a cough, humidified air will help and in some hotels with hot water you can easily fill the bathroom with steam. This is particularly useful in children with croup (which causes a characteristic, but strange-sounding cough).

Small babies are not good at breathing through their mouths and sometimes have difficulty breathing when their noses become congested during a cold, especially when trying to feed. Boil a glassful of water, add a pinch of salt, allow that water to cool and drip couple of drops of this into each nostril. The baby will then sneeze out or sniff in the snot and thus clear the nose.

Cough Without Fever

Honey (by the spoonful or in drinks) has some cough-soothing properties and is a pleasant remedy. Cough medicines may offer some comfort but beware of what you are buying abroad since some contain some bizarre concoctions. If it is available, stick to *simple linctus* (which is a soothing syrup) or make your own with equal quantities of fresh lemon or lime juice, honey and rum or whisky in a little hot water. Inhaling infusions of eucalyptus oil, Vick or tiger balm in hot water is also helpful to some sufferers. Loosening a cough and expectorating phlegm will be aided by drinking plenty of water, tea or similar drinks. Gargling with warm water helps to settle a tickly cough and can be very soothing.

Coughing Up Blood

Blood-stained spit or more profuse blood brought up by coughing is a reason to seek medical help and probably have a chest X-ray. You should also see a doctor if your cough goes on for more than 4 weeks.

Chest Infections and Chest Pain

A chest infection may be indicated by a cough and fever (especially if you produce a lot of discolored thick spit), or a fever with chest pain (especially if it is worse on breathing in) or a feeling of tightness in the chest. Treatment with antibiotics is likely to help. Take *amoxycillin* 500mg three times a day for 7 days, unless you are allergic to it, when *cephradine* 1g twice daily or *erythromycin* 250mg four times a day can be used. Otherwise you can take *trimethoprim* 200mg twice a day (which is safe for people allergic to penicillin but not for those who are pregnant). In addition take *aspirin* (or *paracetamol*) every 4–6 hours to control the fever and pain. If the symptoms do not improve within 48 hours change antibiotics: penicillin takers should add erythromycin.

Smokers suffer many more chest infections than non-smokers; they are also more likely to contract illnesses like legionnaires' disease (*see* p.115).

Severe Chest Pain

Severe central chest pain, especially if crushing in nature, and without an associated fever needs urgent and careful medical assessment and care. Heart problems are most common in males over 50 years of age, especially if they are heavy smokers (more than 20 cigarettes/day) and are over-weight.

'Heart Burn'

A burning pain at the bottom of the rib cage is likely to be indigestion so try taking some antacids. If the pain is severe and not relieved by antacids seek medical help urgently.

Case History (Nepal)

John had been travelling rough in Nepal for 4 months and was feeling very unwell again. He had had very bad luck with his health during this, his first trip to the developing world. He smoked cigarettes. He had three loose stools in the morning and by early afternoon had a splitting headache, a severe stabbing pain in the right side of his chest and aching limbs and back. He thought he had a fever and felt a little disorientated. He had a slight tickly cough. He had taken one aspirin which was beginning to ease the headache by the time I saw him.

He looked very unwell, was trembling and very distressed by the pain in his chest whenever he moved, breathed in deeply or coughed. His temperature was 40°C (104°F). He had pneumonia. He was considerably better after 18 hours of penicillin, lots to drink and regular aspirin (two at a time, every 4 hours) to help get the fever down and control the pain in the chest.

Tuberculosis

Tuberculosis (TB) is a potentially fatal lung infection which is very common among underprivileged people in developing countries who live in overcrowded housing. Good living conditions in the developed world have made TB relatively rare there. Those on a short trip abroad are unlikely to risk infection. The risk is greater for those living abroad long term. TB is spread by infected people coughing over others, but since the disease is not very infectious, TB is only caught after a great deal of exposure over a long period. Walking through a busy market puts you at no risk, but expatriates may catch TB from infected colleagues coughing over them in a small poorly ventilated office or from infected staff at home. The most significant risk is to medical staff looking after the sick in a hospital or refugee camp.

TB can also be contracted from infected cows' milk, but not from insect bites, drinking water, food or crockery and you cannot catch it from touching an infected person. BCG immunization gives approximately 80 per cent protection against TB. Most travellers will have been immunized at school, unless you were born before 1940 in which case you will probably have natural immunity.

The symptoms of TB tend to come on gradually and insidiously and include fevers, often night sweats, a feeling of lethargy, a cough, and eventually the production of blood in the spit. People with TB often look quite well, but the symptom of coughing up blood is a useful clue and it may be worth asking potential staff if they have this problem. Not all long-standing coughs are caused by TB.

Even if you have been sharing a house for several weeks with local coughers, there is no need to worry about TB unless symptoms appear. If you do contract it, treatment is easy and effective, although tablets need to be taken carefully for a full 6 months. In summary, boil any fresh cows' milk which you intend to drink and do not worry about TB unless you notice symptoms. If you feel you may have caught it seek a check-up and chest X-ray when it is convenient.

Hepatitis or Jaundice

Jaundice due to either the hepatitis A or E virus is commonly acquired by travellers and expatriates especially in the Indian subcontinent and in tropical Central and South America. It is one of the many filth-to-mouth diseases (see p.21). It usually begins with non-specific feelings of profound lethargy, lack of appetite, nausea and general feelings of being unwell. As this begins to go away the whites of the eyes and the skin turn yellow and you suddenly realize why you have been feeling tired and run down. At this point you begin earning a great deal of sympathy, yet by now you are feeling much better. It is a variable illness, which leaves some people feeling very debilitated for many months, but it is not dangerous.

Western medicine can offer little to the hepatitis sufferer, although I have heard of several victims who have had dramatic improvements in their symptoms by taking ayurvedic medicines in Nepal (on the recommendation of a Western-trained Nepali doctor) and by taking traditional Tibetan *amchi* medicine in Ladakh. There is an Ayurvedic hospital in Naradevi, Kathmandu and in many Indian cities.

You will have to experiment to see what you can eat and drink as you are recovering. Fatty foods and alcohol commonly upset patients with jaundice and the amount of activity undertaken should be built up slowly. Over-doing it will cause profound fatigue. Rest as much as you need to, avoid alcohol, and if fatty foods upset you, do not eat them. Pregnant women can become profoundly ill with hepatitis E and so must be very cautious about avoiding filth-to-mouth infections. There are now good vaccines against hepatitis A and B (*see* pp.7 and 10), but not against hepatitis E or the other causes of hepatitis.

Problems of the Head and Neck

Headaches

A severe headache of an unusual type or one associated with fever, profuse vomiting or the inability to look at light, needs urgent medical help. Meanwhile drink plenty and, if vomiting, take sips of oral rehydration solution.

A headache can signal dehydration and people new to the tropics are often surprised how much they need to drink. Do not worry about replacing salt lost in sweat.

Carbon monoxide poisoning over weeks from faulty kerosene fires or gas appliances can also cause troublesome headaches. In the space of a few months I saw several expatriates living in Quetta who were being poisoned by their natural gas fires.

If headaches start after a head injury, you must seek medical help promptly. Any recurrent headaches of an unfamiliar type should also stimulate you to seek a proper medical check-up.

Treatments for headaches caused by mountain sickness are covered on p.96. If you are abroad long term and start suffering from recurrent headaches, consider checking whether you need to wear spectacles or whether your glasses prescription needs changing. Think about whether you are over-working, stressed or drinking too much alcohol.

Sinusitis

The sinuses are cavities which are supposed to be filled with air. When they become full of mucus they become painful and there is fever; this is sinusitis. The symptoms are a clogged feeling in the nose and front of the face, often with pain over or behind the eyes and tenderness over the cheekbones. Try inhalations first. Lean forward over a bowl of boiling water containing friars' balsam, or menthol, or eucalyptus or Karvol decongestant capsules.

If these do not work, a decongestant tablet like *pseudoephedrine* (e.g. Sudafed or Actifed in UK and US) or antihistamines such as *terfenadine* (e.g. Triludan in UK,

Seldane in US) or *chlorpheniramine* (e.g. Piriton in UK, Chlor-Trimetron in US) or *diphenhydramine* (e.g. Benadryl) may help. Flying will increase sinus pains so if you have to fly start taking *pseudoephedrine* (e.g. Sudafed) a couple of hours before take-off.

If the sinusitis is making you feel feverish and very unwell, take a 5-day course of *doxycycline* (e.g. Vibramycin) 200mg on the first day then 100mg daily with plenty of water during a meal. Do not use doxycycline if pregnant. *Cotrimoxazole* 960mg twice daily or *co-amoxiclav* 250mg three times a day are good alternatives.

Nose Bleeds

Nose bleeds should be treated by rest and placing cold compresses over the bridge of the nose. Lean forward and pinch the nose, but release the pressure every few minutes. Leaning back will make you swallow the blood and vomit.

Greasing the inside of the nose (for example with Vaseline) sometimes helps to prevent recurrent nose bleeds in very dry environments. This is a problem I have had in the high Andes and Himalayas, which are both cold deserts.

Bleeding from the nose, gums or elsewhere when you are feverish needs urgent medical assessment.

Earache

Earache affecting both ears is unlikely to be due to infection, but is probably caused by congestion of mucus. Steam inhalations plus aspirin often help and sometimes a decongestant such as *pseudoephedrine* (e.g. Sudafed) gives relief. If the earache is on one side only and there is fever, take *penicillin* capsules 500mg every 6 hours at least 30 minutes before food or *trimethoprim* 200mg twice daily for 5 days.

Itchy Ears

Ears which are inflamed or very itchy are probably superficially infected. Infection of the outer ear is common, especially in hot moist climates. Introducing anything into the ear is more likely to stimulate an infection, so never use cotton buds and put nothing in your ear smaller than your big toe! Treat (2–3 times daily) with drops containing a combination of an antibiotic (*neomycin*, *gentamicin*, *chloramphenicol* or *framycetin* with a mild steroid, 0.5 per cent *hydrocortisone* (e.g. Otosporin, Audicort, Framycort in the UK or Cortisporin otic drops in the US).

A useful alternative to antibiotics is drops which acidify the ear canal (aluminium acetate or boric acid both in very dilute form). These work well, are cheap and are less likely to cause allergic problems than the antibiotic combination drops.

Cold Sores

Cold sores on the lips are often reactivated by the sun, so if you are prone to cold sores, pack some *acyclovir* cream (Zovirax in UK and US), (*see* p.73). In filtering out ultraviolet radiation lip screens also help prevent cold sores in those who are prone, although lip salves do not.

Sore Throats and Throat Infections

Sore throats can be a problem in very dry environments, especially at altitude when you may find yourself breathing through your mouth rather than your nose. The best treatment is to suck boiled sweets or pastilles and drink plenty.

In adults, sore throats are usually caused by viruses and so antibiotic treatment is unhelpful. Drink plenty. Gargle every 2–3 hours with one soluble *aspirin* or *paracetamol* (take no more than eight paracetamol in 24 hours) then swallow the gargle. Even gargling with warm water can be soothing. The signs which imply that the infection is bacterial and so treatable with antibiotics are: a fever, swollen painful glands in the neck, obviously inflamed tonsils, not having a cough and probably with white pus on the tonsils.

If you decide to take an antibiotic it must be for a full 10 days (even though the symptoms will settle in a couple of days). Take *penicillin* 250mg four times daily for 10 days or *erythromycin* if allergic to penicillin.

Lassa Fever

Sore throat and mild feelings of being unwell can herald one serious infection: lassa fever. This is a disease acquired in West Africa. The infection often comes from swallowing urine of the multimammate rat (most usually via contaminated uncooked food), but it is highly infectious so can be caught from people too. The incubation period is 3–16 days.

Initially the symptoms are an undramatic sore throat, aches and pains, then after 3–6 days there is a sudden deterioration so that it is clear to all that a very serious illness is present. Those who die from the infection succumb 7–14 days after the onset of symptoms. Seek medical help promptly if you are in or have been in West Africa and develop a sore throat within 3 days of arriving or within 30 days of leaving the region. Lassa fever is one of a clutch of very rare, highly infectious and serious viral haemorrhagic fevers which cause bruising and bleeding.

Hoarse Voice

Under normal circumstances at home, someone suffering from a hoarse voice for more than 3 weeks would be sent for a specialist consultation with an Ear, Nose and Throat consultant. If there is no obvious cause of prolonged hoarseness (like a very harsh dry climate) it would be wise to take this precaution while travelling too.

Abdominal Pain

Severe abdominal pain which goes on for more than 4 hours suggests there is a serious problem which will require proper medical assessment; *see* pp.30 and 41.

Reminder

Accidents are the health hazards which most often kill or seriously harm travellers. About half of the deaths which occur while travelling are due to accidents, while only one per cent is due to infections or tropical diseases. Consider the risks of accidents at all times when travelling. Finally, remember that health problems which affect you at home, like sore throats or toothache, are also likely to occur while you are travelling.

Your First Aid Kit

This chapter suggests what to pack in a first aid kit and the precautions needed when buying medicines abroad. Reasons for not taking antibiotics because of their side effects are given.

First Aid Kit

Most medicines that you are likely to need while travelling will be available over the counter in developing countries, although capitals and big cities are obviously likely to be better stocked than small towns. New drugs and some contraceptive pills are often hard to find in some countries. Preparations for children are also surprisingly difficult to come by, so parents must plan carefully and take professional advice if travelling to remote places with small children.

I generally travel with very few medicines. Many people will wish to carry much more. The more I travel, the less I seem to carry, since, increasingly, I realize that almost anything that I really need is available or there is a reasonable substitute. Here is a list of what I consider is a fairly comprehensive kit. Other advisers may suggest taking everything you are ever likely to need, but this will mean carrying an extra rucksack. Asterisked* items in the list below are those which are scarce or difficult to come by or may be of poor quality in developing countries.

▶ *antimalarial tablets—*chloroquine* is readily available in malarious countries but Paludrine and other prophylactics seldom are

▶ *insect repellent, DEET-based; Autan sticks are convenient and not too messy

▶ *sun-screen and lip screen

▶ soluble *aspirin* or *paracetamol* (*acetaminophen* in US)—these reduce fever, are good first line pain-killers and can be gargled to soothe sore throats (carry *paracetamol* syrup if travelling with children)

▶ sore throat pastilles

▶ *Bonjela or Teejel ulcer preparations for Paludrine-induced mouth ulcers

▶ *calamine lotion

▶ Vaseline or moisture cream or Sudocrem

▶ oral rehydration sachets or
   *measuring spoon to make sugar and salt rehydration solution

▶ antiseptic of your choice (*see* p.104)

▶ crêpe or ace bandage and safety pins

▶ *plasters (which stick and stay stuck when you sweat)

▶ *non-stick dressings (e.g. Melonin)

▶ *micropore tape to stick on the non-stick dressings or to tape sore eyes closed

▶ *Steri-Strips or butterfly closures

▶ injection swabs

▶ cotton buds (10 is plenty)

▶ *dental first aid kit/temporary fillings

▶ a strongish pain-killer like DF118, Distalgesic or *codeine phosphate* (which also calms abdominal cramps in severe diarrhoea) or a tablet containing both *paracetamol* (*acetaminophen*) and *codeine*

▶ antihistamine tablets such as *chlorpheniramine* (e.g. Piriton) or *diphenhydramine* (e.g. Benadryl)

▶ fine tweezers or forceps (for removing splinters and coral)

▶ scissors

▶ artery forceps—have various uses including pulling out thorns, clamping off spurting arteries, repairing tents and removing fish hooks from people and fish

▶ paper clip for releasing blood under a nail (*see* p.175)

▶ *condoms and contraceptive pills

▶ a torch

Extras for some people:

▶ low reading thermometer and space blanket if going to cold places

▶ * *acyclovir* (Zovirax) cream if you suffer from cold sores

▶ *adrenaline* (*epinephrine* in the US) injection (0.5ml of 0.1 per cent or 1 in 1000) if allergic to stings (*see* p.144)

▶ antibiotics if you are going somewhere remote

▶ blunt curved forceps if travelling in tick country

A Bigger, Better Medical Kit?

If you wish to carry a comprehensive medical kit because you are going on a major expedition, get some professional advice. The Royal Geographical Society (RGS) run excellent seminars in London on expedition planning, expedition medicine and independent travel. The RGS also has a library of expedition reports which may be consulted and these are helpful since most report on medical problems encountered in particular places. *Expedition Medicine* (*see* **Bibliography**, pp.215–6) contains information useful to those going on large formal expeditions. It also has a section on expedition medical kits, or see Illingworth (*see* **Bibliography**, p.219) for suggested contents. Alternatively you can buy a custom-made medical kit from Nomad (who have great experience of putting kits together for expeditions, overlanders and individuals), or ready-made kits from BCB, Cotswold or similar companies (*see* **Useful Addresses**, p.212). Some organized overland tours carry a comprehensive medical kit so find out what is on board so that you do not carry unnecessary medical clutter.

Carrying Hypodermic Syringes

If you decide to carry an AIDS kit (*see* p.126) remember that some countries, most notably Malaysia, will assume you are a drug addict unless the syringes are obviously part of a medical kit and/or you are carrying a medical certificate. Diabetics and other legitimate syringe and needle-users must be careful about this. Consider carrying some kind of official document.

Buying and Consuming Medicines Abroad

General Advice

Few third world countries have adequate policies controlling use of medicines. This means that it is possible to buy unsuitable or even dangerous medicines across the counter. Buying medicines abroad is also confusing since some of the trade names are very different to those you will be used to. It is best to stick to *generic* (in *italics*) rather than trade names. Most drugs have at least two names: the trade name which is short, snappy and memorable but which may be very different in different countries, and the *generic* name which is usually written in much smaller print on the packet, may be unpronounceable but should be similar in all countries.

A complication of buying medicines abroad even once you have sorted the name out is finding out what is available. Some pharmacists have assured me that a drug does not exist, but what they meant was that they did not have it and would rather sell me something that they did have. But some medicines, even common and very useful ones, are just not available in some countries. Asian pharmaceutical companies are very fond of manufacturing combinations of drugs and it is best to avoid these. So when buying check:

● That the generic name is correct
● That the preparation contains only one drug
● That the expiry date is still in the future

Very few out-of-date tablets are dangerous (one exception is *tetracycline* which degrades to give toxic products when very out of date), but out-of-date medicines, even aspirin, are likely to be ineffective. Syrups and many liquid preparations have a much shorter shelf life than dry medicines, especially in hot climates so opt for tablets if you can. When taking medicines be sure to take a full course. Do not be intimidated by suggestions from people working in pharmacies that you are buying too many antibiotic tablets. They will be used to dispensing three or four at a time.

Locally Manufactured Medicines

Most medicines you buy abroad are probably of acceptable quality but some drugs are manufactured to very poor standards. I try to buy drugs made by local branches of international drug companies or, in Nepal by the national drug company, Royal Drugs Limited. Swindles or mistakes make a minority of drugs unsafe or ineffective in some developing countries. I have heard of antibiotic capsules being filled with flour in India, but worse there are occasionally extremely dangerous problems. In Bangladesh in 1992 there was an epidemic of fatal kidney disease in children which was caused by contaminated, locally made, *paracetamol* syrup.

Beware of Injections and Drips

In all Asian countries where I have worked, many people consulting a doctor will be offered an injection. Hypodermics have a very powerful placebo effect and people often think that the medicine they are getting in the syringe is somehow much more powerful than it would be in pill or syrup form. It can be dangerous to have unnecessary injections. You are more likely to suffer a major allergic reaction. There is a risk of acquiring an abscess or even hepatitis B and HIV if the needle is dirty. If you are incubating polio (which of course you won't be because you are fully immunized) the injection can cause paralysis of the injected limb. So ask if the medicine is available in tablet form.

I have seen Afghan and Nepali doctors administering intravenous saline infusions to treat 'weakness', but in such small quantities (often 20ml or so) that even if the 'weakness' was due to dehydration, it would not have had a therapeutic effect. The patients thought this treatment was truly marvellous, though, and a very 'strong' medicine, and so doctors continue the practice.

Common Medicines, Antibiotics and Their Alternatives

Pain-killers

Aspirin (*acetylsalicylic acid*) is an under-rated and under-used medicine. It is not only an excellent pain-killer but also helps reduce inflammation and swelling which itself causes pain. In addition, it is the best drug for reducing fevers. Those with stomach ulcers or a lot of indigestion should not take aspirin (or any of the other non-steroidal anti-inflammatory medicines) since they will make these symptoms worse. And it should not be given to children under 12 years of age. The alternative is *paracetamol* (*acetaminophen* or Tylenol in the US). The non-steroidal anti-inflammatory medicines are excellent for treating sprains, strains, wrenches and breaks. Unless symptoms are severe start with *ibuprofen* (e.g. Nurofen or Brufen in UK; Motrin, Advil or Nuprin in US) and if that is not strong enough move on to *naproxen* (e.g. Naprosyn in UK and US or Anaprox in US) or *diclofenac* (e.g. Voltarol). If indigestion starts when taking any of these medicines stop them and use a combination of paracetamol and codeine instead. The prime side effect of *paracetamol, codeine*, DF118, Distalgesic and other simple pain-killers is constipation.

If you have pain which continues for a day or more, pain-killers will be most effective if taken regularly. Allowing the pain to return before you take another pain-killer will make the pain more difficult to control. This is equally true for the pain of terminal cancer or for backache.

Antibiotics

Antibiotics have no effect on viral infections (including common colds). Penicillin, in its various forms is probably the most useful antibiotic for travellers. However, allergy to penicillin is common and allergic people should not take *penicillin, amoxycillin, ampicillin, flucloxacillin, cloxacillin* or *co-amoxiclav* (Augmentin). The *generic* names of the penicillins indicate that they are related drugs: most but not all end in …icillin. The common alternative for penicillin-allergic people is *erythromycin*. All these antibiotics are safe to take in pregnancy.

Flucloxacillin is an excellent antibiotic for clearing skin infections but is not available in much of Asia; *cloxacillin* is the alternative but since it is a different preparation it needs to be taken in a different dose. Usually *flucloxacillin* is taken as 250mg four times a day while *cloxacillin* is taken as 500mg four times a day; because of different pharmacological properties and different molecular weights these doses are equivalent and not, as it may appear, double the quantity of antibiotic. If you are allergic to penicillins, take *erythromycin* instead. The tetracyclines (including *doxycycline*) are good broad spectrum antibiotics for respiratory and other infections and *trimethoprim* is also excellent for respiratory as well as urinary tract infections. Neither should be taken in pregnancy (*see* p.192). Uses and cautions regarding *ciprofloxacin* (which *can* be taken by those allergic to penicillins) are given on p.32. *Metronidazole* (e.g. Flagyl) is a good safe antibiotic for treatment of giardia, amoebae and some dental and gynaecological problems.

Reasons for Not Taking Antibiotics or Other Medicines

A wise physician once said, 'Show me a drug without side effects and I will show you a drug which does not work.' What he meant by this is that there are costs to any treatment and effective medicines often cause some side effects. A doctor's job, in controlling the consumption of medicines, is to weigh up the costs and benefits of any treatment he prescribes. The antibiotic *chloramphenicol*, for example, would very effectively treat tonsillitis or travellers' diarrhoea, but in a minority of patients it will shut down the body's immune system with a fatal outcome. Western doctors, therefore, no longer prescribe *chloramphenicol*, except in very serious infections (such as meningitis) or in the form of eye drops, where the drug does not get into the body in any significant quantity. Travellers should be wary of taking drugs which they do not know, particularly steroids.

Side Effects

Medicines cause side effects, but in general they are trivial and short lived. When prescribing for yourself, consider the length and severity of the illness and compare them to the possible side effects of any drug. Simple travellers' diarrhoea, for example, generally lasts 36–48 hours if you follow the guidelines in this book. Do you therefore wish to take a week long course of antibiotics to treat it? The one dose treatment with *ciprofloxacin* (in addition to plenty of fluids) would seem a good compromise if you decide to opt for antibiotic treatment (*see* p.32).

Antibiotic-induced Diarrhoea, Antibiotic Tongue and Thrush

Antibiotics wipe out the body's protective and useful bacteria. This can have a variety of effects ranging from a mild loosening of the bowels to serious diarrhoea which needs treatment in hospital with intravenous drugs. This is rare but it would be exceedingly unpleasant if it occurred where medical facilities were poor. Another effect of antibiotics is that by killing the body's normal bacteria it can allow troublesome bugs to establish themselves: thrush in the mouth or vagina is a frequent outcome. Attacks of vaginal thrush are common after antibiotic treatment, particularly in warm moist climates.

Sunlight-induced or Photosensitive Rashes

A range of medicines (antibiotics, anti-inflammatories and many others) can make the skin of some people extra susceptible to sunburn. Although this effect soon disappears on stopping the offending drug, it could ruin a holiday. If it is an essential drug, like diabetes treatment, this may add some unwanted complications to your travel arrangements and may deprive you of a high-point of your trip.

Resistance

Profligate use of antibiotics promotes resistance to all antibiotics so that when there is a real need for effective antibiotic therapy, it will not work. This is a powerful argument against taking antibiotics too readily. Antibiotic resistance is much less likely to develop if antibiotic courses are properly completed, so do not change your mind after a few days and certainly do not stop the course before it is completed just because you feel better. Most antibiotic courses are for 5 days, some are longer.

Not All Medicines Suit All People

Certain drugs are unsuitable for some individuals. The most obvious example is drug allergy which usually causes a raised, very itchy, red rash, or less frequently breathing problems, swelling of the face and collapse. Mild diarrhoea or slight stomach ache (which is common in people taking antibiotics) is not a sign of allergy. Many drugs may not be given to children or pregnant women.

Medicines, Alcohol and Contraception

If you drink alcohol when you are taking *metronidazole* (e.g. Flagyl) you will experience unpleasant side effects. It is also unwise to drink alcohol when taking drugs with sedative effects such as antihistamines (especially Piriton). Take special care to avoid combining alcohol, medicines and driving. Some antibiotics render contraceptive pills less safe and it is therefore wise for women taking a course of antibiotics to ask their partner to use condoms until 7 pill days after the end of the course of medicines (*see* p.122).

Taking Medicine While Pregnant

If you are in a malarious region when pregnant, it is particularly important to take antimalarial tablets because if you get malaria you are much more likely to become seriously ill or even die; it will also probably abort the baby. If you do not take antimalarials at any other time please do so when pregnant, but ensure that you take a type which is safe in pregnancy. You can get specialist advice from the London School of Hygiene and Tropical Medicine (℗ 0171 636 8636). *Chloroquine* can be taken in pregnancy. If you take Paludrine or Maloprim you should also take *folic acid* supplements. In most regions therefore you will end up taking Paludrine and folic acid daily, and *chloroquine* weekly.

You should be very careful about taking any medicines during pregnancy, but especially during the first 3 months. *Amoxycillin* and *erythromycin* are safe to take while pregnant and breast feeding. Avoid *doxycycline* (e.g. Vibramycin) and other *tetracyclines* while pregnant and breast feeding and do not take *co-trimoxazole* or *trimethoprim* while pregnant. For further advice, *see* p.124.

Summary

⚠ Never take chloramphenicol (also called Chloromycetin, Catilan or Enteromycetin) unless in the form of eye or ear drops. It is now reserved for the treatment of severe infections, like meningitis, in hospital.

⚠ Do not take steroids or corticosteroids unless they are prescribed by a doctor whom you trust.

⚠ Avoid all injections if possible.

⚠ Do not take out-of-date medicines.

⚠ Be wary of taking any medicines during pregnancy.

Responsible Tourism

The realities of poor or absent medical care in the developing world can be shocking. I was approached in Hala (Sindh) by a man suffering from neurofibromatosis (the Elephant Man's disease): a pendulous piece of flesh from his eyelid hung down to his waist. I found him too revolting to look at. A relatively minor operation would remove his horrendous growth, but would deprive him of the means of earning a good living as a beggar. Perhaps if I had offered him the gift of surgery, he would not have accepted it.

For every case who would refuse surgery, though, there must be 10,000 who would give anything to be helped and it can be hard for visitors to cope with this. In the West—and even with the British health service in the state it is in—we can generally get any treatment we need. Yet the simplest surgery is denied most third-world citizens. Proper medical care with the right medicines is often unavailable to most citizens of the developing world. TB commonly kills people yet treatment is not particularly expensive. It needs to be taken for at least 6 months under proper medical supervision, though and this often is just not possible to arrange. We cannot do much about this, except perhaps give a little money to non-government organizations or charities who are helping. The Save the Children Fund, for example, has an excellent programme of repairing hare lips and cleft palates and there are a range of charities restoring sight with cataract operations.

Surgery for neurofibromatosis or hare lip is, of course, beyond most of us, but because gross disability, handicap and chronic disease is so common, obvious and intrusive in the developing world, we may be seduced into interfering by trying to treat simpler conditions. Yet this kind of dabbling to salve our own consciences is unhelpful.

Case History (Afghanistan)

Long before I ever thought of going to medical school, I drove overland to Nepal with three friends. I was in charge of first aid; my qualifications were an ecology degree and life-saving training. One evening some Afghans approached our campsite and asked for medicine. They mimed the shakes and fever and were clearly asking for malaria treatment. We were carrying a single course of treatment in case any of us contracted malaria in the 6 months we would be travelling. I was at a loss because I desperately wanted to help these poor goat herders but equally I was not going to give away our only course so early in our trip.

Chris stepped in; he was much more widely travelled than the rest of us. He rummaged in the Land Rover and pulled out some Horlicks tablets— sweets which look like medicine—and gave the goatherds the packet. The recipient then went on to ask directions (he was amazingly good at mime). How many should he take? Chris broke a tablet in half and showed he must take half three times a day. The goatherd went off very pleased.

I was enormously impressed at Chris's masterful bullshit which had got us off the hook. I had no idea at the time just what a dangerous disease malaria can be and thought that our 'treatment' was harmless, amusing even. Now I squirm to recall the deceit. Perhaps the goatherd died of his next bout of malaria because he never sought real treatment, thinking that our Horlicks tablets would see him right.

Handing Out Medicines

If you want to 'patch up the locals' while you are travelling, you should think carefully about what you are doing and why. Do a little research and act in a way that may allow you to give something more than a 'quick fix'. If your Western 'quick fix' works, the recipient will lose any confidence he had in the few facilities that are available locally and, more important, he is unlikely ever to learn how to avoid future attacks. If your treatment fails, he will lose confidence and you may wreck opportunities for health workers who follow. Few diseases respond to a single dose of a drug and unless you stay to supervise your treatment you can never be sure that the treatment has been taken properly.

There are often situations where there is a temptation to hand out antibiotics. Even educated Westerners have a very poor record of taking medicines as they should, and villagers who have had little exposure to Western therapy will be most unlikely to take a full course as required. In most places where I have worked, local practitioners, both Western and traditional, prescribe a selection of medicines. One so-called Ayurvedic practitioner in Sri Lanka prescribed for one woman with fever one of each of the following tablets: *amoxycillin* (antibiotic), Valium (tranquillizer), *paracetamol* (to reduce the fever), *propranolol* (heart medicine) and a vitamin capsule. Even qualified doctors sometimes prescribe part courses of antibiotics so there is no lead from the practitioners which will show patients how they should take their medicines. Consequently when villagers acquire a course of antibiotics, they are likely to take one or two and save the rest for when they are ill again. This will promote resistance to antibiotics which means that when someone competent comes to treat a serious infection, the antibiotic may well be useless. The odd thing about antibiotic resistance is that bacteria which have 'learned' how to resist an antibiotic are more likely to become resistant to other unrelated antibiotics. Giving out antibiotics will be harmful in the long term unless you are prepared to stay for a week and supervise taking of the medicine. And indeed if you do feel that your patient is so desperately in need of your treatment perhaps you should make the commitment to stay and make sure that the medicine is taken properly. This may sound hard, but treating people properly is hard.

The big killer in the developing world is diarrhoea; people die of dehydration because they do not realize how much fluid is lost or how to replace it. A traveller who has an interest in helping the people he meets may save lives by teaching villagers how to make and when to use sugar and salt solution; details are on p.29. It is easy to hand out packets of oral rehydration solution, but this on its own will not do much to make the villagers self-sufficient when the next bout of diarrhoea comes. Villagers need to know that it is not a medicine and that one or two packets are useless. Salt and sugar measures (available from TALC, see **Useful Addresses**, p.213) are a good educational tool, but even better is something you yourself might make out of locally available materials (like soft drinks bottle tops for example). If you want to help, give the issue a lot of serious thought before plunging in and allow lots of time (days perhaps) to teach about what you are giving.

If you are desperate to hand out pills, there are some that you can give away with relative impunity and which may even do some good. Many women of child-bearing age who live in developing countries are anaemic. In some regions nearly half of such women are estimated to be significantly short of iron. The causes of this are a combination of poor diet, constant pregnancies and hookworm infestation. The consequences are that these women suffer chronic fatigue so are less efficient workers and bread-winners, they are much more likely to die in childbirth and they will deliver small babies which are less likely to survive. Dishing out handfuls of iron tablets to such women and older girls, then, is a useful thing to do (but realize that iron in overdose is dangerous, especially to young children). Tablets are usually very cheap when bought abroad.

Another relatively harmless medicine to give is *paracetamol* (and possibly—if you are sure they have no stomach problems—*aspirin*). When people suffer from a fever from whatever cause they feel very ill and often ache all over. *Paracetamol* and *aspirin* are very effective in reducing fever, as well as being good pain-killers, so will make people feel a lot better when they catch 'flu and other common illnesses. Even with these drugs, do explain carefully what they are for and what they can and cannot do. Again, you would be doing a service to your patient if you gave them recognizably local tablets. Then they will be able to buy the next supply and possibly avoid being exploited by some unscrupulous practitioner. The poor in the tropics spend a large proportion of their small incomes on medicines, many of which are useless or even dangerous.

Case History (Nepal)

We walked into a Nepali village just after someone had handed out packets of oral rehydration packets. A toddler had opened his packet onto the ground and was licking it off his fingers, while a dog shared it. The donors, who had been Nepali health workers, had failed to communicate the life-saving value of the packets; they had not given the villagers enough time.

Skin Infections

Independent travellers are often asked for help with treatment of skin infections and this is one area where it is easy to treat the problem as presented, teach the sufferer how to treat the next attack and also explain how future infections can be avoided. (Some of this will be more difficult if you are somewhere remote and cannot find an interpreter, but the tourist in the case history below had a selection of interpreters available.) You will often be presented with festering sores which will need a week of *flucloxacillin* treatment to clear them up. Superficial impetigo (*see* p.111) is also very common.

In Nepal little packets of *potassium permanganate* crystals (sufficient to treat perhaps 100 people) cost five rupees (£1=NRp75 in 1994). It is easy to carry a handful of these match-box-sized packets so that if you are asked to treat a superficial skin infection you can produce one. Demonstrate dissolving a few crystals in water then briskly rub the solution into the infected area with cotton wool or a scrap of clean cloth, and leave the packet with the family. If you have an interpreter you should explain that the treatment should be repeated thrice daily for a few days and that future infections can be avoided by promptly cleaning even the smallest wounds then sterilizing with *potassium permanganate*. Even this simple level of 'doctoring' requires time and at least 24 hours keeping an eye on your patient to see if they are following your advice. Local paramedics are often very good at treating skin infections because they are so very common so if there is an accessible clinic it is best to avoid dabbling and refer your 'patient' there.

Case History (Nepal)

A tourist had stopped at a house on a popular trekking route in West Nepal. He was attempting to treat a child with a very unpleasant area of oozing infected skin on her face. He was applying germoline antiseptic ointment to the little girl's cheek. This treatment is ineffective against impetigo, and indeed by further moisturizing the infection, it may even encourage it to spread. No doubt the victim's family would have faith in the clever Western 'cure' and would further delay seeking assistance from a medical post where the paramedic would have plenty of experience of treating impetigo. It is a common complaint in warm climates and at this superficial stage it is easy to treat with cheap, locally manufactured medicine.

The additional delay in seeking medical help has two likely consequences. Firstly, the infection, which is highly contagious, is likely to spread to the rest of the family and also the little girl's playmates. Secondly, impetigo can spread into the eyes.

Summary

- Do not attempt to treat diseases that you know nothing about—you may do more harm than good.

- Consider your motives in trying to treat people. It is fun for you and wins admiration, but it can be destructive for your patients.

- Try to carry locally bought medicines if you intend to treat people. In this way the local people will see that these medicines are useful and healing and have a Westerner's approval. Paracetamol or aspirin, salt and sugar measuring spoons (or possibly oral rehydration packets), iron tablets and potassium permanganate can do a great deal of good for many people.

- If you are carrying a large, comprehensive medical kit, donate it to a clinic or hospital at the end of your trip.

- Resist practising on local people and do not give your medicines to a non-medical local friend.

Living Abroad

Most of the tips and information in this book apply equally to independent travellers and to expatriates. Like independent travellers, expatriates need to take care about food hygiene and water quality, but it is relatively easy for them to protect themselves from infection of the gut. They may be at risk of catching TB (*see* p.179) and so should have BCG immunization (*see* p.7). (Americans will be advised otherwise). The medical risks facing expatriates depend on where you are based (capital cities, rural areas, jungle, desert or refugee camp) and also on your kind of work. Diplomats, businessmen, development consultants, oil prospectors, missionaries, health workers, researchers, volunteers all have their own particular risks, requirements, stresses and support mechanisms.

Malaria

Expatriates are consistently bad at protecting themselves from malaria and other insect-borne disease. Try to find out exactly what the local malaria situation is. Many South American and also Southeast and East Asian cities are free from malaria so if you are city-bound it may be safe not to take any prophylaxis (but realize that you may need to for weekend jaunts). Even if malaria is not a local problem, take precautions against being bitten so as to avoid other mosquito-borne diseases (*see* p.60 for details of dengue). Many expatriates have become blasé about taking malaria tablets. Do not be paranoid about the side effects of antimalarials; they are generally safe and thoroughly tested medicines. I urge expatriates to follow the advice on p.56, so that there are no more unnecessary deaths from malaria. A few expatriates take their antimalarials carefully and then say 'because I am taking my malaria tablets it is safe for me to sit outside at dusk [getting bitten by mosquitoes] while I sip my gin and tonic.' It is not. Nor does the quinine in the tonic give you any protection. It is best to avoid bites.

A Good Home Environment

Expatriates are able to make their immediate environment safer than those of travellers. Homes can be screened against mosquitoes (properly fitting screen doors also exclude snakes and scorpions) and the immediate area around the house can be cleaned so as to discourage mosquitoes, flies and snakes. Thick scrubby vegetation close to the house should be cleared since it is a good hiding place for snakes and provides resting sites for mosquitoes. All standing water should be covered or drained and small quantities in tyres and pots emptied and removed; these and plants which trap water at the point where stems join the trunk (e.g. bromeliads and travellers palms) make excellent mosquito breeding grounds. Plants grow with amazing rapidity in the tropics; you can pick papayas from trees planted only 18 months previously and some vegetables can be cropped in 6–8 weeks. Even if you are not interested in gardening at home it is worth growing your own vegetables, especially since you will be able to contribute to the local economy by employing some help in the garden, and supplying your employees with fresh foodstuffs. Grain stores and chickens encourage rodents which in turn encourage snakes, so keeping chickens has advantages and disadvantages.

Rural areas may have no electricity, no water supply and no sanitation. Expatriates may need to dig a pit latrine, arrange to sink a tube well and consider whether a generator is going to be useful. Fans and air conditioners help to cut down mosquito bites inside, confuse sand-flies and help you avoid prickly heat. Keep an eye on people whom you employ to help you; you are responsible for their welfare. Do they cough up blood? This suggests TB which needs treating (*see* p.179). Advice on such domestic arrangements can be found in the little red Ross Institute book (*see* **Bibliography**, p.216).

Filth-to-mouth Pathogens

While at home, expatriates should be at little risk of filth-to-mouth (faecal–oral) diseases. Ensure a ready supply of boiled and filtered water, teach employees about basic hygiene and make sure that they are healthy. Make your own ice and ice cream and adopt sensible additional precautions when you travel in country away from your adopted home, since then you are a traveller with travellers' health risks.

Psychological Problems

The life of an expatriate appears romantic and attractive. What could be more idyllic than living in a tropical paradise, earning pots of money, and being pampered by a household of servants? The reality is that many expatriates work six and sometimes seven day weeks, because they are under huge pressures to achieve and they are also often away from their families. Pressure of work rarely leaves time to learn a local language and this restricts the social circle to other expatriates and a select number of highly educated locals who are often colleagues and whose senses of humour are completely at odds with their own. The community is small, introverted and often obsessed by trivia. Impartial support and comradeship, which usually can be found among friends at home, is difficult to come by and life can seem terribly isolated. Another factor which contributes to dissatisfaction is that many expatriates move rapidly from contract to contract and from country to country. It is hard for them to adjust to local culture and to make local friends. Even the expatriate community is constantly shifting so that friendships often remain at a very superficial level. Volunteers are sometimes even worse off.

Geography and their lower income can isolate them from expatriates. Local people may not value their contribution since it seems to come so cheap. Volunteers can be completely undermined by the local conditions; they are often closely involved in work where success or failure is immediately very obvious to them. Equally, though, life can be easier and more fulfilling for volunteers because they are able to integrate better and there may be less jealousy from local colleagues. However well integrated a volunteer is, though, it can be very difficult for them to relax.

Pressures at work, and because the family are many thousands of miles away, induce tensions and many expatriates unwind at the end of a long day with a stiff drink. Over the years a dependency develop. Alcoholism is a common problem among expatriates. Workaholism is also common so that when the family is around they feel excluded. Although it is difficult advice to follow, it is healthiest to try to work sensible hours and relax properly with some activity which allows you to switch off from work completely. If deadlines mean you must work long hours at times, compensate with the occasional long weekend away.

Sensible Drinking

A few guidelines will help avoid drifting into drinking too much alcohol:

- ○ Never drink spirits, and preferably no alcohol, before sundown.

- ○ Do not rehydrate with beer or other alcoholic drinks; quench your thirst with water or fruit juices before moving on to alcohol.

- ○ Avoid the habit of unwinding with a drink at the end of every day.

- ○ If you are consistently drinking more than 21 units of alcohol a week you are drinking too much. Women should drink less than 14 units a week (one unit is half a pint of beer, one glass of wine or one small measure of spirits; a bottle of wine is six units).

- ○ Abstain from alcohol during the first 3 months of pregnancy because alcohol increases the chance of miscarriage (current recommendations are to take no more than one unit of alcohol per week throughout pregnancy).

Those who live abroad long term face some special problems which can be something of a shocking revelation to new expatriates. Probably the biggest problems faced by expatriates are not the tropical diseases that many fear, but psychological symptoms. One study of a particular group of long-term expatriates found that 60 per cent of repatriations for medical reasons were due to psychiatric illnesses in the household head or spouse. That is not to say that they had gone crazy, but because of a combination of 'culture shock', stress, isolation, insomnia, depression, possible feelings of horror at the injustices that they are trying to work to correct and perhaps alcoholism, they have no longer been able to cope at work or home. Many others just cope but it is a struggle or aspects of their personal life suffer as a result.

Why do people want to work abroad? A droll colleague in Indonesia developed a classification system which he said fitted all expatriates. Each can be grouped as: mercenary, misfit or missionary, and within 'missionaries' my friend classified non-religious evangelists like myself. I am a health evangelist preaching good hygiene and preventive medicine! This 'missionary' group might seem best suited but in fact these people are very likely to have problems. We are fired with a cause that we know is right (my aim to save lives is an unarguably good cause) but because my mission is so important it can throw me into conflicts. Why don't local staff understand the importance of the work? Why is the local bureaucracy slowing me down? Why don't my expatriate colleagues support my work? Why doesn't my husband understand there are more important things in life than baking bread? If you have a righteous cause it may be difficult to be patient. Depression and disillusionment can then easily become problems. It is important to realize that it is not possible to change the world, but that we must be satisfied with small contributions. We must not fall into the easy trap of blaming employers, local bureaucracy or colleagues for difficulties (local professional staff may also be having problems adjusting to having an over-paid outsider interfering with their work). Do all you can to keep problems in perspective. Even if you have tight contract deadlines, you are more likely to meet them if you have a relaxed approach. Try not to let chronic ill health get a hold. Make sure problems are dealt with promptly and arrange home leave especially to do this if necessary. Finally, realize how much you can learn from local skills, traditional knowledge and ways of working, recognizing that you may well be in contact with two cultures: the rural peasants and educated local people.

Those who are most likely to experience depression and problems of motivation are high achievers, or people who are running away from problems at home, or those who have had previous psychological problems. Spouses who have given up a rewarding occupation to follow their partner or who are worried about children's health and education are also under great psychological pressure. Do not mislead yourself with romantic ideals. Be rational and analyse your motivation and temperament and what kind of work you will be involved in before you commit yourself. Only you can judge.

InterHealth (*see* **Useful Addresses**, p.211) have a lot of experience in giving medical support to expatriates. Many companies which send employees abroad are recognizing the value of counselling services. Some companies provide little or no support (especially for contract staff), however.

Sex and the Single Expat

Expatriates are usually very visible in the communities in which they work and there will be a lot of interest in your activities. If you have a local lover, or even if you have a platonic friend of the opposite sex, everyone will know about it. In some cultures this will cause problems for you if you are a female expatriate. You may be seen as available to all comers and have uninvited nocturnal visitors or may simply lose status at work which is so important in getting things done in Asia. Often there will be worse problems for a local woman if she is known to be liaising with a man to whom she is not married. Asian communities, in particular, are far more prudish in such things than many people realize and such a local woman can become an outcast in a community where she will continue to live after you have gone home.

The more obvious risk is of acquiring AIDS and other sexually transmitted diseases; this is covered on p.125.

Difficulties for Spouses

Spouses can suffer enormously in struggling to adjust to life as an expatriate. Often they have given up an excellent job to travel and so they not only lose a key role, but they also seem to lose all worth too. It can seem as if they are just trailing along with no job, no status, no interests and, perhaps, they are even assumed to be short on grey matter too. Your husbands' colleagues may seem stand-offish, but this is mainly because they seldom know how to strike up a conversation with a house-wife; what interests can they have in common?

Even if unemployed spouses have a useful skill, they are often not allowed to work, even on a voluntary basis. Some will feel they are even ousted by servants from the role of cook and housekeeper. The situation is worse for househusbands since local men will be mystified about how any man can stoop to being kept by a woman. Unemployed childless professional women also have a tough time too. Wives of the working partner's local colleagues will be educated but will have had their children early and will be well adjusted to the role of home-manager and mother; they will be puzzled by a childless wife who has enjoyed a responsible career but has little interest in children, cooking, make-up and clothes. Situations are variable, though, and depend on your skills and where you are. It can be more difficult to find work in big cites with all their rules and bureaucracy but there may be social advantages. Remote rural postings can be hard socially but rewarding professionally and linguistically.

The Ideal Expatriate

The ideally adjusted expatriate who enjoys his time abroad keeps a balanced approach to work by having at least a whole day a week thinking about something completely different. He will have a long-term assignment (2 years or more) in the country and will take time out to sight-see and learn about the culture in which he is living. He will often have an interest which he can follow in different countries: a sport, bird-watching, playing a musical instrument, an interest in fabrics or languages perhaps. He will take some regular exercise and may enjoy a gentle game of tennis, a brisk walk or even jogging. He appreciates a few beers with friends but never drinks alone and seldom touches spirits.

Unemployed spouses take lessons in the local language and thus have an entrée. Language training necessarily involves learning about social customs and enriches the experience of living in a different culture. It also allows enquiries about what things are for, why people are doing what they are doing and how novel foods might be prepared. Villagers are often delighted to find a foreigner to whom they can talk and ask questions. If her role is primarily that of housewife, she will often do her own shopping (rather than sending the cook out daily) which forces her into contact with locals, improves her language skills, enables her to find out what is going on locally and what interests her local neighbours.

Babies and Children

Travelling with children is a delight because they make ready introductions to people who would otherwise not have approached you. Their observations are also often most enlightening and frequently amusing. They can cause a great deal of worry when they become ill and you are far from adequate medical facilities, but as long as they are protected from insect bites, especially around dusk, take their anti-malarial medicines and have had the right immunizations they will thrive. There are two special precautions that parents should take. The first is to ensure that children drink plenty (preferably oral rehydration solution) when they get diarrhoea (*see* p.29) and the second is that they must be protected from the sun (*see* p.70). Small children should wear a shirt and hat as well as sun-cream when bathing in the sea or open air pools. If infants are bottle fed or drink from training beakers, be meticulous about sterilizing them very frequently. Sterilization tablets are often hard to come by but boiling the bottles, teats and cups in water for 15 minutes is effective and can be organized anywhere. Bringing up small children abroad has its complications and it would be wise to contact other expatriate parents so that they can brief you on local child-rearing practices. Attitudes to what you see as important can be very different and if these contrasts are not understood, problems may arise.

Getting rid of disposable nappies is difficult and if put into the ordinary rubbish system they will probably be scattered far and wide. Burn them, or use terry-towelling nappies with liners and plastic over-pants. Nappy liners are quite indestructible and block toilets, but washing them will make a box last ages. Some expatriate parents assume that because they lack a local language, their children cannot play with local friends, but integration and having friends of a similar age is important for a child's normal social development and encourages a unique and invaluable broad-mindedness. Younger children have a remarkable aptitude for languages and will often readily integrate with local children. Indeed many games do not require a great deal of verbal exchange to be great fun. I have been amazed at the number of playground games I recall from my own childhood in Surrey which are played in remote villages in Nepal.

Adolescents who arrive with their parents in a new country are not so adaptable, since they are often going through difficult processes of self-identification. This group can have some big problems particularly if their visit to the country is to be for less than a year. They may need a great deal of time and patience; like the well adjusted adult expatriate, they will cope better if they have a transferable hobby, like an interest in entomology.

Medical Advice From Afar

It is now possible to buy or hire a system of emergency medical support which puts expatriates in very remote situations in touch via satellite telecommunications with specialist doctors. At present these systems cost at least £25,000 but will probably become cheaper as the technology develops. They would be ideal for isolated expatriate communities. RGIT Health run this from 338 King Street, Aberdeen AB2 3BJ, UK ✆ +44 0224 619519.

When You Get Home

The most important thing to remember when you get home is to continue taking your antimalarial tablets for at least 4 weeks. And if you fall ill (especially if this is within 2 months of returning) remind your GP you have been abroad and may have been exposed to malaria. If returning ill to Australia, present yourself to a hospital which specializes in infectious diseases (*see* p.212).

A Post-trip Check-up?

'Should I have a medical check-up when I return from a tropical trip?' Many travellers and expatriates ask this question and quite a number wish to have a formal post-trip check-up by a specialist in tropical diseases.

Generally, if a returning traveller feels well, there is no need to have a medical examination. However, if you are worried you may have malaria (p.54), bilharzia (p.81), HIV (p.125) or Chagas' disease (p.62), go and see your doctor.

Malaria

Falciparum malaria is the only common, life-threatening disease imported from warm countries. Symptoms invariably begin within 3 months of return and most victims have been in Africa or Melanesia (PNG, Solomons and Vanuatu). There is no screening test which will diagnose it before the symptoms manifest themselves and so travellers and doctors must be aware of it as a possible diagnosis. The safety net is not a clever laboratory test, but alert travellers and doctors who act quickly if symptoms of possible malaria begin. There are much rarer, but serious, causes of fever in returning travellers but these will cause problems within a month of return (e.g. lassa fever).

Bilharzia (Schistosomiasis)

This little worm is acquired most often by travellers who have been wading or swimming in African lakes, although it is also a problem in the tropical Americas. A blood test is available to test for the parasite before symptoms emerge and may be worthwhile if you have put yourself at risk. GPs can often organize this. It should be done at least 6 weeks after leaving the bilharzia area.

HIV/AIDS and Sexually Transmitted Diseases

Travellers frequently enjoy casual sex while abroad and will therefore have put themselves at risk of contracting HIV as well as 25 other sexually transmitted diseases. Returning travellers may therefore wish to consider being screened for these problems. Counselling about HIV testing can be arranged through your GP or through a special genito-urinary clinic.

Chagas' Disease

This is a disease of tropical and subtropical Central and South America transmitted by bug bites. It is very rare in travellers, but if you have been exposed to bug bites while sleeping in wattle and daub village housing, a blood test may help to determine if you have been infected. Screening will be justified in only a very few people.

Other Rarities

Leishmaniasis (or kala-azar fever) can present months to years after a bite by an infected old world sand-fly and bronchopneumonia is the most common way in which it manifests itself. The Mediterranean coast is one source of this infection, but it is generally acquired from much further afield (*see* p.61). If you become ill, remind your doctor about your travels.

A blood test (ELISA) can detect filarial worms. These cause elephantiasis, river blindness or loa-loa in west and central Africa, Southeast Asia and South America. If you have no symptoms, do not request screening unless you have been home for more than 6 weeks. If you have symptoms, seek medical help promptly.

Stow-away Worms

Diseases and parasites are often imported from the tropics and sub-tropics, especially by people who have been abroad for relatively long periods. Most of them pose little threat to the infested individuals or to the general public in contact with them. Passing an earthworm-sized *Ascaris* worm is revolting but she will have done you no harm and will probably have been alone. Most infestations will die out in time, or if they do start causing problems (as they may on rare occasions) they can be treated easily.

Two parasites do rarely cause serious problems. In a minority of those they infest, tapeworms can end up in the brain. Amoebae commonly infest travellers and often cause no symptoms at all. However, in a minority they can cause a liver abscess; more frequently amoebae cause dysentery but you will know if you have this and will no doubt seek treatment. Unfortunately screening will be most unlikely to detect these problems before they cause symptoms of brain or liver invasion. Travellers should think about this and realize the benefits of avoiding infestations by eating safe, properly cooked food.

What Do Stool Checks Reveal?

Some doctors advocate screening faeces for parasite eggs or cysts. This may reveal an infestation but they generally only need treating if they are causing symptoms, or squeamishness. If you do have symptoms which someone thinks may be due to worms or *Giardia*, it is important that three stool samples are sent and that they are taken on different days. Only if three samples are negative is it likely that the traveller is free from parasites. Both *Giardia* and worms produce eggs and cysts intermittently so one clear sample does not necessarily mean your are free from parasites.

Lingering intestinal problems are common after a tropical trip, particularly in people returning from South Asia. Often no cause is found and the symptoms settle in time.

Summary

⊕ Remember the risk of serious malaria and seek medical help urgently if you fall ill within 3 months of returning from the tropics—even if you have taken your antimalarial tablets.

⊕ Antimalarial tablets should be continued for at least 4 weeks after returning from abroad; they do not absolutely guarantee that you will avoid malaria, but if you are unlucky enough to get it, you are less likely to die of it.

⊕ Other diseases imported from the tropics are unlikely to be serious, but seek a medical opinion if you notice a rash, new lumps or bumps or are unwell. Remind your doctor that you have been abroad.

⊕ Do not worry about your health on your return; if you feel well, you almost certainly are well.

Health and Immunization Information and Travel Clinics

British Airways Travel Clinics, ✆ 0171 831 5333 for the nearest. They sell malaria prophylaxis memory cards as well as treatment packs.

Hospital for Tropical Diseases, 4 St. Pancras Way, London NW1 0PE. Touch-tone phone health line (charged at 36p/minute cheap rate) giving advice relevant to specific destinations on ✆ 01839 337733.

Thomas Cook Travel Clinic, 45 Berkley St, London W1A 1EB, ✆ 0171 408 4157.

Malaria Reference Laboratory: countries of risk and prophylaxis, ✆ 0891 600350; avoiding bites, ✆ 0891 600274. In 1994 this cost 36p per minute cheap rate or 48p per minute at all other times.

Nomad Travel Pharmacy and Vaccination Centre, 3–4 Wellington Terrace, Turnpike Lane, London N8 0PX, ✆ 0181 889 7014, 📠 0181 889 9529. These are not computer-linked.

Nomad Travel Shop, 4 Potters Road, New Barnet, Herts EN5 5HW, ✆/📠 0181 441 7208.

Independent Medical Centre/Bridge the World, 47 Chalk Farm Road, Camden, London NW1, ✆ 0181 444 4070.

MASTA, Medical Advisory Services for Travellers, at the London School of Hygiene and Tropical Medicine, Keppel Street, London WC1 7HT, ✆ 0891 224 100 or 0171 631 4408. They offer immunization and other information but are not a travel clinic. They sell AIDS kits and other useful items including neat DEET and anti-mosquito anklets

Centers for Disease Control in Atlanta, Georgia are the central source of travel health information in North America with a touch-tone phone line and fax service. They publish each summer the invaluable *Health Information for International Travel* available from CDC (Attention Health Information), Center for Prevention Services, Division of Quarantine, Atlanta, GA 30333, USA, ✆ (404) 332 4559.

InterHealth is a specialist travel service providing comprehensive care for aid workers, volunteers and missionaries: clinical consultations, advice, an immunization service and a full range of health equipment. Contact Dr Ted Lankester or Jackie Hall on ✆ 0171 729 4230 or 📠 0171 729 3569; from April 1995 they are at Partnership House, 157 Waterloo Road, London SE1 8UU.

International Association for Medical Assistance to Travellers (IAMAT), 736 Center Street, Lewiston NY 14092, USA, ✆ (716) 754-4883, and Gotthardstrasse 17, 6300 Zug, Switzerland; a non-profit foundation that provides lists of English-speaking doctors abroad as well as foreign health information.

Useful Addresses

Medic Alert Foundation International, Turlock, CA 95380-1009, USA, ☎ (209) 668 3333, (800) 344 3226.

British Diabetic Association, 10 Queen Anne Street, London W1M 0BD, ☎ 0171 323 1531. Publishes leaflets and advice for travelling diabetics.

Australian Medical and Vaccination Centres

These clinics are all members of the International Association for Medical Assistance to Travellers. They do not give advice over the phone; ring for an appointment before attending:

2nd Floor, 393–397 Lt. Bourke St, Melbourne, Victoria 3000 (☎ 03 602 5788).

7th Floor, Dymocks Bldg, 428 George St, Sydney, NSW 2000 (☎ 02 221 7133).

6th Floor, Australian Airlines Bldg, 247 Adelaide Street, Brisbane, Queensland 4000 (☎ 07 221 9066).

5th Floor, Connor Bldg, Queen Elizabeth Hospital, Woodville Road, Woodville, SA 5011 (☎ 08 347 0296).

Level 5, Capita Centre Stage III, 1 Mill Street, Perth, WA 6000 (☎ 09 321 1977).

Australian hospitals which specialize in treating infectious and tropical diseases are the Fairfield Hospital in Melbourne (which also has a good travel health section), Westmead Hospital (Sydney), Queen Elizabeth Hospital (Adelaide), Royal Perth (Perth), Royal Darwin (Darwin) and Royal Hobart (Hobart).

Some Suppliers of First Aid and Medical Kits

MASTA (*see* above).

Nomad (*see* above) can supply a range of kits and also stock a good selection of water purification devices.

BCB Ltd, Clydesmuir Road Industrial Estate, Tremorfa, Cardiff CF2 2QS, ☎ 01222 464463, 🖷 01222 491166.

Jungle Para-Medical Services, 2 The Byeway, Weald Village, Harrow, Middlesex HA3 7EF.

SAFA Ltd, 59 Hill Street, Liverpool L8 5SA, ☎ 0151 708 03977.

Cotswold, Broadway Lane, South Cerney, Cirencester, Glos GL7 5UQ, ☎ 01285 860612, 🖷 01285 860483. Shops in London, Reading, Manchester, Southampton and Betws-y-Coed with a good range of water purification devices, plus some first-aid packs, mosquito nets, blister relief kits, etc.

Dental Projects Ltd, Blakesley Lodge, 2 Green Street, Sunbury-on-Thames, Middlesex TW16 6RN.

Oasis Mosquito Nets, 1 High St, Stoke Ferry, Kings Lynn, Norfolk PE33 9SF, ☎ 01366 500466, 🖷 01366 501122. Sells mosquito nets, insectacide and repellents, including the useful non-DEET Gurkha, which is good for those with sensitive (or sunburnt) skin or children.

Other Information Sources

Expedition Advisory Centre, Royal Geographical Society, 1 Kensington Gore, London SW7 2AR, ✆ 0171 581 2057, 📠 0171 584 4447.

South American Explorers Club, 126 Indian Creek Rd, Ithaca, NY 14850, USA, ✆ 001 607 277 0488; or PO Box 3714, Lima 100, Peru, ✆ 00 51 1431 4480; or PO Box 21–431, Eloy Alfaro, Quito, Ecuador, ✆ 00 593 2566 076; or subscription information via Bradt Publications, 41 Nortoft Rd, Chalfont St Peter, Bucks, SL9 0LA.

Globetrotters Club, BCM/Roving, London WC1N 3XX, for contacts and meetings.

Stanfords (books and maps), 12–14 Long Acre, London WC2E 9LP.

TALC, Teaching Aids at Low Cost, PO Box 45, St Albans, Herts AL1 4AX.

Glossary

I have tried to avoid technical or medical terms as much as possible but occasionally it seemed helpful to introduce them. Those which are used are defined below:

AIDS	Acquired immunodeficiency syndrome which is caused by HIV.
bilharzia	Schistosomiasis (*see* p.81.)
bromeliads	The family of plants to which the pineapple belongs; water collects in them where mosquitoes can breed.
bug	A precise entomological term describing a group of flat-backed insects with piercing mouthparts. I have avoided describing pathogens which cause illnesses as bugs to avoid confusion with the insects.
diarrhoea	Abnormally frequent and fluid bowel actions; usually adults passing more than three abnormal motions a day are said to have diarrhoea.
diuretic	A substance which makes you pass more urine than normal.
endemic	A species of animal, plant or pathogen indigenous to a particular geographical region.
epidemic	A disease which attacks abnormally large numbers of people in one place at one time.
ETEC	Enterotoxigenic *Escherichia coli*, the bacteria which cause travellers' diarrhoea.
faecal–oral disease	One which is transmitted from an ill person's faeces to someone else's mouth thus making them ill too; filth-to-mouth disease.
***generic* drug name**	The name of a medicine which should make it

universally recognizable; trade names often vary depending on the country of manufacture whereas *generic* names are often the same or nearly the same.

genus	A group of closely related animals or plants.
haemorrhagic	Adjective used to describe a group of diseases where the main problem is malfunction of the body's blood clotting system. This means that disastrous bleeding can occur without any injury. Without treatment the patient bleeds to death internally. Fortunately it can be treated in hospital with transfusions of blood products (usually plasma and platelets).
HIV	Human immunodeficiency virus; the virus which causes AIDS.
host	An animal or plant on or in which a parasite lives.
immunization, active	Priming the body's immune system by administering a harmless part of a pathogen or inactivated (e.g. boiled) pathogen; such vaccines can confer immunity for life.
immunization, passive	Injecting blood products which already carry some immunizing properties which protect for only a matter of months.
mortality	Death rate.
ORS	Oral rehydration solution which is the treatment for diarrhoea (*see* p.29).
pathogen	A 'germ' (viruses, bacteria, protozoa or worms) that causes disease.
prophylaxis	Avoiding disease through preventative measures or tablets.
schistosomiasis	Bilharzia (*see* p.81).
serotype	A virologists' term used to distinguish similar viruses which provoke different immunological reactions.
STD	Sexually transmitted disease.
topical preparations	Medicines which are put on the skin surface rather than taken internally.
trypanosomiasis	Disease of animals and man cause by trypanosome parasites. In the Americas these cause Chagas' disease and in Africa, sleeping sickness (*see* p.62).
vector	An animal, usually a biting insect or tick, which transmits disease to man.

Bibliography

I have drawn on standard medical texts and journals which are not listed here, so this is not a comprehensive reading list. It includes literature which supports some of the comments I have made (particularly when they have been controversial) or provides fuller descriptions of particular problems. My own work has been published under the name J. M. Wilson.

General

Hatt, John (1993) *The Tropical Traveller*. Penguin. Full of exceptionally useful advice on many aspects of independent travel including insurance, money and equipment.

General Medical

Behrens, R. H. & McAdam, K. P. W. J. eds (1993) Travel Medicine *British Medical Bulletin* **49** (2) also published by Churchill Livingstone. A specialized expert review by the British experts of travel medicine. Excellent and useful source.

Centers for Disease Control in Atlanta, Georgia (1994) *Health Information for International Travel*. Single copies are available from CDC (Attention Health Information), Center for Prevention Services, Division of Quarantine, Atlanta, GA 30333, USA; multiple copies are sold by the Superintendent of Documents, US Government Printing Office, Washington DC 20402; best English language publication for up-to-date international disease risk information.

Dawood, R. ed., (1992) *Travellers' Health*. Oxford University Press. Each section is written by an expert so quite a good text for professionals (Behrens, R. H. & McAdam, K. P. W. J., is better but costs £50) but many lay-folk find it intimidating.

Department of Health, Central Office of Information (1994), *Health Advice for Travellers: Anywhere in the World*. HMSO (leaflet T5): includes forms CM1 and E111 which enable holders (who will be British residents) to obtain emergency medical treatment in the European Community. Available free via freephone 0800-555-777 or from BAPS, Health Publications Unit, Heywood Stores, Manchester Road, Heywood, Lancs OL10 2PZ. Although updated yearly, the advice tends to lag behind current thinking.

Dessery, B. K. & Robin, M. R., (1992) *The Medical Guide for Third World Travelers*. KW Publications, San Diego, California. Good on North American travel clinics and New World health hazards but thin on health information worldwide. British doctors would disagree with some advice offered. Snake bite advice is dubious.

Juel-Jensen, B. ed. (1994) *Expedition Medicine*. Expedition Advisory Centre of the Royal Geographical Society, London. Ringbound. Costs £8.50 from RGS. Useful but aimed mainly at those going on large military style expeditions

Ross Institute of Tropical Hygiene, (1978) *Preservation of Personal Health in Warm Climates*. Pocket sized; good for expatriates; guidance on building latrines and much more.

Walker, E., Williams, G. & Raeside, F., (1993) *ABC of Healthy Travel*. British Medical Association. An excellent, but simple and accessible review aimed at doctors.

Werner, D., (1979) *Where There is No Doctor*. MacMillan (available from TALC). A useful but large and heavy book for settled expatriates. Covers every medical problem including how to set bones. Snake bite advice is dubious.

'Homework'

Anon (editorial) (1992) Typhoid vaccination: weighing the options. *Lancet* **340** 341–2.

Bezruchka, Stephen (1988) *The Pocket Doctor*. The Mountaineers, 306 Second Avenue West, Seattle, WA 98119, USA.

Hoke, C. H., Nisalak, A., Sangawhips, N. *et al.* (1988) Protection against Japanese encephalitis by inactivated vaccines. *New England Journal of Medicine* **319** 608–14.

Oades, P. J., Buchdahl, R. M. & Bush, A. (1994) Prediction of hypoxaemia at high altitude in children with cystic fibrosis. *British Medical Journal* **308** 15–18.

Ruff, T. A., Eisen, D., Fuller, A. & Kass, R. (1991) Adverse reactions to Japanese encephalitis vaccine. *Lancet* **338:** 881–2.

WHO (1994) *International Travel and Health: Vaccination Requirements and Health Advice.* World Health Organization Publications, Geneva, costing SFR 15 or US$13.50 (also in UK from HMSO). An annually updated pamphlet which now includes a comprehensive supplement on the malaria prophylaxis required for each country where it occurs.

'Travel Broadens the Mind...' and 'A Diet of Worms?'

Anon (1994), Prevention and control of hepatitis A. *Drugs and Therapeutics Bulletin* **32** (2) 9–11

Chiodini, P. L. (1994) A 'new parasite': human infection with *Cyclospora cayetanensis*. *Transactions of the Royal Society of Tropical Medicine and Hygiene* **88** 369–371.

DuPont, H. L., Ericsson, C. D., Matherson, J. J., Marani, S., Knellwolf-Cousin, A-L., Matinz-Sandoval, F. G. (1993) Zaldarine maleate, an intestinal calmodulin inhibitor, in the treatment of travellers' diarrhoea. *Gastroenterology* **104** 709–15.

Mayle, Peter (1990) *A Year in Provence.* Pan Books.

Farthing, M. J. G. (1993) Travellers' diarrhoea : mostly due to bacteria and difficult to prevent. *British Medical Journal* **306** 1425-6.

Rosenberg, M. L., Hazlet, K. K., Schaefer, J., Wells, J. G. & Pruneda, R. C. (1976) Shigellosis from swimming. *Journal of the American Medical Association* **236** 1849–52

Swerdlow, D. L. *et al.* (1992) Waterborne transmission of epidemic cholera in Trujillo, Peru : lessons for a continent at risk. *Lancet* **340** 28–32.

Van der Reis, L., Eyherlde, L. & Freilicher, J. (1994) Acute enteric infections and H_2 blockers. *Travel Medicine International* **12** (3) 89–91.

Weber, J. T., Levine, W. C. *et al.* (1994) Cholera in the United States 1965–1991. *Archives of Internal Medicine* **154** 551–6.

Wilson, J. M. & Chandler, G. N. (1993) Sustained improvements in hygiene behaviour amongst village women in Lombok, Indonesia. *Transactions of the Royal Society of Tropical Medicine and Hygiene* **87** 615–16.

'Getting Bitten to Death?'

Axmann, A., Félegylízi, C., Huszár, A. & Juhász, P. (1994) Long term malaria prophylaxis with Lariam in Cambodia. *Travel Medicine International* **12** (1) 13–18.

Bradley, D. (1993) Prophylaxis against malaria for travellers from the United Kingdom.

British Medical Journal **306** 1247–52.

Calder, L. & Laird, M. (1994) Mosquito travellers, arboviruses and the used tyre trade. *Travel Medicine International* **12** (1) 3-12.

Drummond, R. (1990) *Ticks and What You Can Do About Them.* Wilderness Press, Berkeley, California. Useful but only covers the North American species.

Harrison, G. (1978) *Mosquitoes, Malaria and Man: a History of Hostilities Since 1880.* John Murray.

'Heat and Dust, Sun and Sand'

Anon (1990) Topical sunscreens *Drug and Therapeutics Bulletin* **28** (16) 61–63.

Howarth, S. E., Wilson, J. M. *et al.* (1988) Wells worms and water in western Madagascar. *Journal of Tropical Medicine and Hygiene* **91** 255–64.

Layton, A. M. & Cunliffe, W. J. (1993) Phototoxic eruptions due to doxycyline: a dose related phenomenon. *Clin. Exp. Dermatol.* **18** 425–7.

Tomchik, R. S., Russell, M. T., Szmant, A. M. & Black, N. A. (1993) Clinical perspectives on seabathers eruption, also known as 'sea lice'. *Journal of the American Medical Association.* **269** (13) 1669–72.

'High, Cold and Dark'

Bartsch, P., Merki, B., Hofsteeter, D., Maggiorini, M., Kayser, B. & Oelz, O. (1993) *British Medical Journal* **306** 1098–101.

Bradwell, Jo & Cooper, Martin (1994) 'Reducing deaths and illness from acute mountain sickness'. *Climber and Hillwalker* March/April.

Edwards, P. Q. & Billings, E. L. (1971) Worldwide patterns of skin sensitivity to histoplasmin. *American Journal of Tropical Medicine and Hygiene* **20** 288–319.

Frankland, J. C. (1974) Studies on the responses of healthy English speleologists to exposure to histoplasmosis infection. *Transactions of the British Cave Research Association,* **1** (3) 153–7.

Pollard, A. J. (1992) Altitude induced illness. *British Medical Journal* **304** 1324–5.

Shlim, D. *et al.* (1989) *Journal of the American Medical Association* **261** 1017–1019.

White, A. J. (1984) Cognitive impairment of acute mountain sickness and acetazolamide. *Aviation, Space and Environmental Medicine* July 598–603.

Wilkerson, J. A. ed. (1985) *Medicine for Mountaineering.* The Mountaineers, 306 Second Avenue West, Seattle, Washington, WA 98119, USA.

The British Cave Research Association publish their Transactions quarterly and these carry articles useful to those planning caving expeditions. There have also been several issues devoted almost entirely to cave rescue, and medical care in caves, e.g. *Transactions of the British Cave Research Association* **2** (2) August 1975 and **8** (4) December 1981; *Cave Science* **11** (3) November 1984.

'Skin'

Hardy, D. B. (1993) Cashew nut dermatitis: traveller beware. *Travel Medicine International* **11** (1) 9–11.

McCrae, A. W. R. & Visser, S. A. (1975) *Paederus* in Uganda: outbreaks, clinical effects, extraction and bioassay of the vesicating toxin. *Annals of Tropical Medicine and Parasitology* **69** 109–120; excellent review paper on rove beetle blistering.

'Dangerous and Unpleasant Animals'

Alexander, J. O'D. (1984) *Arthropods and Human Skin*. Spring Verlag, Berlin. Contains a useful chapter entitled scorpion stings.

Bewes, P. C. (1994) Management of wounds *Journal of Wound Care* June 205–7.

Bradt. H. & Rachowieki, R., (1982) *Backpacking in Mexico and Central America*. Bradt Publications. To be reissued as *Backpacking in Central America* in 1995.

Caras, Roger (1975) *Dangerous to Man*. Penguin.

Dutta, J. K. & Dutta, T. K.(1994) Rabies in endemic countries. *British Medical Journal* **308** 488–9.

Freiberg, M. & Walls, J. G. (1984) The world of venomous animals. TFH publications, NJ: ISBN 0-87666-567-9. A good book with colour pictures of dangerous species.

Keegan, H. L. & McFarlane, W. R. eds. (1963) *Venomous and Poisonous and Noxious Animals of the Pacific Region: a Collection of Papers Based on a Symposium in the Public Health and Medical Services Division at the 10th Pacific Science Congress*. Pergamon Press, Oxford. Fascinating tome.

Peters, W. (1992) *A Colour Atlas of Arthropods in Clinical Medicine*. Wolfe Publishing, London. Marvellous book but expensive and not for the squeamish.

Warrell, D. A. (1987) *Venoms and Toxins of Animals and Plants* in *The Oxford Textbook of Medicine*. Oxford University Press, edited by D. J. Weatherall, J. G. G. Ledingham & D. A. Warrell. The best review of the consequences of venomous bites, etc. but frightening clinical descriptions unmitigated by information on actual risks; lists antivenom sources.

Wilson, J. M. (1987) The scorpion story. *British Medical Journal* **295** 1642–4.

Wilson, Jane (1990) A sting in the tail in: *Lemurs of the Lost World*. Impact Books.

'Your First Aid Kit'

Illingworth, R. (1981) Medical equipment for expeditions. *British Medical Journal* **282** 202–5.

'Living Abroad'

Foyle, M. J. (1994) Expatriate children: selection, preparation and typical needs. *Travel Medicine International* **12** (3) 93–7.

Peppiatt, R. and Byass, P. (1991) A survey of the health of British missionaries. *British Journal of General Practice* **41** 159–62.

'When You Get Home'

Conlon, C. J., Peto, T. & Ellis, C. J. (1993) Post-tropical screening is of little value unless the traveller feels unwell. *British Medical Journal* **307** 1108.

foot problems, *see* feet
fractures, treatment 170–1
freshwater fish 150
frostbite
  mountaineering and 98
    treatment 98–9
  superficial 98
frostnip 98
fugu 46
fungal infections, skin 110
fungi, poisoning from 44
funnel-web spiders 139
Fybogel, for constipation 40

gad-flies 135–6
game, hazards 132
Gamow repressurisation bag 96
gangrene 154
gastro-colic reflex 30
gastroenteritis 20
  see also diarrhoea; travellers'
    diarrhoea
generic name, of medicines 14,
  188
genital problems 118–25
  female 111, 120–5
  male 119–20
geography worm 109–10
Giant hogweed 76
  skin blistering 112
Giardia 39, 210
  filth-to-mouth disease 21
  treatment 39
Gila Monsters 154
glasses (spectacles) 174
glossary 213–14
glucose, in oral rehydration
  solutions 29, 30
gnathostone worms 46
goats' milk 23
grass snake 154
Great Indian rhinoceros 156
guinea worm 39
gut diseases 40–2
  see also specific diseases;
    travellers' diarrhoea

haemorrhage
  subconjunctival 173
  see also bleeding
haemorrhoids (piles) 41
hair loss 16, 57
Hamadryad 154
harvest mites 137

Havrix, hepatitis A vaccine 7
head
  injury 165–7
  itchy 109
  problems 181–4
headaches 181
head lice 109, 135
health information
  addresses 211
  sources, *see* information
    sources
health problems, special 12–14
  see also specific
    disorders/conditions
heart burn 42, 179
heat
  acclimatization 70
  fluid requirements 70
  hazards 70–5
  loss, mountaineering and 97
heat exhaustion 73–4
  treatment 74–5
heat illnesses 73–5
heat stroke 74–5
heels, cracked 114
hepatitis A 83, 172, 180–1
  filth-to-mouth disease 21
  immunization 7
hepatitis B 4, 127, 163
  immunization 10–11
hepatitis E 21, 124, 180–1
Heracleum mantegazzianum,
  skin blistering 76, 112
herring worms 45
high altitude, *see* mountaineering
hippopotamus 155
histoplasmosis
  as cave disease 100–1
  geographical distribution
    100–1
HIV, *see* human
  immunodeficiency virus (HIV)
honey bees 144–5
hookworm 37
hornets 144–5, 145
Hospital for Tropical Diseases 18,
  211
house-flies 143
hover-flies 143
human immunodeficiency virus
  (HIV) 4, 163, 208
  screening test (post-trip) 208
  see also AIDS
huntsman spiders 139

hymenoptera (thin-waisted
  insects) 144–5
  see also bees; wasps
hyoscine (Buscopan) 17, 30
hyperventilation 178
hypodermic syringes, carrying
  188
hypotension, postural 166–7
hypothermia, mountaineering
  and 97

ibuprofen (Brufen) 190
  muscle sprains/strains 169
  sun sensitivity and 73
immunizations 5–14
  against tropical and other
    diseases 6
  further help and information
    sources 18
  rabies, pre-trip 11, 157
  for special or occupational risks
    10–12
  for specific geographical areas
    8–10
  for trips to developing countries
    6–8
  see also specific diseases
Imodium, for diarrhoea 32
impetigo 111
Independent Medical Centre/
  Bridge the World 18, 211
Indian cobra 154
indigestion 42, 179
infants
  breast fed 14
  breathing problems 178
  living abroad 205–6
  travelling with 14, 205–6
infections
  bladder 118
  chest 177, 178
  eye 172
  from snakes 154
  from swimming 83
  skin, *see* skin infections
  throat 183
  tick-borne 66–7
  travellers' diarrhoea 20
influenza, immunization 12
  symptoms, *see* malaria
information sources 18, 213
  on immunizations 18
  mountaineering 99
  useful addresses 211–12

inhaled objects 175
injections, dangers 189
insect repellents 53–4, 138
insects
  biting 135–40
    treatment 105
  eye irritation and 173
  in jungles, tropical forests and
    scrub 75–6
  stings 13
  swimming dangers from 136
  thin-waisted 144–5
  see also specific insects
insurance
  in European Union
    countries 3
  medical and accident 3
InterHealth 203, 211
International Association for
  Medical Assistance to
  Travellers (IAMAT) 212
intrauterine contraceptive device
  (IUD) 121
intravenous drips, dangers 189
iodine 26
  tincture of 104
irritation, insect, of eyes 173
Isphaghula husk 40
itches 107–11

Japanese encephalitis 9, 50
  geographical distribution 51
  immunization 9
jaundice 180–1
jellyfish, stings from 79, 80, 146
  treatment 147
jet lag 16–17
jigger fleas 114, 130, 131, 132,
  134
  removal 131
jungles, hazards 75–6

kala-azar fever 61, 209
kidney stones 13, 118
King cobra 154
knee injuries, in mountaineering
  87–8
Komodo Dragon 154
krait 153
Kwells (hyoscine) 17

lactulose, for constipation 40
lakes, bathing dangers 80–3
larva migrans 109–10

Lassa fever 183
laxatives 40–1
leeches 64, 132
  aquatic 83, 140
  bites 140
  removal 131
Legionnaires' disease, showers
  and 115
leishmaniasis 61, 209
leprosy 46, 113
leptospirosis 83, 159
  cave disease 101
libido 118
lice 109, 132, 135
  body 109, 135
  head 109, 135
  pubic 118–19
  sea 78–80
lindane 108, 109, 119
Lister Institute of Preventative
  Medicine 144
liver flukes 46
living abroad 200–6
lizards, poisonous 155
Lomotil 32
London School of Hygiene and
  Tropical Medicine 192
long-haired caterpillars 141
Lyme disease 66, 111

maggots, skin-invading 132
magnesium sulphate paste 107
malaria 50, 54–9, 177, 208
  avoidance methods 56, 200
    three 'A's' 56
  case histories 58, 59, 177,
    194–5
  cerebral 58, 59
  cure 58–9
  diagnosis 58
  expatriates and 200
  geographical distribution 51,
    55–6
  immunization 8
  number of cases 54
  post-trip 59
  post-trip check-up 208
  precautions against 56, 200
  in pregnancy 56, 124, 192
  prevention 56–7
    see also antimalarial tablets
  symptoms 55
  transmission 55
  treatment 58–9

case histories 194–5
Malaria Reference Laboratory 57,
  211
malathion 108, 109, 119
mamba 153
mammals, hazardous 155–9
  see also animals
mangrove flies 135–6
manioc (cassava) 43
marine creatures, see under sea
MASTA (Medical Advisory
  Services for Travellers) 18, 57,
  211
meat 22
  toxoplasma infection from 38
  undercooked 38
mebendazole, for threadworms
  38
mebeverine (Colofac) 30
medical advice, emergency
  medical support system 206
Medical Advisory Services for
  Travellers (MASTA) 18, 57,
  211
medical check-up 5
  post-trip 208–10
Medic alert bracelet 13, 212
Medic Alert Foundation
  International 214
medical insurance 3
medical kits
  comprehensive, for major
    expeditions 187–8
  suppliers 212
  see also first aid kit
medical treatment
  emergency 3
  risks 125–7
medicines
  alcohol and 192
  buying and consuming abroad
    188–9
  complications 188
  common and alternatives to
    189–90
  contraception and 192
  for diarrhoea 32–4
    prevention of 28
  generic names 14, 188
  handing out to 'locals' 195–6
  locally manufactured 189
  mountain sickness prevention
    94–5
  pregnancy and 192

medicines cont'd
  reasons against taking 190–1
  side-effects 190–2
  sunburn and 191
  sun sensitivity and 73, 191
  taking notes on 14
  unsuitability 192
Medina worm (guinea worm) 39
Mediterranean fevers 50
Mediterranean spotted fever 50
mefloquine 57
melanoma, malignant 112
melatonin 16
men, genital problems 119–20
meningitis 9
  immunization against 9
  'meningitis belt' 9
Meningococcus, immunization 9
menstruation
  delayed 123
  tampons and 123
metronidazole 190
  Giardia treatment 39
miconazole 110, 113
mifepristone 121
milk 23
mini-pill 122
miscarriages 124
mites 64
  Australian whirligig 137
  bites 137–9
    prevention 138
  chigger 130, 132, 137
  harvest 137
  Mauritian red poison 138
  scrub typhus 51, 137
moles, skin cancer and 112–13
mosquitoes 50, 64, 135
  avoidance 53, 54, 200–1
    repellents 53–4
    screens 53, 200
  bites 52, 104
    avoidance 53, 54
    hypersensitivity 52–3
    itching and treatment of 52
  breeding 61
  diseases transmitted 50–9, 60, 64
    see also malaria, Japanese encephalitis, yellow fever, dengue, etc
  electric devices to repel 53
  resting position 52

moths, unpleasant habits 142
motion sickness 17
mountaineering 86–99
  contraceptive pill and 96
  exposure and treatment of 97–8
  frostbite 98–9
  haemorrhoids associated 41
  hazards 96–9
    serious 86–99
  information sources 99
  knee injuries 87–8
  medical conditions preventing 87
  pregnancy and 97
  walking problems 87–90
mountain sickness 90–6
  acute (AMS) 90
  at-risk groups 93
  avoiding 93–4
  children 93
  diagnosing 91
  mild, symptoms 90–1
  moderate to severe, symptoms 92
  prevention with medicines 94–5
  treatment 95–6
mugger crocodile 151
muscle-cramp 170
muscle strains, treatment 169–70, 170
musk phasmids 141

Nairobi eye, skin blistering 112
nalidixic acid, for bloody diarrhoea 33
nappies, disposal 206
naproxen (Naprosyn) 169, 190
nausea 40
neck, problems 181–4
nettles 76
  sea, stings from 146
'nightsoil' 23
Nile crocodiles 132, 151
nitrofurantoin 120
Nomad Travel Pharmacy and Vaccination Centre 4, 18, 211
Nomad Travel Shop 211
non-steroidal anti-inflammatory medicines 169, 170
  see also ibuprofen (Brufen), naproxen, diclofenac norfloxacin, for bloody

diarrhoea 33
nose
  bleeding 182
    in mountaineering 89
  broken 171
noxious animals 130–5, 141–3
noxious plants 76
noxious sea creatures 78, 132
nutrition 46–7
  see also diet
nystatin 110, 113

obesity 13
octopuses 146
oedema, in mountaineering 88
onchocerciasis (river blindness) 51, 82
oral contraceptives, *see* contraceptive pills
oral rehydration solution (ORS) 29, 166–7, 196, 205
  case histories 196–7
  home-made 29–30
  volume needed 30
  see also fluid replacement
Oriental schistosomiasis, geographical distribution 51
Oroya fever 176
oxygen reduction, harm due to 12–13, 90

pacemakers 13
pain
  abdominal 41–2, 184
  muscle, relief 169, 170
pain-killers 189–90
paludrine, *see* proguanil
paracetamol (acetamimophen) 176, 190
  as pain-killer 190
  responsible tourism and 196–7
  for sore throats 183
paratyphoid A, B and C 21
parrots 159
pathogens, filth-to-mouth disease 21, 201
Pediculus humanus capitis 109
Pediculus humanus humanus 109
penis, discharge from 119
peppermint oil 30
periodic (Cheyne–Stokes) respiration 92–3
periorbital cellulitis 173

Permethrin 108, 109
pesticides, poisoning from 43–4
photosensitivity 73, 191
pigs, attacks by 159
piles (haemorrhoids) 41
pink eye 172
piperazine, for threadworms 38
piranhas 83, 150
plague 63, 159
  from fleas 135
  geographical distribution 51
  immunization 11
plants, noxious 76
Plasmodium 55
Plasmodium falciparum 55, 208
  see also malaria
Pneumococcus, immunization
  10
pneumonia
  case history 179
poisoning
  food, *see* food poisoning
  strychnine fruits 43
poison ivy 108
poison oak 108
polio
  filth-to-mouth disease 21
  immunization 6
Portuguese-man-o-war, stings
  from 146
post-coital contraception 121–2
postural hypotension 166–7
potassium permanganate crystals
  104, 168, 197
povidone iodine 104, 157
pregnancy 14, 47
  alcohol drinking and 202
  dietary precautions 124
  malaria 124
    antimalarial tablets 47, 124,
      192
    avoidance 56, 124, 192
  medicines and 192
  mountaineering and 97
  travel and 124
  vitamins and diet in 47
preparation (pre-trip) 2–5
pressure effects, in flight 15–16
pre-trip preparation 2–5
prickly heat 107–8
primroses, skin blistering 112
proguanil (Paludrine) 40, 47, 57
  side-effects 57
pseudoephedrine 15, 181

psychological problems,
  expatriates 201–2, 203
pubic lice 118–19
puffer fish, poisoning 46
python 154

Q-fever, in milk 23
queasey symptoms 40
quinine 58

rabies 11
  cave-related disease 101
  from bats, case histories 158
  from dog bites 106, 132,
    157–9
  immunization 11, 158
    post-bite treatment 158
    pre-trip 157
  incubation period 158
ranitidine 42
rapids (in rivers), coping with
  80–1
rashes 104, 107–11
  allergic 108
  groin/crutch 110–11
  itchy 107
  photosensitive/sunlight-
    induced 191
rat fleas 63, 64
rats, health risks 159
recovery position 166
Red bugs 137
red eye 172–3
red-flies 135–6
red poison mites, of Mauritius
  138
red scorpion 144
red tide poisoning 45
Regulan, for constipation 40
repellents, insect 53–4, 138
reptiles, dangerous 151–5
  case histories 151
  see also snakes
respiration
  normal rate 178
  periodic (Cheyne–Stokes) 92–3
  see also breathing
resuscitation 162, 163–5
RGIT Health 206
rhinoceros 155
river blindness (onchocerciasis)
  51, 82
rivers, bathing dangers 80–3
Rochalimaea henselae 159

Rocky mountain spotted fever 67
rodents, health risks 159
rotaviruses 21
roundworm 37
Rove beetles, skin blistering 112,
  141
Royal Geographical Society (RGS)
  Expedition Advisory Centre 3,
  187
RU486 (mifpristone) 121
rufous funnel moth caterpillars
  142

saat ispagol 40
safety, after accidents 163–4
sahib's knee 87–8
salads 23
  poisoning from 44
Salmonella 21
salt
  needs 47
  in oral rehydration solutions
    29–30
salt tablets 47, 170
saltwater crocodile 78, 132, 149,
  155
sand-fleas, *see* jigger fleas
sand-fly 61, 64, 135
sand-fly borne diseases 61
sand-fly fever 50
sanitary towels, disposal 123
sanitation, poor and disease from
  21–2
Sarcoptes scabiei 108
scabies 108–9
scalds 168–9
schistosomiasis, *see* bilharzia
scorpion fish 147
scorpions 143–4
  antivenom 144
  dangerous 132
  geographical distribution
    143–4
  screens to exclude 200–1
screw worms 130
scrombrotoxic poisoning 45
scrub typhus mites 132, 137
  geographical distribution 51,
    132
SCUBA diving 77–8
sea
  hazards 77–80
  noxious creatures in 78, 132
  stinging from 80

throat
infections 183
something stuck in 174–5
sore 177, 183
thrush 120, 191
tick-borne diseases 50, 63–7
tick-borne encephalitis
European 66–7
immunization 10
tick-borne fevers, geographical
distribution 51
tick paralysis 67
ticks 63–7, 132, 135
preventing attachment 65
removal 65, 131
toe-biters 136
toe nails
bleeding under 175
care 88
toilets, squat 115
tongue, antibiotic 191
tourniquets, dangerous for snake
bites 153–4
toxoplasma 38
travel clinics 18, 211
travellers' diarrhoea 20
causes and transmission 20
prevention 22–8
treatment 28–34
see also diarrhoea
travelling
with adolescents 206
with babies 14, 205–6
with children 14, 205–6
travel sickness 17
trichinella 38
Triludan (terfenadine) 181
trimethoprim 120, 179, 190
trip planning 2–5
tropical diseases, immunization 6
tropical forests 75–6
tropical plants, dangerous 76
tropical sprue 46
tetracycline for 34
tropical ulcers 104, 111

tse-tse flies 62–3, 64
tuberculosis (TB) 179–80
immunization 7
symptoms and management
180
transmission/spread 180
tularaemia 136, 159
Tumbu flies 130–1
Tunga penetrans 131
tylenol, *see* paracetamol
typhoid
filth-to-mouth disease 21
immunization 7–8
infection risk 8

ulcers
on genitals 119
tropical 104, 111
ultraviolet (UV) radiation 71,
71–2
see also entries beginning sun
urine, blood in 118

vaccines, *see* immunizations
Valoid (cyclizine) 17
vectors and vector-borne diseases
50–68
diseases, treatment and vector
habits 64
geographical distribution 51
see also specific vectors
vegetables, growing 201
vehicles, drowning inside 80
vitamin pills, diet and 46
voice, hoarse 183–4
Voltarol, *see* diclofenac (Voltarol)
vomiting, blood 42
treatment 30

walking, problems 87–90
walking sticks (insects) 141
wandering spiders 139
wasps 144–5, 145
sea, stings from 146
water 4, 26–7

boiled 201
diarrhoea and 20, 26
expatriates and 201
filtered 201
filters 27–8
purification units 27–8
see also drinking water
water buffalo 159
water cress, wild, dangers of 44
water scorpions 136
weever fish, venomous 148
Weil's disease 83, 159
wind chill, in mountaineering
88–9
wolf spiders, bites 138
women
genital problems 111, 120–5
sexually transmitted disease in
125
women's health 120–5
World Health Organization 33,
157
worms 36–9
case history 38–9
filarial 60, 209
geographical distribution 36
imported/stow-away 209
life cycle 36
transmission mechanisms 36
see also specific worms
wounds
stitches for 167
treatment 167–9
wrenches, treatment 169–70

yellow eyes 172
yellow fever 8, 50
geographical distribution 51
immunization 8–9
yoghurt 23

zaldarine maleate, for diarrhoea
33
Zovirax (acyclovir) 73, 183